For the End of Time

For the End of Time

The Story of the Messiaen Quartet

REBECCA RISCHIN

■

This is the story of a quartet for all time,
based on the Apocalypse and written in apocalyptic times,
music for the future, defiant of the past,
music for the moment, and for eternity.

CORNELL UNIVERSITY PRESS

Ithaca, New York

First published 2003 by Cornell University Press

Printed in the United States of America

Library of Congress Cataloging-in-Publication Data

Rischin, Rebecca, 1967–
  For the end of time : the story of the Messiaen quartet / Rebecca Rischin.
      p. cm.
Includes discography (p.), bibliographical references (p.), and index.
  ISBN 0-8014-4136-6 (alk. paper)
  1. Messiaen, Olivier, 1908– Quatuor pour la fin du temps. 2. Prisoners of war as musicians—France. 3. Prisoners of war as musicians—Germany. 4. World War, 1939–1945—Prisoners and prisons. 5. Music—First performances—Germany. I. Title.
  ML410.M595R57 2003
  785'.24194—dc21

                                                                2003011589

Cornell University Press strives to use environmentally responsible suppliers and materials to the fullest extent possi-ble in the publishing of its books. Such materials include vegetable-based, low-VOC inks and acid-free papers that are recycled, to-tally chlorine-free, or partly composed of nonwood fibers. For further information, visit our website at www.cornellpress.cornell.edu.

Cloth printing   10 9 8 7 6 5 4 3 2 1

To the quartet that transcended its time, 15 January 1941

"Je suis né croyant."
[I was born a believer.]

OLIVIER MESSIAEN

"C'est la musique qui a été ma bonne fée."
[Music was my good fairy.]

ETIENNE PASQUIER

"Un prisonnier, c'est fait pour s'évader."
[A prisoner is made to escape.]

HENRI AKOKA

"Le seul souvenir de la guerre que je veux garder,
c'est le *Quatuor pour la fin du Temps*."
[The only memory of the war that I wish to keep
 is the memory of the *Quartet for the End of Time*.]

JEAN LE BOULAIRE

Contents

Acknowledgments

I am forever indebted to those who agreed to be interviewed for this book—who provided me with precious photos and documents as well as their fascinating testimony: the Akoka family, Jeannette, Lucien, Philippe, and Yvonne; Jean Lanier Le Boulaire; Yvonne Loriod-Messiaen; and Etienne Pasquier. It is their experience that made this story, their voices that empowered this history so that it could be retold, and their faith and devotion that finally enabled this project to be realized.

For granting me access to her precious archive of photos and documents of the prison camp, Stalag VIII A, I am immensely grateful to Hannalore Lauerwald. I would also like to thank Dominique Akoka, Michel Arrignon, Guy Deplus, David Gorouben, Yvette Lanier Le Boulaire, Roger Muraro, and Kent Nagano, whose commentary provided additional important insights into this fascinating piece. In addition, I would like to acknowledge Éditeurs Durand for granting me permission to include my own translation of the preface to the *Quatuor pour la fin du Temps*. I am also appreciative of the librarians of the following institutions who graciously assisted me: the Archives Nationales de France, the Bibliothèque Nationale, the Centre de Documentation de la Musique Contemporaine, the Centre de Documentation de la Résistance et de la Déportation, the Centre Pompidou, the Hoover Library at Stanford University, and the Alden and Music/Dance Libraries at Ohio University. I also thank Leslie Sprout of the University of Iowa for sharing with me her important findings on the *Quartet*'s Paris premiere.

Except where indicated in the notes, all of the translations are my own. For their generous help in transcribing and proofreading interviews, as well as in writing French correspondence, I am grateful to my friends, the brilliant Morel sisters, Ginette and Renée, and to Jean-Pierre Bobineau. I would also like to thank the music faculty of Florida State University who encouraged me in the realization of my doctoral treatise, "Music for Eternity: A New History of Olivier Messiaen's *Quartet for the End of Time*" (1997), which was the starting point for the creation of this book: James Croft, John Deal, Jeff Keesecker, Patrick Meighan, John Piersol, and, especially, my mentor, Frank Kowalsky. I am also grateful to Florence Lewis for her creative suggestions.

It has been an honor and a pleasure to work with the staff of Cornell University Press. I especially thank my editor, Catherine Rice, for her thoughtful insights and faithful encouragement, as well as Karen Laun, production editor, and Eric Schramm, copy editor, for their meticulous copy editing. I also thank Susan Barnett, copy supervisor, Melissa Oravec and Nancy Ferguson, editorial assistants, and John Ackerman, the director of Cornell University Press.

This project was made possible in part through the aid of two important grants, a 1993–94 Harriet Hale Woolley Scholarship, which enabled me to reside for a full year at the Fondation des Etats-Unis in Paris, where I could freely conduct research, and a 1994–95 Florida State University Dissertation Fellowship, which enabled me over the course of a second year to pursue this project to its fruition—in the United States as well as in Europe.

I am extremely fortunate to have a wonderful family of sisters and extended relatives. In conclusion, I would like to thank my parents for their remarkable historical and literary insights and their unending love and support throughout this enterprise.

Quartet for the End of Time
(Quatuor pour la fin du Temps)

MOVEMENT TITLES AND
INSTRUMENTATION

OLIVIER MESSIAEN

for violin, clarinet in Bb, cello, and piano

1. Crystal Liturgy
   Liturgie de cristal
   (entire quartet)

2. Vocalize, for the Angel Who Announces the End of Time
   Vocalise, pour l'Ange qui annonce la fin du Temps
   (entire quartet)

3. Abyss of the Birds
   Abîme des oiseaux
   (clarinet alone)

4. Interlude
   Intermède
   (violin, cello, and piano)

5. Praise to the Eternity of Jesus
   Louange à l'Eternité de Jésus
   (cello and piano)

6. Dance of Fury, for the Seven Trumpets
   Danse de la fureur, pour les sept trompettes
   (the entire quartet)

For the End of Time

Invitation

It is 6 June 1994. I am outside 237 rue du Faubourg St. Honoré, a faded brownstone building in the eighth *arrondissement* of Paris, ten minutes by foot from the Arc de Triomphe and the Champs Élysées.

I look for his name, Pasquier, E. At the sound of the bell, I push open the door. The building, a lovely turn-of-the-century structure, has no elevator. Arriving out of breath at an apartment on the fifth floor, I am greeted by a frail, white-haired gentleman in a beige suit.

"Mon Dieu! How did you make it up the stairs?" he jokes. "I've been climbing these five flights of stairs for over fifty years—with my cello!" In tiny steps he leads me into the living room, where, on the wall above a baby grand piano, hangs what appears to be a viola. "That was my first cello," he says. "As I was only five when I began—I had to play a small one. If you look closely you'll notice a scratch there. I tripped over it, so it had to be repaired."[1]

On the wall to the right of the piano hangs a portrait of a dark-haired woman in a strapless dress and a mink stole. "That's my wife," he says. "She was a wonderful woman, very kind, very devoted, and very beautiful. She was a singer, a first-prize winner from the Paris Conservatory. She passed away ten years ago. We were married for fifty-four years."

So began the first of my five meetings with Etienne Pasquier. I was not the first nor would I be the last to interview him, for Etienne Pasquier was one of the most renowned cellists of his generation and the last to personally experience almost an entire century of French chamber music.

In spite of his eighty-nine years, he has remarkable powers of recall. Laughing, he tells of his first encounter with Camille Saint-Saëns:

In my little village of Tours, I went to a concert featuring Saint-Saëns on the piano. When my mother asked me what my impression was, I said: "Oh, il joue bien, M. Saint-Saëns, mais il ne va pas en mesure."

I was eleven years old, and I said about the great Saint-Saëns: "He doesn't keep a steady tempo!" "But it's on purpose that he does that," said my mother. "Oh, I don't think so," I answered. [He laughs.]

He goes over to the piano and retrieves a press release for the Trio Pasquier, formed in 1927 with his brothers, Jean and Pierre. "The most famous group in the world devoted to the literature written for one violin, one viola, and one cello," it reads.

Unexpectedly, he pulls out his wallet and removes from a pocket a faded card. "I guard this with my life," he says. Inside is an invitation. In French it reads, "Stalag VIII A, Görlitz. Premiere of the *Quartet for the End of Time* by Olivier Messiaen. 15 January 1941. Performed by Olivier Messiaen, Etienne Pasquier, Jean Le Boulaire, and Henri Akoka" (see figs. 1–2).

Proudly, he reads aloud the inscription on the reverse side of the invitation:

> To Etienne Pasquier—the magnificent bedrock of the Trio
> Pasquier!—I venture to hope that he will never forget the rhythms,
> the modes, the rainbows, and the bridges to the beyond cast by his
> friend into sonorous space; as he brought so much finesse, precision,
> emotion, faith itself, and technical perfection to the execution of my
> "quatuor pour fin du Temps" [*sic*] that the listener must have
> thought that he had played such music his entire life!
> Thank you, and with all of my affection,
>
> OLIVIER MESSIAEN[2]

■

This is the story of a quartet for all time, based on the Apocalypse and written in apocalyptic times, music for the future, defiant of the past, music for the moment, and for eternity.

Olivier Messiaen's *Quatuor pour la fin du Temps*, or *Quartet for the End of Time*, is a signature work within the musical, political, and cultural history of the twentieth century. Yet surprisingly, this quartet for violin, clarinet, cello, and piano, composed and premiered in a German prison camp during the Second World War, has inspired little published scholarship. In fact, this monumental chamber work in eight movements, lasting nearly an hour, has garnered less scholarly attention than have many of the composer's less celebrated compositions. If numerous biographies of Messiaen invariably include an examination of the *Quartet for the End of Time*, in most of them, the discussion of the compositional history of the *Quartet* serves merely as a brief introduction to an extensive theoretical analysis of the work. The majority of authors who have chosen to recount the history of the *Quartet* have relied on secondary sources or on the published statements of the composer alone. Few have interviewed the three other performers and their families, searched out witnesses to the historic premiere, or examined the documents relating to Stalag VIII A, the camp for prisoners of war where the premiere took place.

This book examines for the first time the fascinating history of the *Quartet for the End of Time*: the events that led to its composition and first performances; the experiences of the musicians in Stalag VIII A; and the responses of the prisoner musicians to their situation, the premiere, and the era in which they lived. The book reveals the contradictory accounts given by Messiaen and witnesses to the first performance regarding several important issues: the order in which the piece was composed, the size of the audience at the premiere, the condition of the instruments, and the reasons for the composer's liberation. It discusses the composer's interpretive preferences and the musicians' problems in execution and how they affected the *Quartet*'s premiere and subsequent performances. It describes the musicians' life in the prison camp and explores the composer's relationship with the German camp officials and his fellow musicians, aspects of the camp experience that Messiaen noticeably passed over in his retelling. The fortunes of Messiaen's fellow musicians before and after the momentous premiere are some of the most intriguing aspects of the history of the *Quartet*. Until now, the biographies of these musicians have gone unexplored. This book, then, is the narrative of a remarkable *collectif*—of the principals from the premiere performance of the *Quartet for the End of Time*—whose testimonies, together with those of the Messiaen circle, change our understanding not only of this musical composition, but of the culture of the prison camp in World War II.

Like the *Quartet* itself, this book consists of eight "movements," chapters, of varying length and character. Chapters 1–3 examine the events leading up to Messiaen's captivity; his chance encounters with a cellist, a clarinetist, and a violinist; the prison camp circumstances and the musicians' evolving friendship; the procurement of instruments; and the difficulties encountered in the execution of the *Quartet*. The fourth chapter, "*Intermède*," an interlude, as in the *Quartet*, examines the work's musical content. Chapter 5 recreates the dramatic circumstances of the famous premiere. Chapters 6 and 7 recount the liberation of three of the musicians from Stalag VIII A and the heroic escape of the fourth, the Paris premiere, and Messiaen's subsequent career as a composer and pedagogue. Chapter 8, "Into Eternity," narrates in the first person the author's conversations with two of the musicians who premiered the *Quartet* and with surviving members of the Messiaen circle and their relatives, so as to transmit the living discourse "into eternity."

That walk up five flights of stairs to Etienne Pasquier's apartment, where he pulled from his pocket the invitation to the premiere of the *Quartet for the End of Time* in January 1941 in a prison camp in Silesia, became an invitation to retell the story of how this Messiaen quartet came into being.

■

Who was Messiaen? Although he dutifully answered his questioners and provided personal information in interviews and in prefaces and notes to his works, Messiaen remains an enigma.

A devout Catholic, Messiaen combined a passion for his religion and an interest in mysticism with a love of nature and the supernatural. An ornithologist and rhythmician as well as a composer, he mixed sounds as a painter mixes colors, associating specific shades with certain modes and chords. Drawing on Gregorian plainchant, church modes, and ancient Greek and Hindu rhythms, he interwove Christian symbolism with "sound-color" and transcriptions of birdsong, creating an eclectic musical language that was uniquely his, an intricate puzzle of seemingly disparate parts that miraculously make musical sense.

Born on 10 December 1908 in Avignon, France, to Pierre Messiaen, a teacher of English and translator of Shakespeare, and Cécile Sauvage, a poet, Olivier Messiaen was drawn to mystery, marvel, and poetry at an early age. A childhood fascination with the plays of Shakespeare, "a super-fairy-tale," influenced his embrace of Catholicism, in which he found "the marvelous multiplied a hundredfold, a thousandfold."[3] His mother, who made her pregnancy the subject of a collection of twenty poems, *L'âme en bourgeon* (The budding soul), had premonitions about his artistic predispositions while he was still in the womb, said Messiaen. "That's why she said, without knowing I would become a composer, '*Je souffre d'un lointain musical*' [I suffer from an unknown, distant music]."[4]

It was the score to Debussy's *Pelléas et Mélisande*, a gift from his harmony teacher Jehan de Gibon, that Messiaen claimed had "the most decisive influence" on him.[5] This influence manifested itself at the Paris Conservatory, where Messiaen, studying with Marcel Dupré, Maurice Emmanuel, Paul Dukas, and others, took first prize in five disciplines: counterpoint and fugue (1926), piano accompaniment (1927), organ and improvisation (1928), history of music (1928), and composition (1929); he also won second prize in harmony (1924).[6]

In 1931, at the age of twenty-two, Messiaen became the youngest titular organist in France when he was named principal organist at the Trinity Cathedral in Paris (see fig. 3).[7] Five years later, he was appointed to the faculties of the Ecole Normale de Musique and the Scola Cantorum. The same year, together with composers Yves Baudrier, André Jolivet, and Daniel Lesur, Messiaen founded La Jeune France, a group united by the common objective of "sincerity, generosity, and artistic good faith."[8] The group did not last long, for World War II brought an end to its activities. On 25 August 1939, Messiaen was called to military service (see fig. 4). Then, in the summer of 1940, he was captured by the Germans and sent to a camp for prisoners of war.[9]

Messiaen's account of the work's premiere in the camp has become a legend. In his own words:

> Conceived and composed during my captivity, the *Quartet for the End of Time* was premiered in Stalag VIII A, on 15 January 1941. It took place in Görlitz, in Silesia, in a dreadful cold. Stalag was buried in snow. We were 30,000 prisoners (French for the most part, with a few Poles and Belgians). The four musicians played on broken instruments: Etienne Pasquier's cello had only 3 strings; the keys of my upright piano remained lowered when depressed.[10] . . . It's on this piano, with my three fellow musicians, dressed in the oddest way—I myself wearing a bottle-green suit of a Czech soldier—completely tattered, and wooden clogs large enough for the blood to circulate despite the snow underfoot . . . that I played my *Quartet for the End of Time,* before an audience of 5,000 people. The most diverse classes of society were mingled: farmers, factory workers, intellectuals, professional servicemen, doctors, [and] priests. Never before have I been listened to with such attention and understanding.[11]

It is an extraordinary story, and yet the absence of studies of the compositional history of the *Quartet* is surprising considering the massive outpouring of books and films on World War II; the *Quartet*'s popularity with performers and audiences alike; the numerous recordings of the piece—far exceeding those of any other composition by Messi-

aen; and the *Quartet*'s renown in the Western canon as one of the great
chamber works of this century, its premiere ranking with the 1913 premiere of Stravinsky's *The Rite of Spring* as "one of the great stories of
twentieth-century music."[12]

While the era of World War II has brought forth many significant
compositions by Strauss, Schoenberg, Hindemith, and Stravinsky, and
the war itself has inspired countless musical works—from the symphonies of Shostakovich to the requiem masses of Britten and Ka-
balevsky and the compositions on the Holocaust by Schoenberg, Pen-
derecki, Morton Gould, Lukas Foss, and Steve Reich—little music has
emerged as a direct expression of the prison camp ordeal. Compositions
written in prison and concentration camps, such as those by Czech
composers Pavel Haas and Viktor Ullman, continue to be discovered,
but the *Quartet for the End of Time* is the only one by a major composer found thus far.

Even more intriguing, while many World War II–inspired works have
understandably been absorbed with the problem of the *Deus Absconditis*
(the absence of God), Messiaen's *Quartet* is not. The message the *Quartet*
radiates is not one of despair, but, on the contrary, one of resounding reaf-
firmation. Admittedly, Messiaen did not face extinction, like the Jews.
One might even say that "God was with him." Still, in an environment
that provoked depression and suicide among many of his fellow inmates,
the source of Messiaen's inspiration is compelling. The *Quartet* was inspired by the first six verses from the tenth chapter of Revelation. The title
page of the piece refers to the verse in which the Angel of the Apocalypse
raises his hand to heaven and declares that there will be no more time: "*en
hommage à l'Ange de l'Apocalypse, qui lève la main vers le ciel en disant:
'Il n'y aura plus de Temps'*" [in homage to the Angel of the Apocalypse,
who raised his hand to heaven, saying, "There will be no more Time"].[13]
Attesting to the eternal freedom of the spirit over the temporal captivity of
the body, the piece illustrates how captivity paradoxically set free a work
that became a testament to creativity, to the unshakeable faith of a devout
Catholic, and to the aspects of belief exemplified in the lives of Messiaen's
fellow musicians who premiered the *Quartet*.

The *Quartet* is unique in several other respects as well, most obviously in its instrumentation for clarinet, violin, cello, and piano. The
Quartet for the End of Time, Paul Hindemith's quartet (1938), and Tōru
Takemitsu's *Quatrain* (1975) and *Quatrain II* (1977) are among a hand-
ful of pieces written for this instrumental combination. Both the instrumentation of the piece at its first inception and the relationship of

the instrumentation to the circumstances of the *Quartet*'s composition, questions that for many years have been put aside, are brought to the fore in this book.

The *Quartet* has been considered "the single most significant work" that Messiaen composed, in that it was "the technical source from which all of his subsequent output was directly to spring."[14] Certainly, the *Quartet* marked two significant turning points in the development of the composer's style. It was one of the first compositions into which Messiaen incorporated identifiable birdsong, an element that would appear and reappear in many of his subsequent compositions. It was also one of the first of Messiaen's compositions to include a treatise on rhythm, and as such prefigured his first major theoretical work, *The Technique of My Musical Language* (1944).

Although the *Quartet* is widely regarded as one of the great chamber works of the twentieth century, it is Messiaen's only significant such work. Of Messiaen's seventy published compositions, only five are chamber works, three of which preceded the *Quartet*. "It was not much of a preparation for a work occupying four players for nearly an hour, especially one from a composer whose only important instrumental works for several years had been organ cycles,"[15] notes Messiaen scholar Paul Griffiths. Even more ironic for a composition of such stature is that it emerged almost accidentally. The piece might never even have been conceived in its specific instrumentation had Messiaen not chanced upon the three musicians who became his fellow performers. Moreover, the *Quartet* would never have been realized had it not been for the music-loving officers in Messiaen's prison camp, who, as it shall be seen, went out of their way to accommodate the needs of this celebrated composer.

Finally, the compositional and performance history of the *Quartet* is unique, for it embraces not only a quartet of music, but a quartet of singular musicians, each one of whom was unusual in his own way, each one of whom was involved not only in the art of making music but in the art of relating to one another, and in the art of surviving imprisonment in a cruel and turbulent time.

■

In its polarities of clamor and silence, of terror and calm, the *Quartet for the End of Time* refutes the clichés of captivity, and in its audacious affirmations demands that the silence surrounding its creation be shattered.

This is the *Quartet* for the end of an era. This is a story for the end of a time. Read it in its entirety without pause, chapter by chapter, movement by movement, as you would listen to the *Quartet* itself, and ascend to that unknown place sought by the final note of Messiaen's violin, that place where you carry away a feeling of a true and eternal vision, of a quartet for all time, of the *Quartet for the End of Time.*

CHAPTER I

The Quartet Begins

On 1 September 1939 Germany invaded Poland. Two days later, Great Britain and France declared war on Germany. The most destructive world war in history had begun. Just over a week earlier, after completing *Les corps glorieux*, Olivier Messiaen was drafted into the army, but due to poor eyesight he was found unfit for active service.[1] Instead, he was sent to work as a furniture mover in Sarreguemines and then as an orderly (medical auxiliary), first in Sarralbe and then in Verdun.[2] Along with thousands of others, he would eventually be captured and imprisoned.

Numerous musicologists have traced the beginnings of the *Quartet for the End of Time* to Stalag VIII A, where Messiaen supposedly encountered the three musicians whose presence dictated the choice of instrumentation for his composition. In fact, the history of the *Quartet* began somewhat earlier and did not develop in the order in which it has been repeatedly claimed to have unfolded. Although the *Quartet* was born in Stalag VIII A, it was actually conceived in Verdun, where Messiaen met two musicians, Etienne Pasquier and Henri Akoka, who would unknowingly contribute to the shape of musical history.

■

Like Messiaen, Pasquier was no ordinary soldier. Born on 10 May 1905 in Tours, Pasquier was a child prodigy who started playing the cello at the age of five in what he called *"une boîte à musique"* (a music box). His mother would give piano lessons in one room, his father would give violin lessons in another, and he and his brothers would practice in the bedrooms. "Everyone was making music."[3]

With his two older brothers, Jean and Pierre, who played the violin and the viola, respectively, Etienne began an international career. In 1918, just as World War I was coming to a close, the thirteen-year-old Pasquier entered the Paris Conservatory, where he was to receive the

9

premier prix in cello in 1921. In the same year he became the youngest member of the Concerts Colonne orchestra.⁴ Then, in 1927, one year after completing his military service, he and his two brothers, Jean and Pierre, founded the Trio Pasquier (see figs. 5–6).⁵ With a career that spanned forty-seven years, this ensemble would perform with such world-renowned musicians as Marguerite Long and Jean-Pierre Rampal and commission trios by Jean Françaix (1934), Bohuslav Martinu (1935), André Jolivet (1938), Darius Milhaud (1947), Florent Schmitt (1948), and Gabriel Pierné (1952).⁶

In 1929, at the age of twenty-four, Etienne Pasquier married singer Suzanne Gouts and joined the Théâtre National de l'Opéra (Paris Opera Orchestra), where, a year later, he was appointed assistant principal cellist. Nine years later, his career took a fateful turn.

"I was mobilized on 3 September 1939," Pasquier began, recalling the events leading up to his first encounter with Olivier Messiaen,

> and so I went, as a soldier, to Lorraine, in the eastern part of France. In 1940, I got permission to be released. It had been so cold in Lorraine that I developed a severe earache, and, instead of returning immediately to the front lines, I was taken to the Val-de-Grâce hospital in Paris. When I returned three weeks later, I was transferred to the citadel of Vauban at Verdun, where, because of the lull in the battle at Verdun, a French general, Utziger, had created a theater orchestra for the soldiers. I was a corporal—of music, that is. Four other Frenchmen were under my command, one of whom was Olivier Messiaen. And it was there, at the citadel of Vauban at Verdun, that our friendship began.⁷

The meeting of these two musicians ignited an instantaneous camaraderie. Messiaen, who had already developed an interest in ornithology, asked Pasquier, who distributed the duties, to arrange their military watches together so that they could listen to the awakening of the birds at dawn. Pasquier recounted these episodes with humor and affection: " 'Look. A faint glimmer, over there. It's dawn,' Messiaen would say. Little by little, light began to appear. 'Listen carefully. Once the sun comes out, pay attention.' " Pasquier continued:

> The moment was still. Then, all of a sudden, we heard, "Peep!" A small cry of a bird, a bird giving the pitch, like a conductor! Five seconds later, all the birds started singing together. Like an orchestra! "Listen to them!" said Messiaen. "They're giving each other assignments. They'll reunite tonight, at which time they'll recount what

they saw during the day." So, every time Messiaen had his night-
watch, I would go with him, and it would start all over again.
"Tweet! Peep!" A few seconds would go by. Then, suddenly, the
whole orchestra of birds would be singing! It was deafening. Then the
singing would stop, but later, like a genuine military regiment, the
birds would return in the evening to report what they had observed.[8]

Here, near Verdun, the chorus of birds that Pasquier found deafening
inspired the composition that would later become the third movement
of a monumental work. But, in the person of the clarinetist Henri
Akoka, the piece had a human inspiration as well.

■

Born on 23 June 1912 in Palikao, Algeria, into a musical family, Henri
Akoka was the second of six children (see figs. 7–8).[9] His father, Abraham, a self-taught trumpeter, moved his family to Ponthierry, France, in
1926 in the hopes that his children would become professional musicians.[10] There, Abraham Akoka, together with Henri, who had already
begun to study the clarinet, and his older brother, Joseph, who played the
tuba, earned money playing in a band associated with the wallpaper factory where they were employed. Only fourteen, Henri also found work
playing for silent films, where live musicians were often used.[11] At the
encouragement of his teacher, Monsieur Briançon, a clarinetist in the
Garde Républicaine, the premier French military band, Henri auditioned
for the Paris Conservatory, where he received the *premier prix* in clarinet in June 1935. In 1936, he joined the Orchestre Symphonique de la
Radio–diffusion de Strasbourg, where he played for *les déjeuners concerts* [noon concerts]. Soon after he became a member of the Paris-based
Orchestre National de la Radio. But the outbreak of war interrupted his
tenure. In 1939, Akoka was mobilized and sent to play in a *théâtre aux
armées*, a military orchestra at the citadel of Vauban near Verdun.[12]
There, another fortuitous encounter took place.

■

"I had never before met Henri Akoka," said Etienne Pasquier. "I was
in the Opera. He was in an orchestra at Radio France. But during the
war, a military orchestra was installed in Verdun. He had been called
there and that's how the two of us got to know each other."[13] Messiaen

and Akoka became fast friends as well. Prodded by Akoka, who had brought his instrument with him, Messiaen immediately went to work.

Thus, recalled Pasquier, it was not at Stalag VIII A that the *Quartet for the End of Time* began, but at Verdun. There, where listening to the waking of the birds had become a daily ritual, Messiaen began writing his famous "Abyss of the Birds" for unaccompanied clarinet. But Akoka had not even had the chance to read Messiaen's composition, when, on 10 May 1940, Germany launched a blitzkrieg against Belgium, Luxembourg, and the Netherlands. The three musicians were forced to flee. On 20 June, before they could reach their destination, they were captured in a forest by the Germans and sent on an arduous forty-three-mile march to the vicinity of Nancy.[14] With gratitude, Pasquier recalled how Akoka encouraged him to persevere during this long hike, supporting him during his spells of exhaustion:

> This is a man who was completely loyal and kind to me. He was younger; he was more robust, and he helped me walk for miles and miles.[15] I probably owe him my life because, when the Germans imprisoned us, they sent us in the direction of Nancy. There were 70 kilometers to do by foot. We had nothing to eat. I would walk, and from time to time, I would collapse from hunger. But Akoka would lift me up and would guide me until I was self-sufficient again. He never once abandoned me. . . . This was a man with a big heart, who played very well.[16]

It was only after their march to the open field near Nancy, where the Germans quartered their prisoners before transporting them to the prison camp in Germany, that Akoka first played the "Abyss of the Birds." While Akoka played and Messiaen listened, Pasquier, who had been unable to bring his cello with him, assumed the function of the "music stand":

> It's in this open field that Akoka sight-read the piece for the first time. I was the 'music stand,' that is to say, I held the score for him. He would grumble from time to time, as he found that the composer gave him difficult things to do. "I'll never be able to play it," he would say. "Yes, yes, you will, you'll see," Messiaen would answer.[17]

■

Although the other movements of the *Quartet* had yet to be written, and a violinist had yet to appear on the horizon, a singular relationship between Messiaen, Pasquier, and Akoka had already begun to form. It is clear from Pasquier's recollections how unique these men were in temperament and how much their personality differences produced contrasting reactions to their shared ordeal.

In spite of his obvious talent and the fame and fortune that he had acquired as a member of the renowned Trio Pasquier, Etienne remained charmingly modest. Moreover, despite the severe physical and emotional hardships that he endured during the war, he retained a lovable sense of humor virtually to the end.

Akoka also had an infectious sense of humor. His son Philippe recalled that his father often spoke in a coded language. "Now, I'm going to practice my clarinet," for example, meant, "Now, I'm going to take a nap."[18] This candidly casual attitude toward practicing is also evident in Pasquier's description of Akoka's reading of "Abyss of the Birds," in which Akoka "grumbled" from time to time about the piece's difficulties. If, even today, with the extraordinary technical demands of contemporary music, the *Quartet for the End of Time* is considered an extremely difficult work, at that time, when technical standards were lower and Messiaen's style so original, it surely must have seemed far more so, and Akoka's frustrations perfectly understandable.

What is certain is that Akoka's playing style had an enormous influence on Messiaen's future musical preferences. Like his teacher at the Paris Conservatory, Auguste Périer, Akoka played a Couesnon clarinet and a Couesnon mouthpiece with a Périer facing.[19] No doubt due both to the mark of his clarinets and mouthpiece as well as to his own concept, Akoka played with a brighter, thinner, more "metallic" sound than that of modern-day clarinetists, typical of the French school at the time. The memory of this brighter sound subsequently influenced the way Messiaen preferred clarinetists to play his composition. In 1963, when Guy Deplus, formerly professor of clarinet at the Paris Conservatory, made his first recording of the *Quartet* under Messiaen's supervision, the composer asked him to make one change in dynamics in "Abyss of the Birds" to compensate for the difference in timbre between his sound and that of Akoka. Deplus explained:

Messiaen retained Akoka's particular sound in his mind.[20] And when he worked with our quartet, he was taken aback, because my sound was different. For example, in "Abyss of the Birds," when the theme from the beginning returns in the low register of the clarinet [see where the theme returns on a low F#, marked, as in the beginning, "Lent, expressif et triste"—"Slow, expressive, and sad"], it's marked *piano*, but Messiaen said to me: "No. With you, it needs to be louder." Because sounds are darker now, so they project less. Even when Akoka played *piano*, he projected more. With me it was different. And so Messiaen asked me to play *mezzo-forte* here rather than *piano*.[21]

Michel Arrignon, Deplus's successor at the Paris Conservatory, recalled that Messiaen made a similar modification in dynamics in the same passage of "Abyss of the Birds" when his group, the Quatuor Olivier Messiaen, made its first recording of the *Quartet* under the composer's supervision.[22]

Though musically, Messiaen and Akoka frequently found points of agreement, philosophically they were on different planes. The clarinetist's apparent matter-of-factness innately conflicted with the composer's seemingly ascetic Catholicism. In statements made by their wives, Yvonne Loriod and Jeannette Akoka, these philosophical differences between Messiaen and Akoka are striking. They describe a scene in which the prisoners, parched and famished after their forty-three-mile march to Nancy, batter one another over a sip of water. Yvonne Loriod, a devout Catholic like Messiaen, cited her husband's disdain at the sight of what he viewed as human pettiness:

> They suffered for several days without water or food until finally they arrived at a place where water was distributed.
>
> And then an extraordinary episode followed in which thousands of soldiers literally fought each other in order to get a drink of water. Messiaen was seated in a little courtyard and he began to take out of his pocket a score, some music, which he began to read. There was one other man, also seated, also reading, who'd refused to join in this struggle for water and his name was Guy-Bernard Delapierre [an Egyptologist]. Well, the two men got talking and they said to each other, "Look, we are brothers, because we have placed the finer things of life above this struggle for earthly food."[23]

Alluding to the same incident, Mme. Akoka, by contrast, emphasized the virtues of her husband's pragmatism as opposed to what she and Henri perceived as the uselessness of Messiaen's religiosity:

> Messiaen would say: "Look how they're behaving. They're fighting over a drop of water." And Henri would answer: "But all we have to do is bring some containers so that we can distribute the water."

Messiaen was very Catholic and would kneel down and pray, and Henri would say to him: "Praying won't help. What we have to do is act, to do something for these people here."[24]

Yet, in spite of their philosophical and temperamental differences, Messiaen and Akoka got along marvelously, claimed Lucien Akoka. Messiaen adored Henri "because he was spirited and witty, and because he was a remarkable clarinetist. He had a rare sense of humor. Everyone with whom he came in contact was fascinated by Henri." Messiaen, "like the others," said Lucien, "was captivated"—so thoroughly that he wrote a piece for him.[25] Philippe Akoka credited the birth of the *Quartet* not simply to his father's musical and personal appeal, but also to his prodding of Messiaen:

> This insistent side of Henri I remember well. He said that, in captivity, Messiaen had lost the will to compose. He told me many times: "I would push him. Write something for me. We have time on our hands. We're prisoners. Write some music." And it's in this way, according to my father, that the *Quartet* was born. Because the clarinet was the only instrument that they had on hand.[26]

Thus, the *Quartet* was born of a succession of fortuitous encounters, two of which occurred before Messiaen had even arrived in Stalag VIII A. The encounter with Delapierre also had an indirect impact on Messiaen's career. An aficionado of classical music, Delapierre had asked to borrow Messiaen's score of Stravinsky's *Les Noces* (The wedding) in the open field near Nancy. Three years later, the two men met again—at the Egyptologist's home, where the composer held analysis courses on contemporary music.[27] Among the first works to be analyzed in these courses was the *Quartet for the End of Time*.[28]

The final series of fortuitous encounters that furthered the creation of the *Quartet for the End of Time* occurred in Stalag VIII A, where Messiaen, Pasquier, and Akoka were sent after their brief stay in the open field near Nancy. As new dimensions were added—notably a violinist named Jean Le Boulaire—a musical composition as well as a relationship among four men, each one remarkable in his own way, began to evolve. Ironically, the prison camp of Stalag VIII A liberated the composer and his fellow musicians, providing them with the means to real-

ize the composition and premiere of seven more pieces, which, together
with "Abyss of the Birds," constituted an eight-movement quartet and
the beginning of a musical legacy.

■

Musicologists have claimed that the fourth movement, *"Intermède"*
(Interlude), the trio for violin, clarinet, and cello, was the first movement of the *Quartet* to be composed, that it was written as an experi-
mental piece for three musicians whom Messiaen met in Stalag VIII A,
and that it then became the compositional "germ" out of which the
seven other movements of the *Quartet* would be generated. It would appear, then, that Messiaen had not given any thought to composing a
quartet for violin, clarinet, cello, and piano prior to his arrival in Stalag
VIII A.

Such claims are not unfounded, for they are based upon actual testimony given by the composer. The composer repeatedly affirmed that
the *Quartet* was as much practically composed as it was religiously inspired. Moreover, he stressed that its unusual instrumentation was
purely incidental, and that his decision to write for this particular combination reflected no special affinity for these specific instruments.
Rather, insisted Messiaen, the instrumentation was the simple result of
coincidence: his fortuitous encounter with a violinist, a clarinetist, and
a cellist.[29]

In his conversations with one of his interviewers, Antoine Goléa,
Messiaen elaborated:

> In Stalag there happened to be a violinist, a clarinetist, and the cellist
> Etienne Pasquier. I wrote for them at once a short trio without any-
> thing larger in mind, which they played for me in the lavatories, be-
> cause the clarinetist had brought his instrument with him and the
> cellist had been given a gift of a cello with three strings. Emboldened
> by these first sounds, I retained this little piece as an interlude and
> added to it in succession the seven movements that surround it, thus
> carrying the total number of movements of my *Quartet for the End
> of Time* to eight.[30]

About the order in which the *Quartet* was composed, Messiaen was
unequivocal, so it is no wonder that scholars have repeatedly asserted

that "*Intermède*" was the first movement to be composed. Nowhere in these interviews did Messiaen mention that he composed the clarinet movement in Verdun. Instead, he claimed that it was one of seven movements added "in succession" to the "*Intermède.*" He also did not mention that he had met the cellist and clarinetist prior to his arrival in Stalag. Instead, he omitted the Verdun episode entirely: "Au Stalag se trouvaient avec moi un violoniste, un clarinettiste et le violoncelliste Etienne Pasquier" (In Stalag there happened to be a violinist, a clarinetist, and the cellist Etienne Pasquier).[31]

But in the Pasquier version, Messiaen met Akoka and Pasquier well before his arrival in Stalag VIII A, and "Abyss of the Birds" was composed and read for the first time well before the other movements, not in Germany, but in France. Since Akoka was the only one of the four original performers of the *Quartet* who had brought his instrument with him, this version of the order of the *Quartet*'s composition makes complete sense and is the most persuasive.

This discrepancy regarding the genesis of the composition is addressed for the first time in Anthony Pople's *Messiaen: Quatuor pour la fin du Temps* (Cambridge Music Handbooks), which quotes Pasquier's recollection of Akoka's initial reading of "Abyss of the Birds." In an interesting analysis, Pople speculates about the order of the composition, based on the testimony of Messiaen and Pasquier and the development of musical material. "If the two accounts are to be reconciled," he writes, "one must surely conclude that the music which Akoka sight-read in a field simply formed the basis for a more developed piece that Messiaen finalised in Stalag VIII A at a later date."[32]

The question remains, however, why Messiaen would fail to mention crucial facts about the genesis of his own composition. Certainly, the creative process is complex, and perhaps the order in which the piece was conceived was different from the order in which it was actually written. It is also possible that the physical and emotional hardships that Messiaen endured during the war may have caused certain events to become effaced from his memory. And yet, it seems unlikely that a man of Messiaen's genius would unknowingly omit such important information as the roots of his work's inspiration, especially when this information makes for such an interesting story.

The most obvious reason for these different versions is that it makes for a shorter story that is easier to explain to interviewers. By incisively recalling the events leading up to his imprisonment in Stalag and skipping over the details in Verdun, Messiaen could focus immediately upon the *mise-en-scène*—the prison camp where the *Quartet* was premiered—and then smoothly proceed to recount the most climactic event—the premiere itself.

By stating that the *"Intermède"* was the first movement to be composed, and that it was written for three musicians whom he met in Stalag VIII A, all roughly at the same time, Messiaen also could preclude any doubt that from the very beginning it was intended as a composition for a quartet and not for some other ensemble. Since the piano was the last instrument to arrive in Stalag, the trio for violin, clarinet, and cello served as the core movement and instrumentation to which the piano was then added.[33] But the historical evidence presented in this chapter could be taken to suggest otherwise. When Messiaen composed "Abyss of the Birds," he could not have been sure that he would have access to any other instruments anytime soon. Had those instruments not been procured, "Abyss of the Birds" would now stand as an independent composition for unaccompanied clarinet rather than as a movement within a larger chamber work. Except for the 1938 *Quartet* by Hindemith, with which in 1941 Messiaen was not yet familiar,[34] the instrumentation of violin, clarinet, cello, and piano was without historical precedent. Given that Messiaen did not meet Le Boulaire until he arrived in Stalag VIII A, could he have intended to write a trio for clarinet, cello, and piano, the genre made famous by Beethoven and Brahms? Pasquier is not sure, although he has said that when he, Messiaen, and Akoka arrived in Stalag, they "were looking" for a violinist, a statement which seems to confirm that, from the beginning, Messiaen had intended to write a quartet for violin, clarinet, cello, and piano.[35]

Another reason why Messiaen may have claimed that *"Intermède"* was the first movement of the *Quartet* to be composed is that it also makes for a neater analytical discussion of the work. Let us not forget that Messiaen was a renowned pedagogue and theorist as well as a composer. In explaining to his students the genesis of the *Quartet* it makes sense, from a compositional standpoint, that a less complex and less ambitious movement might serve as the starting point—the prelude to rather than the interlude for—a much greater composition. *"Intermède"* is the lightest movement and rhythmically and harmonically the simplest as well. It also contains thematic fragments, *"rappels mélodiques"* [melodic recalls] that Messiaen suggested served as a foundation for material in some of the other movements.

The final reason why Messiaen may have offered a different version of the compositional history of the *Quartet* is that he may simply have desired to be diplomatic. Messiaen's version of the story implicitly attributes equal importance to the roles of the violinist, the cellist, and the clarinetist in the inspiration of his *Quartet*. On the other hand, if Messiaen told Pasquier's version of the story, had he stated that the clarinet movement had been written first, then the composer would have been seemingly granting Henri Akoka a more prominent role than that assigned to Etienne Pasquier and Jean Le Boulaire.

The genesis of the *Quartet* is complicated by the fact that two of its movements were reworked from earlier pieces. The fifth movement, "*Louange à l'Eternité de Jésus*" (Praise to the Eternity of Jesus), for solo cello with piano accompaniment, was taken from a section of *Fêtes des belles eaux* for *ondes Martenots* (1937), and the eighth movement, "*Louange à l'Immortalité de Jésus*" (Praise to the Immortality of Jesus), for solo violin with piano accompaniment, was reworked from the organ work *Diptyque* (1930). Messiaen never mentioned whether he composed the fifth and eighth movements with the overall form of the piece in mind (their similarities—both are "songs" in E major that contemplate eternity and thus give the piece symmetry), or whether he transcribed them from earlier pieces at a later stage, due to pressure to complete the composition.[36]

From a diplomatic standpoint, it would make sense that these movements were composed earlier, for, after "Abyss of the Birds," Messiaen would want to reassure the cellist and violinist that they too would get solo movements. This theory makes sense from a practical standpoint as well, for, like "Abyss of the Birds," the fifth and eighth movements could have been rehearsed without a piano. Indeed, Messiaen's decision to employ the full ensemble of instruments in only four movements—the first, second, sixth, and seventh—may have been pragmatic as well as aesthetic. Though the sixth movement, written entirely in unisons, and the middle section of the second movement for string duo with piano accompaniment, could have been rehearsed without a piano, the first, seventh, and outer sections of the second are far too rhythmically complex to have been rehearsed with only violin, clarinet, and cello.

These are just some of the possible explanations for the discrepancies between Messiaen's account of the origins of the composition of the *Quartet* and the account presented here. As we proceed, more questions will arise.

Curiously, the story of the composition of the *Quartet* has been virtually unquestioned. In spite of the numerous allusions to the piece in

Technique of My Musical Language (1944) and the wealth of published interviews with Messiaen, we know very little about the *Quartet*'s creation. This absence of knowledge only magnifies the composer's elusiveness; his omissions serve to preserve the myths surrounding the piece and the mystery surrounding the man.

CHAPTER 2

The Quartet in Prison

L ess than two months after the German invasion of May 1940, France surrendered. By 25 June 1940 an armistice had been signed. The terms of the truce provided for a quasi-sovereign French state, in which Germany would occupy the northern two-thirds of France extending along the Atlantic Ocean, while Southern and Mediterranean France would remain under French control with the town of Vichy as its capital. Article 3 of the agreement demanded that the French government aid the German authorities in exercising the "rights of an occupying power" in the Occupied Zone. It ordered French officials and public servants to "conform to the decisions of the German authorities and collaborate faithfully with them."[1] Collaboration, "a banal term for working together, was to become a synonym for high treason after the occupation had run on for four years."[2] While France's surrender and the Vichy government's collaboration directly compromised that country's glorious libertarian past and implicated that great nation in the deportation and execution of France's Jews, ironically, surrender and collaboration also facilitated the creation of Messiaen's *Quartet for the End of Time.*

■

On 25 June 1940, five days after Olivier Messiaen, Etienne Pasquier, and Henri Akoka had been captured, the armistice took effect. After being quartered for approximately three weeks in the open field near Nancy where Akoka read "Abyss of the Birds" for the first time,[3] the musicians and their company were transferred to Stalag VIII A, a German camp for prisoners of war of enlisted rank located on a five-hectare lot (approximately twelve acres) in the town of Görlitz-Moys in Silesia, Germany.[4]

Messiaen's description of his arrival in Stalag VIII A has become the symbol of his determination to survive and ultimately compose under such harsh conditions:

> Upon arriving in the camp of Görlitz, in Silesia, called in military jargon Stalag VIII A, like all the other prisoners, I was at once stripped of my clothing.[5] Naked though I was, I continued to guard with a fearsome look a satchel containing all of my treasures, that is to say, a little library of pocket orchestral scores that would be my consolation when, like the Germans themselves, I suffered from hunger and cold. This eclectic little library ranged from the *Brandenburg concerti* of Bach to the *Lyric Suite* of Berg.[6]

That "fearsome look," Messiaen said in a later interview, was directed toward an armed soldier who tried to confiscate his music: "There was a soldier with a submachine gun who wanted to take away my satchel. I gave him such a terrible look that it was he who was afraid, and it was I, who, completely naked, got to keep my music."[7] Yvonne Loriod's description imbues the scene with additional pathos:

> Imagine the picture: Messiaen, completely naked with this little satchel of four or five scores of Stravinsky, Debussy, and others that he clutched to his heart because he didn't want them to be confiscated. And he struggled with the German officers, who wanted to take away his music. He was so mean to this one German officer that the officer was afraid and let him keep his scores.[8]

Although in its retelling the moving description may have acquired an element of dramatization, it nevertheless illustrates an important point that will recur throughout this story. How much Messiaen actually struggled with the German officer to keep his scores may not be certain, but what is sure is that the officer allowed him to keep them. This incident would actually foreshadow the composer's subsequent treatment in Stalag VIII A. Not only was Messiaen treated kindly, he was encouraged to compose, and the performance of his music was not only facilitated, but celebrated.

■

Between the years 1939 and 1945, approximately 120,000 prisoners of war passed through Stalag VIII A.[9] The first to enter the camp on 7 September 1939 were 8,000 Poles, followed by 2,000 more just a few days later. As the war continued, they were joined by Belgians, French,

Serbs, Russians, Italians, British, and Americans.[10] During the time that Messiaen was there, there were approximately 30,000 prisoners in Stalag VIII A, the majority of them French.[11] Most of these prisoners, however, were not housed on the grounds of the camp, but lived in outlying *commandos*, annexes where they were sent to work on farms and in mines and factories. Thus, at any given time, only about a thousand prisoners actually lived in the camp itself.[12]

When the first prisoners of war arrived in Stalag VIII A in September 1939, the camp was in its earliest phase of construction. The Polish prisoners, who slept in tents intended for 300–500 men, were forced to build barracks. Germany's unexpectedly rapid conquest of France compounded the lodging problem, for suddenly thousands of French prisoners of war had to be accommodated. By December 1939, the move from tents to barracks had begun, although tents were still being used as late as the end of 1940.[13] Thus, when Messiaen, Pasquier, and Akoka arrived in the summer of 1940, Stalag VIII A was still under construction (see fig. 9).

The sudden surge of French prisoners that summer also created food shortages. For many months, until the Red Cross arrived, inmates of Stalag VIII A barely subsisted. Even after the intervention of the Red Cross, the food rations were insufficient. Yvonne Loriod claimed Messiaen had nothing to eat all day except a bowl of soup with whale fat at noon and that he and his fellow prisoners consoled each other by reciting menus and recipes to each other: "So Monsieur Pasquier would say, 'Do you remember, Olivier, duck *à l'orange*? You see, it's made like this: you sauté this, and then you boil that. . . . '"[14] Pasquier recalled that a typical day's fare was ersatz (a coffee substitute) for both breakfast and lunch, accompanied by one piece (per day) of black bread "with a lump of fat on it," and nothing at all for dinner. That lasted for a few weeks, recalled Pasquier, until the Red Cross managed to get packages to them. Subsequently, they were regularly served a stew of boiled potatoes, turnips, and cabbage. But for many weeks, he said, they were "dying of hunger." The Germans did not intend to starve their prisoners to death, claimed Pasquier, but were not prepared for the sudden influx of so many French prisoners. "We could have adequately fed 100 men. There were thousands!" said Pasquier.[15]

Still, even after the intervention of the Red Cross, the physical condition of the prisoners of war, though obviously not as appalling as that of the deportees, was extremely precarious. Most of the prisoners became dangerously thin. Pasquier, who was slim to begin with, lost approximately twenty pounds.[16] Some prisoners lost their hair and teeth. Messiaen also developed chilblains due to the extreme cold and malnutrition.[17]

The Red Cross helped prisoners send and receive mail. However, the Germans inspected all incoming and outgoing mail and permitted packages only to Western Europeans. The latter were also allowed to send and receive a greater number of letters than the Eastern European prisoners.[18]

By the beginning of 1941, just in time for a brutal winter, fifty-six barracks had been built.[19] Each of the prisoners' barracks, approximately 55 yards long and 10 yards wide, was furnished with three-tiered bunk beds and wooden benches and tables. In the middle of each barrack was a washing area of approximately eleven square yards, with running water that drained into an outside ditch.[20] Although the barracks were heated by an earthen stove, most prisoners still suffered from the cold. Pasquier joked that the barracks were actually heated by "living furnaces"—the inmates.[21] Each barrack had enough beds for approximately 175 men,[22] although some apparently had enough *couchettes* for as many as 222 persons (see figs. 10–11). Prisoners were usually separated by nationality, but sometimes also by profession or by camp occupation. Clergymen, for example, were placed in a separate barrack. Messiaen, housed in barrack 19A with other French and Belgian prisoners,[23] often took refuge in the barrack of Catholic priests in order to read in peace and quiet.[24] Pasquier lived with the cooks, as he and about forty other prisoners had the privilege of working in the kitchen, where they could prepare their own meals. The kitchen duty also enabled him to sell potatoes to other prisoners and to steal bread, sugar, and even *fromage blanc* (similar to yogurt or sour cream) that he shared with his comrades. He was never caught.[25]

By the beginning of 1941, the camp had twenty barracks for prisoners, two for camp officials, and twelve for watchmen. In addition, there were several latrines, two infirmaries, two kitchens, a canteen, a barrack of showers, a barrack for directing mail, and even one barrack designated as a theater and another as a chapel and camp library (see figs. 12–13).[26] A later plan shows a more developed camp, with a sports field where prisoners played soccer, handball, volleyball, and ping pong,[27] as well as several more barracks (see fig. 14).[28]

In general, conditions in Stalag VIII A improved as German victories mounted and as France continued to collaborate. In the fall of 1940, the Stalag library had only 500 volumes. One year later, its collection had increased to 6,000, and by 1943, to 10,000. A small ensemble of Polish musicians grew into a twenty-four-piece multinational classical orchestra conducted by a Belgian prisoner, Ferdinand Caren (see fig. 15).[29] There was also a jazz band.[30] Their programming was rigorously controlled; patriotic music was prohibited. From 1941 to 1944 the camp officers organized art exhibitions under the direction of prisoner Albert Moira. There was also a monthly newspaper put out by the prisoners, *Le lumignon* (The Light), though, of course, its content was censored (see fig. 16).[31] Jules Lefebure, a prisoner in Stalag VIII A from April 1941 to April 1943, described the camp as "a veritable university" with academic conferences and courses in English and German.[32]

Compared to the descent into nothingness of the concentration camps, the "civilized" ambience of Stalag VIII A, with its many cultural and recreational outlets, may come as a surprise, but it explains how the composition and premiere of the *Quartet for the End of Time* were realized. Not all the prisoners of Stalag VIII A had access to the same privileges, however. After Messiaen's departure, the camp was split into two sections, one predominantly for West Europeans, the other for Russians and Italians. The Russians arrived on 5 January 1942, while the Italians, who began arriving in December 1943 following the fall of Mussolini, were regarded as traitors and placed with the Russian prisoners as punishment.[33] All the cultural and recreational resources—the theater, chapel, library, kitchen, canteen, and sports area—were on the Western European side. This differential treatment of prisoners according to nationality is clear from prisoners' testimonies. "Sometimes, I saw Poles who were treated very badly, who wouldn't obey orders," recalled Pasquier. "They would strike them with clubs. But strike the French, never."[34]

It seems, however, that in Stalag VIII A, as in many other prison camps, preferential treatment was partially determined not only by nationality but by profession, and musicians were especially privileged, a disposition probably due to Germany's long musical tradition, as Philippe Akoka pointed out: "The Germans had respect for music and musicians. This is the only favorable thing that I can say about them. They loved music very deeply, and so musicians were given a relatively free ride."[35] Henri's brother Lucien, a trumpeter interned for five years in Stalag IX A in Ziegenhain, Germany, recalled that musicians received more food as well as more coal, which is why one of his fellow inmates, François Mitterrand, a lawyer who became president of France from 1981 to 1995, used to frequent the musicians' barracks:

Everyone suffered in the prison camps, but the musicians had several advantages. Among the prisoners, all the professions were represented, but in my camp the artists were privileged. I myself remember that instead of having a loaf of bread for six, we had a loaf of bread for four. We didn't have any meat, but the soup that they gave us everyday was a little thicker. We got a little more coal to keep warm. We had a lot of things that other prisoners didn't have. We were lodged in special barracks. That is why Mitterrand, who was a prisoner in our camp, was always with us, in the musicians' barracks. Because it was warmer in our barrack. During the winter of 1941–1942, it was -30° Celsius [-22° Fahrenheit].[36]

But Lucien viewed the good treatment of musicians on the part of the Germans more cynically than did his nephew. In Lucien's camp, where an orchestra of approximately fifty musicians was created under the direction of the esteemed Jean Martinon,[37] the Germans gave musicians instruments and rehearsal space in order to show the world, namely the Red Cross, that they were taking good care of their prisoners, and to ensure France's continued collaboration:

The Germans, wanting to have a good image, delegated certain officers to look after the musicians. They set up a rehearsal hall for us and gave us instruments. They provided me with a trumpet. They gave violins to the violinists. Where did these violins come from? I think that they came from Germany, because at this time, in 1941, they hadn't yet run off with everything that they had been able to steal. The Germans didn't take instruments away; on the contrary, they gave them to us. They wanted us to arrange concerts for the German officers and for the prisoners. "We're taking care of the prisoners," they'd say. "You have no choice but to collaborate."[38]

The Germans, due to their musical tradition, exhibited respect for musicians. "One must admit," said Loriod, "that the Germans, though Nazis, were musicians."[39] However, as is now commonly known, the Nazis were also experts in the dissemination of propaganda. The best example of the way the Nazis used musicians as tools of propaganda is the camp of Theresienstadt, conceived by Reinhard Heydrich, one of the devisers of the Final Solution, as a "transit ghetto" for Jews heading for the death camps. Artists were gathered in this ghetto to convince Red Cross delegations that Jews were being well treated.[40]

As in Lucien Akoka's camp, Stalag IX A, musicians in Stalag VIII A also received preferential treatment. Prisoners in Stalag VIII A who were not sent to work in the *commandos* (labor areas located outside the camp) were generally employed as tailors, cobblers, cooks, or orderlies, or were made to do the camp laundry.[41] Musicians, however, at least the ones in Messiaen's circle, often were relieved of the more disagreeable duties. Soon after his arrival in Stalag VIII A, Pasquier, for example, was sent to a granite mine in Strigau, a *commando* approximately sixty miles from the camp, where he was an excavator in charge of loading wagons with stone for funerary monuments. "We were twenty-eight in a room which was built for ten. We were one on top of the other," said Pasquier. "And I nearly lost a finger with a chainsaw."[42] Upon the intervention of one of his comrades, actor René Charles, who told the camp officials that if Pasquier continued working in the granite mine, he might risk his musical career, Pasquier was ordered back to the camp. There he was assigned the privileged position of camp cook, the job that he held for the rest of his captivity. The cellist attributed the special treatment he received to the press releases that he had brought with him, which excerpted newspaper reviews from all over the world (see fig. 17): "I was brought back to the camp upon orders of the camp administration, because my two brothers and I were already known as musicians in Germany! I had press releases. . . . I could have stayed there in Strigau for many years, working in the mines, but I was brought back to the camp upon the order of the commandant."[43]

The special treatment that Messiaen received in this camp is even more remarkable. He was allowed to go on watch in the wee hours of the morning so that he could have peace and reflect on his composition. This is how one early morning, recalled Loriod, Messiaen saw the aurora borealis, the extraordinary colors in the sky that no doubt intensified his fascination with color, a fascination that he would eventually express in his music.[44] Messiaen recalled doing chores twice a day,[45] but Charles Jourdanet, one of Messiaen's comrades who was present at the famous premiere in Stalag VIII A, wrote, "I can testify that he who we affectionately called 'the French Mozart' was relieved of all chores by the barrack members themselves."[46] Pasquier corroborated Jourdanet. Once it became known that Messiaen was a famous composer, said the cellist, he was immediately exempted from prisoners' duties and placed in a barrack so that he could compose in peace.

Messiaen was recognized by the camp authorities. He had already had his music played *before the war*! All of the critics agreed that he was absolutely extraordinary. When the Germans learned of this, they put him in a barrack and told him: "Compose. You're the one who's a composer, so compose. We won't let anyone disturb you." So, we would bring him things to eat. It was out of the question for Messiaen to work. He was composing all the time.

A guard was placed at the entrance to Messiaen's barrack in order to prevent people from entering. "They were like that, the Germans," added Pasquier.[47]

Loriod agreed that Messiaen was allowed to compose in peace and quiet, but hers is a less benign version. She asserted that Messiaen was locked up to compose not in a barrack, but in one of the camp latrines:

> So, what is remarkable and what my husband would say is that, since he was viewed as a very quiet man, one who wouldn't hurt any-one, who asked for nothing, a German officer said to him: "Sir, I see that you're a musician and so from time to time I'm going to give you a piece of bread, and pencils and manuscript paper as well. And so that you will have some peace, I am going to lock you up in the la-trines, so that you can be left to work quietly." Imagine how moving it must have been! Poor Messiaen, in the prisoners' toilets, used by 3,000 people. They weren't very clean. And he was locked up in the toilets so that no one would bother him, so that he could write the *Quartet*. You see what kind of suffering he underwent.[48]

Whether Messiaen composed in the barracks or the latrines, "what I know is that we were not allowed to disturb him,"[49] said Pasquier. Certainly, the description of Messiaen composing the divinely inspired music of the *Quartet* in the prisoners' latrines evokes quite a different image than that presented by Pasquier. In the former, the German officer is portrayed almost as a saint, whereas in the latter, he is portrayed as a human being who inflicts punishments and bestows rewards. Both from Messiaen's testimony and from that presented by other prisoners in the camp, it seems that Pasquier's version might be closer to the truth. This does not mean that Messiaen never composed in the camp latrines, but simply that the motives of the German officer seem to have been sincere.

■

In countless accounts of the history of the *Quartet for the End of Time*, reference is made to the German officer who gave Messiaen the

supplies with which he wrote his beloved composition. Messiaen remembered: "Outside of some required chores, I was soon able to enjoy
relative tranquility, the Germans considering me to be someone perfectly inoffensive. . . . Moreover, as they've always respected music,
wherever it is to be found, not only did they let me keep my scores, but
an officer gave me pencils, erasers, and manuscript paper."[50]

For years, however, the German officer described above went unnamed. Then, in an interview in 1991, one year before his death, Messiaen revealed the identity of the mysterious man:

> A German officer who was not part of Stalag but who was a lawyer in
> civilian life—I don't know anything else about him except that he
> was called Monsieur Brüll—secretly brought me a piece of bread two
> or three times, and, something marvelous, he knew that I was a com-
> poser, and he brought me manuscript paper, pencils, and erasers. And
> this enabled me to work.[51]

If the Angel of the Apocalypse inspired Messiaen to compose, Monsieur Brüll could be said to be the angel's emissary, providing Messiaen
with the means to realize his artistic inspiration. Brüll not only helped
Messiaen's quartet members; he was one of the few officers who went
out of his way to protect Jewish prisoners.

A lawyer by profession, Hauptmann Karl-Albert Brüll was born to a
German father and a Belgian mother. His father was president of the
Catholic Youth of Silesia. From his mother, a citizen of Liège, Belgium,
Brüll learned French, which he spoke fluently. In Stalag VIII A, Brüll
was employed as a guard.[52] He was unarmed.[53]

David Gorouben, a French prisoner in Stalag VIII A, never met
Olivier Messiaen, as he was sent from the camp in 1941 to work in
downtown Görlitz as a leather craftsman, but he knew Hauptmann
Brüll quite well. Taken prisoner on 21 June 1940, Gorouben was trans-
ferred to Stalag VIII A, where he worked as an interpreter for six
months, having learned German from a cousin who was a high school
German teacher in Paris. It was there in the camp that he met Karl-
Albert Brüll.

"Brüll was a German Nationalist, but an anti-Nazi," wrote Gorouben. "As early as 1940, he told me that Germany would lose the war,
and so he raised my morale." Brüll helped many prisoners of Stalag VIII
A. Because of his fluency in French, however, he was of particular help
to the French and Belgian prisoners. Like the other Francophones in
the camp, Gorouben was grateful to find an officer who spoke his na-

tive language. He was especially relieved, moreover, to come upon a German officer who was sympathetic to the plight of Jews, for Gorouben, born in Paris, was of Russian-Jewish origin. Brüll apparently helped Gorouben and many other Jews in the camp, advising them not to attempt to escape, for if they were caught, he said, they might risk being deported: "We became very good friends as he would seek out many of the Jewish prisoners to advise and help us as much as he could. He advised me not to escape and told me that as long as I had the uniform I was protected, whereas if I returned to France, I would risk being arrested and deported. I therefore stayed in Görlitz for five years."[54]

Given the thoroughness of Hitler's Final Solution, one might wonder how a Jew was able to remain undetected in a camp such as Stalag VIII A, when the majority of European Jews eventually wound up in camps such as Auschwitz-Birkenau, entrance to which virtually ensured extinction. It must be recalled, however, that Jews were not barred from the French military until 3 October 1940, after the defeat of France, when a series of anti-Semitic measures were enacted by the Vichy government.[55] Gorouben was mobilized in September 1939. His *double appartenance* seems to have been in his favor, for he was considered to be a West European residing in France, and, once in the camp, was exempt from the fate of East European Jewish prisoners, 1,523 of whom were deported from Stalag VIII A to Lublin en route to their eventual "unknown destination" on 4 February 1941. According to Hannalore Lauerwald, author of *Im Fremden Land*, a documented history of Stalag VIII A, not a single West European Jewish prisoner at Stalag VIII A was deported: "They could circulate just as freely as their comrades, protected by the uniform of their fatherland."[56] Jews like Gorouben, therefore, seemed to be relatively safe in the camps for prisoners of war. French Jewish civilians, on the other hand, were less fortunate. Systematic mass deportations of Jews in France's Occupied Zone began in May and June 1942.[57]

The Vichy government's role in the persecution of the Jews might seem tangential in a book about Messiaen's *Quartet for the End of Time*. In fact, it is directly relevant. Had Messiaen and his fellow musicians not been ready to perform the *Quartet* until one month later, on 15 February rather than on 15 January, and had the Nazis demanded the deportation of West European as well as East European Jewish military prisoners from Stalag VIII A on 4 February 1941, then the premiere of the *Quartet* might never have taken place. Why? Simply because Henri

Akoka, the clarinetist for whom the work was written, was Jewish. This fact has hardly been mentioned in any publication about the *Quartet for the End of Time*, although the composer himself was aware of it. As we shall see, the tale of Akoka's survival contains as many miraculous twists and turns as the story of the Messiaen *Quartet* itself.

CHAPTER 3

Preparing the Premiere

W ith the assistance of the German officer, Karl-Albert
Brüll, Messiaen was well on his way to realizing the
composition of the *Quartet*. But for the premiere,
one vital role yet to be assigned was resolved with the arrival of a violinist, Jean Le Boulaire (see fig. 18).

Eugène Jean Le Boulaire was born on 2 August 1913 in Saint-Ouen-sur-
Seine, France, into a family of four children.[1] His father, like Pasquier's,
Messiaen's, and Akoka's, had been summoned to fight in World War I, and
these early ugly images of war, combined with Le Boulaire's own later experiences in World War II, profoundly affected him. "My first recollections as a child were of men maimed and gassed, horrible men that we
called *'les gueules cassées'* [broken faces]," he wrote. "My school buddies
were for the most part war orphans. Many others besides myself lived the
same horrors and I prefer that it all be forgotten."[2]

At the age of seven, Le Boulaire began lessons on the violin, an instrument whose "800 grams of wood made wonderful sounds that captivated [him],"[3] and at fourteen he entered the Paris Conservatory. Although he and Messiaen never met during their years at the
Conservatory, Le Boulaire was aware of the young composer's presence.
Unfortunately, unlike Messiaen, Le Boulaire did not receive a *premier
prix*. "This failure," he wrote, "was very difficult to forget."[4]

Having served in the military from 1934 to 1936, Le Boulaire was re-
mobilized in 1938. He described the events leading up to his captivity
in the summer of 1940:

> A desperate flight of the French army. After the Battle of Dunkerque
> [June 1940], we fled to England. From there, we traversed the south of
> England and were sent back to France via Brest [in Brittany]. You can
> see the detour that we made. We began struggling to return to Paris.
> It's then that we were taken prisoner in conditions that were ab-
> solutely so rotten, so ugly that I don't even want to talk about them.[5]

Le Boulaire was then sent to Stalag VIII A, where Messiaen, Pasquier, and Akoka were being held. Aside from cleanup duties, which were required of Akoka and, at first, of Messiaen as well, Le Boulaire had few chores.[6] To escape from boredom, he took refuge in books or in shower baths: "It was infernal to live there. Life was totally monotonous. We were condemned to die of boredom. There was nothing to do. I spent my time chasing after books. Trying to read something, do something, and, if possible, to take a shower. [He laughs.] That was the great occupation."[7]

But Le Boulaire had gotten a lucky break in the barracks assignment, for he found himself in the very same bunk as a certain French clarinetist.[8] It was Henri Akoka who informed him that Messiaen was in the same camp.[9] Word was passed on to the composer, and before long the trio became a quartet. The four instrumentalists, alas, had only one instrument—Akoka's clarinet. Pasquier and Le Boulaire had been unable to bring their instruments and Messiaen obviously had no piano.

Some musicians who were prisoners were able to buy instruments with money earned doing small jobs in the camp, while others shared instruments supplied by the Red Cross.[10] Le Boulaire described the situation:

> There were 40,000 [actually about 30,000] men there and there were four or five violins, one or two cellos, and one piano, you understand? The only personal instrument was Akoka's clarinet. The English, the Poles would also ask for a little music and so we had to share all this. This resulted in a horrible situation. How could one manage to play something like Messiaen's *Quartet* under these conditions? It was very difficult.[11]

In the case of the *Quartet* musicians, "quite probably," said Abbé Jean Brossard, a French priest interned in Stalag VIII A from October 1940 to February 1945[12] who was present at the premiere, "the instruments were furnished by the camp authorities, all too happy to show their magnanimity and their taste for great music."[13]

Pasquier and Le Boulaire corroborated Brossard's conjecture. Le Boulaire attributed their acquisition of instruments to Brüll, the same officer who provided Messiaen with pencils, erasers, and manuscript paper. Pasquier said the instruments were provided by the camp commandant, a man he did not mention by name, but who was probably Alois Bielas, the German commandant of Stalag VIII A from 7 August 1940 to 2 July 1943:[14]

We were extraordinarily lucky to have a camp commandant, a German, who loved music, who understood the situation. Incidentally, I never met this man. A prisoner's life is like a goldfish's in a pond. You always see the same faces.[15]

When the camp commandant realized that there were musicians (I had press releases), he arranged for Messiaen to have a piano, for Le Boulaire to have a violin, and for me to have a cello.[16]

Pasquier was afforded the privilege of selecting an instrument himself. In a charming story, he recalled going with two armed guards to a dealer in downtown Görlitz to buy a cello, bow, and rosin using the sixty-five marks that the prisoners had generously donated out of their earnings from chores. When he returned to the camp at six o'clock, the end of the workday, the prisoners were elated, he said, and they begged him to play for hours:

Oh! They cried for joy. In my whole life, I have never seen such enthusiasm. They made me play until the curfew. And I noticed something. These people, who, from a musical point of view, were completely uneducated, sensed that I was not meant to play popular tunes. They were very enthusiastic when I played the "Swan" of Saint-Saëns [from Carnival of the Animals], the "Air" from Bach [suite for unaccompanied cello]. They went wild. I later played for them a popular tune as well, "Les mignons d'Arlequin." So, this was a good sign. These were people who sensed immediately that I was a serious musician.[17]

As the camp authorities had not yet been able to obtain a piano, aside from the unaccompanied clarinet movement that Akoka had already begun to practice, the musicians could rehearse only the fourth movement, the trio, in its entirety, which they read for the first time in one of the barrack washrooms.[18]

Not until a piano arrived was the quartet able to attack the entire piece from beginning to end, and only then was the composer granted the pleasure of hearing his masterpiece performed.[19] From that moment on, however, the camp theater became the center of these four men's musical existence.

■

Soon after the signing of the armistice between France and Germany on 25 June 1940, the camp authorities designated Barrack 27 for plays, concerts, and movies. The larger half of the barrack was transformed into a theater, with enough wooden benches for the seating of approximately four hundred people; the lavatories became a stage, and the rest of the barrack served as a dressing room.[20]

Messiaen, along with artists Henri Marty, Lucien Vial, René Vernett, and P. Legrand, among others, was instrumental in the founding of this theater.[21] With the help of the camp authorities, Feldvebel Pluscher and Lagermeister Vogl, the theater was equipped with sets, costumes, wigs, musical instruments, and more.[22] The theater troupe created a repertoire that ranged from classical to contemporary, including comedies, satires, operetta, and French plays (see fig. 19). Female roles, naturally, were played by men.[23] One prisoner recalled that there was even a ballet.[24] On 24 November 1940 the theater gave its inaugural performance in the presence of the camp commandant and several officers, as well as hundreds of prisoners.[25]

At the time that Messiaen, Pasquier, Akoka, and Le Boulaire were in the camp, the full classical orchestra and jazz band that would later dominate the concerts in this theater had not yet been formed, but actor René Charles had obtained permission from the camp authorities to organize weekly chamber music concerts and variety shows.[26] And so, every Saturday evening, prisoners crowded into Barrack 27, in search of refuge from the daily monotony.[27] The classical concerts began at six o'clock and were followed an hour later by variety shows organized by Charles, featuring singers, instrumentalists, comedians, storytellers, and acrobats.[28] One ticket cost twenty pfennigs and all shows ended in time for the nine o'clock curfew.[29] Pasquier recalled the consistently high attendance at the classical concerts: "We would tell everyone, 'Don't come until 7 if you don't like classical music.' But they would all arrive at 6! To listen to classical music—people who had no musical education whatsoever! The barrack was always full."[30]

Barrack 27 was also used as a movie theater and lecture hall. The movie showings, organized by the camp authorities, usually featured propaganda films,[31] but the lectures presented by the prisoners embraced a variety of topics. One of the most famous was given by Messiaen himself. Aware of the composer's religiosity and of his interest in the Apocalypse, a Catholic priest had invited Messiaen to speak on the importance of color in the Book of Revelation before a group of other prisoner priests, who, the composer claimed, "incidentally approved of [his] commentaries."[32] "I was very surprised to be listened to so attentively," said Messiaen. "It was this conference, this angel [crowned with a rainbow] finally, that rekindled my desire to compose."[33] The lecture, a precursor to the *Quartet*, entitled "Colors and Numbers in the Apocalypse," certainly must have ignited ecclesiastical curiosity about this "composer/priest" from France, for on 15 January 1941 the clergy showed up en masse, recalled Abbé Jean Brossard, who was present at both the lecture and the musical premiere.[34]

Not long after Messiaen's lecture, the German officers brought into the camp an "upright piano that was extremely out-of-tune, whose keys intermittently stuck."[35] It was this piano that was used for all concerts and variety shows, and on which Messiaen premiered the *Quartet*, following a number of other performances by members of the ensemble (see fig. 20). Pasquier recalled the evening that he, Messiaen, and Akoka played Beethoven's Trio, Op. 11, for clarinet, cello, and piano, to a packed house of prisoners, who afterward waited eagerly for the chance to exchange a few words with the composer:

> December 1940, Stalag VIII A, in Görlitz in Silesia, the end of a musical performance granted to the war prisoners. Outside it is bitter cold and pitch black. But a group of music-lovers wait for one of the artists to emerge, the one who is the driving force behind this concert. His name is Olivier Messiaen, the famous composer and organist at Trinity Cathedral in Paris. In spite of the freezing wind, he responds graciously to the many requests for meetings that are being addressed to him. I am right next to him, exhilarated from having performed the Beethoven Trio with him and Henri Akoka. Fortunately, the camp commandant understood the importance of the presence of this young and already famous master. He would give a lot of time to his fellow prisoners and would comfort them. That, the officer knew well.[36]

An unnamed prisoner who was present at the premiere of the *Quartet* also recalled attending an earlier performance at which the group played a transcription of Beethoven's Seventh Symphony: "This performance moved me, I who, until that moment, had been totally ignorant of classical music."[37]

As time went on, Messiaen became something of a celebrity in Stalag VIII A. Prisoners besieged him with requests for consultations. "There were all these people who would come to ask Messiaen for advice," claimed Pasquier, "because he was an exceptional musician. But he was also a poet! His mother was a poet and his father was an English translator, the most respected in the field." Like star-struck paparazzi, undeterred even by freezing cold temperatures, the prisoners implored the devout composer for inspiration:

> In the camp there were intellectuals, musicians, painters. There were thousands of prisoners, you see. And they would come to arrange interviews with Messiaen. You should have seen it: we were dressed in rags. We had to wait outside in the dreadful cold, and yet people would stand in line to make an appointment with Messiaen. There he was, surrounded by these men who were practically in tatters, standing in a terrible cold that made everyone shiver. But there . . . they would wait patiently in the hopes of getting an appointment with Messiaen. It was absolutely extraordinary.[38]

Other prisoners begged Messiaen and his musician colleagues for autographs, but there was little time to sign them. One autograph, dedicated by Messiaen and Pasquier to André Foulon, secretary of the Stalag theater, has been preserved by Yvonne Loriod (see fig. 21).

With the arrival of the camp piano, Messiaen and his fellow musicians suddenly became quite busy, and meeting the requests of all of the prisoners sometimes became difficult for the composer. Rehearsing with his quartet and making the necessary changes to his composition had to be his first priority. As the four men tackled this extraordinarily difficult work, their technique, their musicality, their relationship, and their thinking became transformed. At the center of their musical universe revolved a mysterious composer whose brilliance reflected wonder and radiated light, but whose unshakeable faith in the face of the seemingly hopeless surroundings often raised puzzling questions.

■

Sometime in November, when the piano finally arrived, the musicians began rehearsing the entire piece as a full quartet.[39] Every evening at six o'clock, Pasquier would leave the kitchen and hurry over to the theater barrack for rehearsal.[40] The camp commandant allowed the musicians four hours of practice a day,[41] which enabled them both to rehearse as an ensemble and to work on their individual parts. Often the German officers would observe them quietly, approaching them with respect after rehearsals.[42]

The musicians also took advantage of Saturday afternoon leisure when prisoners were permitted at least two hours of free time. "At one o'clock, instead of going back to work, we could relax a little and then go to the theater barrack to rehearse, said Pasquier."[43] Messiaen also was able to practice and revise his composition at night while the other prisoners were sleeping. "I think I remember that the kind-hearted Brüll played a great part in this," wrote Le Boulaire.[44] Brüll also helped to provide a comfortable rehearsal environment for the musicians, granting them privileges not accorded their comrades:

> Many men died in captivity. Temperatures of 25° below zero [-13° Fahrenheit] were common. But the barrack in which we rehearsed was better heated than the others, bizarre as it may seem, because this German officer gave us wood. We could warm ourselves up, which was virtually unprecedented for prisoners in these camps. I remember that. We could warm up our fingers. This was already a big advantage. It might not seem enormous, but it was an advantage that a lot of others didn't have.[45]

The rehearsal conditions, however, were far from ideal, acknowledged Le Boulaire: "The 'barrack' 27 for concerts was accessible to all, and thus the site of an often indescribable, deafening mixture of languages. We had great difficulty finding a moment of tranquility where the piano was located."[46] One can imagine the musicians' frustration during rehearsals of the plaintive "Louange" movements in these conditions.

Le Boulaire also recalled brutality in the camps. "When the guards were very strict, there were some very bad incidents. Young men were executed for stealing three potatoes!" But toward musicians, the violinist admitted, the German officers behaved "with total propriety": "I don't know if it was like that everywhere, but to me, the German officers were perfectly behaved. I don't recall there being the slightest brutality. On the contrary, they did everything to help us."[47]

■

With the aid of the camp authorities, three major obstacles to the realization of the premiere of the *Quartet* had been overcome: the lack of instruments, rehearsal space, and time to practice. But the greatest obstacle remained: Messiaen's extremely difficult composition, which has daunted musicians under the best of circumstances.

Those preparing the premiere, however, had the advantage of the composer as both pianist and coach. Messiaen later included some of his comments at these rehearsals in the *Quartet*'s preface:

Read, first of all, the "Commentary" and the "Brief Theory" above. But do not become preoccupied with this in the performance: it will suffice to play the music, the notes, and the exact values, and to faithfully follow the dynamics indicated. In the non-metered movements such as "Dance of Fury, for the Seven Trumpets," you can, to help yourselves, mentally count the sixteenth notes, but only at the beginning of your work: this process may encumber the public performance; you should, therefore, mentally retain the feeling of the rhythmic values, no more. Do not be afraid to exaggerate the dynamics, the accelerandos, the ritardandos, everything that renders an interpretation lively and sensitive. The middle of "Abyss of the Birds," in particular, should be full of imagination. Sustain implac-ably the two extremely slow movements, "Praise to the Eternity of Jesus," and "Praise" to his "Immortality."[48]

Simply reading Messiaen's composition and playing it together were formidable tasks, said Le Boulaire:

The first great difficulty was to read the piece. It wasn't easy. The second was to play it together. That wasn't easy either. From the ensemble standpoint, we had a lot of trouble. Messiaen would give us cues, but that did not make it any less difficult. There are some extraordinary young people today, who certainly manage much better than we did. But we, Pasquier included, ran across something that we had never seen before, and we all stumbled a little.[49]

What Messiaen hated most was being a prisoner of the dictates of conventional rhythm, said Le Boulaire. He would often say, " 'I don't like being binary. I don't like walking on two feet, in steps, in rhythm.' He was unhappy in this sort of rhythmic straitjacket. It annoyed him." But Messiaen's unusual rhythms and frequent elimination of meter posed great challenges to the other three musicians of the quartet, who, as Le Boulaire recalled, felt lost when liberated from the prison of conventional expectations:

Where Messiaen is right is where he says that we're prisoners of rhythm. Aurally, it was very difficult for us to find a straight path in the midst of all these winding roads, in this tangled rhythm, at moments tangled with no point of reference, with no rhythm at all. No longer having our little measure in 4/4 or 3/4 time, we were a little lost.[50]

Even before his arrival in Stalag VIII A, Akoka had encountered some of these difficulties, as mentioned earlier. The excruciatingly long phrases and protracted crescendi in "Abyss of the Birds" necessitated the utmost in breath control from the clarinetist. The composer also asked Akoka for extreme pianissimos in the altissimo register. When reading the piece for the first time in the open field near Nancy, Akoka doubted that he would ever overcome the obstacles facing him on the musical page. Pasquier recalled:

> In the movement for solo clarinet, "Abyss of the Birds," Messiaen asked for unbelievably high notes! And Akoka would protest: "It can't be done." And Messiaen would watch and listen and say: "But yes! You're getting there."[51] . . . Messiaen also wanted Akoka to expand the sound. . . . "It's impossible!" the clarinetist would protest. "But you're doing it! You're getting there!" Messiaen would reassure him.[52]

Even the world-class cellist admitted that Messiaen's music pushed him beyond his limits: "Never were such things asked of a cellist before. I had to acquire a new technique in order to play it."[53] Intonation, in particular, was difficult, said Pasquier, as were the swift leaps from the high register to the low. "And then the system of harmonics. You see, all these harmonics [in the first and fifth movements especially] are very difficult to do."[54]

Le Boulaire was awestruck by the paradoxes of Messiaen's musical style, particularly the composer's juxtaposition of dissonance and consonance evocative of the apocalyptic duel between "monsters and cataclysms" and "adoring silences and wonderful visions of peace":[55]

> There are two ways of appreciating Olivier Messiaen. There's the mystic and there's the man, and the *Quartet* is split between these two things. There's the pure man, that is, the bird-lover, the nature-lover, but there are also some extremely harsh things, which makes one understand very well why there was so much criticism of Messiaen: at moments, it's unlistenable. It's severe, jolting. There's no harmony, no song, no melody, just this harshness. . . . So, we were a little dumbfounded by his music, because, amid all this severity, suddenly, a song would arise.[56]

Most likely, the composer made changes after the initial readings, as the piano did not arrive until later. Le Boulaire recalled seeing the composer revise many of the rhythms, although otherwise, he said, Messiaen kept to himself: "Basically, he was immersed in his own dream and wouldn't come out of it."[57] Pasquier recalled going to the composer's barrack many times to answer technical questions about the cello part;[58] it was the cellist who decided upon many of the bowings, articulations, and fingerings that appear in the published score.[59]

In rehearsals, claimed Pasquier, Messiaen was extremely demanding. To try to render what the composer wanted was frequently difficult:

> Messiaen would demand paroxysmal dynamics. He would say to the clarinetist: "Hold the note until you can't blow anymore at all. Enlarge the sound." Or, he would tap on the piano. He wanted terrifying fortissimos, especially in "Dance of the Seven Trumpets" [the sixth movement].[60] He wanted terrifying effects, but he also wanted very subtle ones. And the rhythms had to be absolutely precise.[61]

In the fifth movement, for cello and piano, the composer insisted that Pasquier adhere to the tempo indicated, despite the cellist's protests that, at such a slow tempo, it was virtually impossible to sustain the bow: "He wanted it *very* slow. Even a slowness that verges on the impossible. So, I would debate with him, because you cannot manage to sustain the bow at that tempo. 'But yes, you're doing it,' he would insist."[62]

To explain the birdcalls in the *Quartet*, Messiaen often whistled, giving indications at the piano or imitating the sound of the clarinet, which Le Boulaire called Messiaen's "instrument of love":

> Messiaen adored the clarinet. He told me so, and he told Akoka as well. And whenever he explained a passage containing a birdcall, he would hum, imitating the clarinet's very sweet sound. He told me that he would spend hours, entire mornings listening to birds. And when he gave indications of birdcalls he would whistle. He whistled very very well. He would also give indications at the piano, saying: "This is a nightingale." And I don't know if it was because we were trying to penetrate his mind or what, but somehow we would manage to hear a nightingale at the piano.[63]

Messiaen made several comments about violin fingerings, but mainly, claimed Le Boulaire, he was uncompromising about rhythm:

> Messiaen asked for different fingerings, to glissando or not to glissando, to emphasize a certain note or part of a phrase. Rhythmically, it had to be absolutely steady. These pylons, this "granite," can not waver [alluding to the composer's commentary on the sixth movement in the preface]. He was uncompromising about that. I under-

stood, and I did my best to observe those rhythms. Because it was the only way the piece could be.[64]

Regarding the eighth movement, for violin and piano, Le Boulaire remembered Messiaen insisting that he adhere to the tempo indicated, just as the composer had demanded of Pasquier in the fifth movement. The tempo had to be "inhumanly slow," said Le Boulaire, in order to establish the atmosphere of the great beyond conveyed by the movement's title, "Praise to the Immortality of Jesus": "This slowness is not annoying. On the contrary, I have the impression that this world that we don't know must be, in effect, something rhythmic but extremely calm, calm, calm. It's a sort of superiority to silence. What I find beautiful is this musical silence. One has already left the earth at this moment."[65]

Messiaen was also particular about sound in this movement, said Le Boulaire. "He spoke often of elevation, of ascending." The movement is not traditionally violinistic, he pointed out. It transcends virtuosity. Instead of exploiting the technical agility of the violin, observed Le Boulaire, Messiaen combined slow tempo with the violin's color and high tessitura to create an atmosphere of the beyond, the aura of eternity with which the *Quartet* concludes. The clarinet, cello, and piano writing are similarly unidiomatic. "His music wasn't about instrumentation; it was about something far beyond that. That's where the great genius of Messiaen lies."[66]

■

As the rehearsals of the *Quartet* proceeded, the personal relationships among the performers began to mirror their music-making. Like good chamber musicians who listen, anticipate, and react to one another, who, when well-acquainted with one another's playing, can rely on spontaneous inspiration rather than on pre-planned cues, these men conversed, argued, reflected, and acted, merging dissent into unity while still sounding their individual differences of opinion.

The musicians of the *Quartet* represented a wide range of religious, philosophical, and political views. At the center of this musical circle was Messiaen, whose *Quartet* inspired all but whose religious convictions his colleagues did not share. Around Messiaen, the devout Catholic, revolved Pasquier, raised Catholic but ideologically agnostic; Le Boulaire, also raised Catholic but staunchly atheist by his own admission; and finally Akoka, the secular Jew and ardent Trotskyist. Yet these four men shared a musical mission that united them and spawned a friendship that transcended their differences. Guiding this mission was Messiaen, who, out of respect, was placed slightly apart by the others, said Le Boulaire:

> Our friendship in the prison camp was very warm. I was very close to Akoka and Pasquier, a little more distant from the latter, nevertheless. But with Messiaen, there was a bizarre harmony between us. He was only three years older than I. We could have easily been friends, but we weren't. As bizarre as it may seem, we had respect for this comrade whom we sensed was well above us, superior to us. We all realized that Messiaen was exceptional, and so he was always placed a little bit above us. Respectfully, we listened to him.

Indeed, Messiaen, composer, ornithologist, rhythmician, and devout Catholic, was exalted in the eyes of others. "I fully confess that it's the mystery of this man that I still carry with me," said Le Boulaire. "But that's what is so attractive about Messiaen. He was elusive, a man who lived in his own personal sphere. And that's why I admired him."[67] To other prisoners, destabilized, demoralized, dehumanized by their captivity, Messiaen must have seemed mysteriously at peace. If he was not rehearsing with his comrades or meeting with those prisoners who had arranged consultations with him, he was sequestered in a barrack in order to compose his *Quartet* without interruption. And "every Sunday," said Pasquier, "Messiaen was invisible."[68] On that day the composer was to be found praying in the camp chapel.

To the prisoners and camp authorities of Stalag VIII A, then, Messiaen was awe-inspiring, not simply because of his musical genius, but also because of his seemingly unshakeable faith. As often as his comrades must have attempted to understand his enigmatic music, as much as they must have pondered the root of Messiaen's compositional, poetic, rhythmic, and ornithological genius, they must have wondered what mysterious power enabled this curious man to continue believing in a greater good when the immediate world seemed to be teetering on the edge of an apocalypse. Of course, no one yet knew how prophetic the *Quartet for the End of Time* would be. For the secular musicians of the *Quartet*, who worked and spoke with the composer on a virtually daily basis, and who, like their fellow prisoners, were sometimes prone to despair, this enigmatic genius had a "Messiaenic" effect.

"We had faith in Messiaen," said Pasquier, "and we had faith that the war would come to an end." Denying that he was ever demoralized in

captivity, Pasquier claimed that he was "saved by [his own] optimism. . . . There was propaganda but it never influenced me. I was so
convinced that the Germans would lose in the end. I had a brother who
was always very pessimistic but my morale was very high."[69] "I never
doubted that we would throw the Germans out the door. I was sure that
they would lose. . . . I was about thirty-five years old. I still had my
strength."[70]

Always there was Messiaen, the composer who, though "persuaded
that [he] had forgotten everything about music, that [he] would never
again be capable of doing another harmonic analysis, that never again in
[his] life would [he] be able to compose,"[71] found solace when hungry
and cold in his little backpack of holy scriptures and musical scores.
"Messiaen would say that one had to believe in the music," recalled
Pasquier when questioned about the composer's comments during the
rehearsals of the *Quartet*. "We were all good friends. Yes, those were
the days. No, I never lost hope, never."[72]

For Le Boulaire, who was much more pessimistic, Messiaen "radiated a sort of light":

> I'm going to confess something. I am a man who does not believe at
> all. I don't believe in God. I believe that Christ was a man who ex-
> isted, but that's all. Yet when I heard Messiaen's music, I suddenly
> thought that it was possible that there was something. For thousands
> of reasons: his way of expressing himself, his kindness, his gracious-
> ness, his deep studies of music, his love of birds, of wind, of nature.
> . . . All this made an extraordinary impression on me. I stumbled
> upon the question of the divine, but with Messiaen's music I sud-
> denly said to myself: "God . . ."[73]

Although Le Boulaire never argued his religious position with Messiaen, he admitted that the composer made him question his own lack of
faith and brought him solace in his greatest moments of despair:

> I admit that . . . well, I cried certain evenings. But all of a sudden,
> Messiaen would begin to sing. That's what made me really stumble
> over the question of the divine. I would never have dared to broach
> this question with him. Because I would have been derided, and
> moreover I probably wouldn't have understood his argument. But
> when I came upon a man like Messiaen, something occurred that I
> didn't understand, that I still don't understand and that still poses a
> question mark for me. I attribute it to his profound consciousness.

It's he who invented this faith. On music we were in complete agreement, but on the spiritual plane, he posed a question to me that I had never raised anywhere else.[74]

In starkest contrast of all to Olivier Messiaen stood Henri Akoka, who differed from the composer not only in his religion but in his self-formulated philosophy and political ideology. Pasquier recalled that in Stalag VIII A, Messiaen's mantra was "I have faith in God," while Akoka's was "I have faith in Man."[75] "That sums up the basic difference between their natures," explained Lucien Akoka. "Henri was the antithesis—the total opposite—of Messiaen. Messiaen accepted his lot, because God had willed it. But Henri would say, 'We have to get out of here.' While Messiaen was praying, Henri was preparing what he needed to escape."[76]

Henri actually tried to escape twice from Stalag VIII A and, on his second try, succeeded. Lucien claimed that Henri encouraged Messiaen to go with him the first time, but that at the last moment, Messiaen backed down:

Henri said to Messiaen, "Well, Olivier, we're prisoners. We have to escape immediately. I will take care of the provisions, but we're going to have to walk quite a bit." After a few months, the time it took to acquire provisions and a compass, Henri went to see Messiaen: "So, shall we go tomorrow?" "No," Messiaen answered. "I'm staying here, because God has willed that I be here."[77]

Akoka went anyway. In September 1940, he, René Charles, and a Polish prisoner fled the camp, hiding during the day and walking at night, separating whenever they arrived in a village and reuniting whenever it was safe.[78] Akoka, Charles, and the Polish prisoner had traversed nearly 350 miles. They were only about 13 miles from the Czechoslovakian frontier when, one week after their departure, they were caught.[79] In his usual manner, Akoka attempted to win over the German officers with his talent and wit, claimed Le Boulaire:

I don't know how he managed to do it, but Akoka found a way to escape with his clarinet. He had lost half his clothes but not his clarinet. And I think that, when he was caught, he was brought to the office of the camp commandant and managed to charm him with this clarinet, playing the solo from *Pré aux Clercs*. And not once did he lose his instrument.[80]

Akoka was allowed to keep his clarinet and was put in solitary confinement for a couple of weeks, recalled Pasquier. There, in the camp prison, Akoka was treated fairly well:

> It was the only place that was heated, so he was very comfortable there [he laughed]. We would bring him things to eat. He was always reading. He was a great reader, and he was nice and warm for two weeks. He would have liked it to continue, because people left him alone, he didn't have to work, he could read what he wanted, and he ate well [he laughed].[81]

"Being Jewish, Henri was risking a lot," said Lucien. "Many Jews who were caught would disappear; no doubt, they were sent to concentration camps."[82] But Messiaen's hesitance about escaping should not be seen as a sign of a lack of courage. Physically, Henri was hardier than Messiaen and his comrades. "Henri Akoka had incredible energy. . . . He was younger; he was more robust." He wasn't tall, but he was very sturdy. "He found things to eat and he would bring them to us,"[83] recalled the cellist, reiterating how Akoka helped him to walk on the long march to the open field near Nancy, supporting him "until the moment at which [he] was able to make it on [his] own."[84]

Akoka's determination to escape reflected an unwavering resolve. "This was a man who knew how to make decisions,"[85] said Lucien. Henri's son Philippe described his father as "someone who always had '*la pêche*' [the need to get going]." He had an optimism and a sense of humor that helped him get through the war as well as through other difficult times in his life. "My father was never demoralized for a moment in his life," insisted Philippe:

> The very first day that he arrived in the prison camp, he was already thinking about how to escape. He had already made a plan. He tried to escape twice. Moreover, he always spoke to us with joy about this period, even though it was a very difficult time in his life. He would recount his escapes with a lot of humor. He always saw the positive side of life . . . whereas Messiaen had this slightly despondent side.[86]

Akoka also had a rebellious streak in his character that impelled him to break rules, which were, to him, simply a symbol of the despised status quo. "Akoka was a revolutionary. He was a Trotskyist," said Pasquier. "He would say, 'We can succeed only if we're in permanent revolution.' "[87] The clarinetist distributed Trotskyist pamphlets at the Citroën and Renault factories and persuaded his parents to hide Trotskyist refugees in their home during the 1936 war against Franco.[88]

Naturally, Henri's revolutionary ideas conflicted directly with those of the religiously and politically conservative Messiaen, and Henri's politics often spilled into his conversations with the composer. "Henri would try to persuade people. He would try to rally people to his cause. That was his nature. He would never give up,"[89] said his sister Yvonne. Yet, surprisingly, the pious composer who rarely raised his voice[90] was enchanted by this outspoken revolutionary. Lucien attributed Messiaen's fondness for his brother to Henri's unique spirit and wit as well as to his obvious musicianship.[91] Philippe said that "Henri had such charisma, such personality, that no one could remain indifferent to what he said."[92] Moreover, Henri was extremely cultivated and well read, qualities that, in combination with his radical political views, made him a compelling conversationalist. Virtually self-educated, having left school at the age of fourteen to work as a professional musician, Henri was a great reader of Joyce and Shakespeare. The latter he could recite from memory—in English, noted Philippe.[93] Lucien remarked:

> Henri was eminently intelligent. He had read tons of books. He had only a *certificat d'études* [a French diploma that one gets at age fourteen][94] but he knew Montaigne, Rabelais, and all the classics! Henri was very erudite. He also had a great personality and was extremely cultivated. And Messiaen noticed this very quickly. Philosophically, he must have sometimes been in opposition to Messiaen. But Henri must have provided him with some very convincing arguments.
> Henri had something unique, given his political orientation. And Messiaen was captivated.

Messiaen's affection for Henri was mutual. "Henri was very curious about new things," said Lucien Akoka. "He loved modern art. That's why he liked Messiaen's music so much. . . . Because Messiaen was *the* twentieth-century composer, and Henri was a very cultivated man."[95]

"Akoka was Jewish, but he was not religious," recalled Pasquier. "Nevertheless, he and Messiaen, the absolute Catholic, were very good friends." Recalling a statement by Messiaen, Pasquier explained why: "It's funny. Akoka, who believed in revolution, who believed in humanity, and Messiaen, who believed in God, were very good friends . . . because Messiaen would say: 'You see, both of us have faith; it's just not the same kind.' "[96]

So the circle of faith would find its most pivotal completion when the *Quartet for the End of Time* was premiered on 15 January 1941. What would mark the final cadence for this quartet would become a momentous event, a quartet for the end of a time.

CHAPTER 4

Intermède

Before recounting the famous premiere on 15 January 1941, we will take a brief intermission to explore the *Quartet*'s musical content. As in Messiaen's composition itself, this fourth "movement" serves as an interlude and differs in style from the others. It may be helpful to read Appendix A, "Composer's Preface," before this "*Intermède*."

■

Messiaen was a complex man of wide intellectual and aesthetic interests that are directly reflected in his eclectic musical style. Four diverse elements pervade Messiaen's *Quartet for the End of Time:* Catholic doctrine, rhythm, sound-color, and birdsong. Cited in the *Quartet*'s preface and discussed in the composer's subsequent personal commentary, these four elements are fundamental to a basic comprehension of the *Quartet*'s musical language.

■

"I have the good fortune to be a Catholic," said Messiaen. "I was born a believer, and the Scriptures impressed me even as a child. The illumination of the theological truths of the Catholic faith is the first aspect of my work, the noblest, and no doubt the most useful and most valuable—perhaps the only one I won't regret at the hour of my death."[1]

Catholicism guided Messiaen's music as it guided his life. Nearly half his published works allude to biblical, theological, or liturgical subjects. One of Messiaen's most beloved books from the New Testament was the Revelation of Saint John the Divine, in which an angel forecasts the Apocalypse, the destruction of the world, and its subsequent redemption by the Birth, Passion, and Resurrection of Christ. Filled with spectacular images of monsters and cataclysms and colorful visions of rainbows, emerald seas, and a celestial city built of blue sapphires and violet amethysts, the story captivated the composer as a child, said Yvonne Loriod. "When Messiaen was little, he read Shakespeare. 'A super-fairy-tale,' he called it. But when he discovered the Apocalypse, he said it was the most enchanting, the most awesome, and the most wonderful of fairy tales."[2]

The *Quartet for the End of Time* is the second of eight compositions by Messiaen inspired by Revelation. The movement titles and the composer's commentary in the preface, as well as the title of the composition itself, evoke from Revelation one or another of its contrasting paired images of terrifying cataclysm and religious triumph. The following passage, which opens the preface, was the direct source for his inspiration:

> "And I saw another mighty angel coming down from heaven, wrapped in a cloud, with a rainbow on his head; his face was like the sun, and his legs like pillars of fire. . . . Setting his right foot on the sea and his left foot on the land . . . and, standing on the sea and on the land, he raised his right hand toward Heaven and swore by He who lives forever and ever . . . saying: 'There will be no more Time; but in the days when the seventh angel is to blow his trumpet, the mystery of God will be fulfilled.'" (Revelation of Saint John, Chapter 10)[3]

One cannot miss the parallels between the angel's forecast of doom and the portentous events in Europe between 1939 and 1945. To so many survivors of its devastations, World War II was Armageddon. In Stalag VIII A, "in the endless boredom of that camp," as Roger Nichols has written, ". . . it must frequently have seemed . . . that the Angel's prophecy had been fulfilled."[4]

Yet Messiaen denied that the Apocalyptic allusions in his *Quartet*, notably the title itself, bore any relation to his captivity.[5] Moreover, he said, the *Quartet* was never intended to actually depict an apocalypse. The quotation alluded to in the title was "simply a point of departure" for his composition, written for the instruments and instrumentalists that he had on hand.[6] Still, the parallels are ironic, and, the composer conceded, the war did indirectly rekindle his interest in the New Testament story, for the physical deprivation that he experienced in captivity led him to have colored dreams—quasi-hallucinations—that reminded him of the colorful images presented in Revelation. These images drove him, in turn, to reread certain passages:

Curiously, as I had nothing to eat, I would have dreams with colored visions. . . . And because I was having all these colored visions . . . I reread the Apocalypse, and I saw in the Apocalypse that there were a lot of colors, notably two complementary colors, green and red. There was an emerald sea before the celestial throne—this is the color green—and then there was red in several places. Finally, there was an extraordinary being, an angel crowned with a rainbow—the symbol of all colors—and this tremendous angel, . . . immense, greater than our planet . . . lifted his hand toward the heavens and said: "There will be no more time."[7]

The angel crowned with a rainbow was both savior and muse. The source of inspiration for Messiaen's *Quartet*, it was also his source of consolation in the face of hunger, cold, and demoralization in Stalag VIII A, as the composer confessed:

It was an era of dreadful despair. . . . I found myself in Silesia, a prisoner of war. . . . I was persuaded that I had forgotten everything about music, that I would never again be capable of doing another harmonic analysis, that never again in my life would I be able to compose. However, since my mobilization, I had had in my backpack a little book containing, in spite of its very small size, the Psalms, the Gospels, the Epistles, Revelation, and the *Imitation*.[8] This little book never left me; it followed me everywhere. I read and reread it constantly, and I paused upon this vision of Saint John, the angel crowned with a rainbow. I found in it a glimmer of hope.[9]

Crucial to understanding the title of the *Quartet*, said Messiaen, is the translation of the angel's famous words, *"Il n'y aura plus de temps"* (There will be no more time). The quotation appears in many versions of the New Testament as *"Il n'y aura plus de délai"* (There will be no more delay). Messiaen elevated the statement to the sublime, to evoke the idea of eternity:

There are people who understand "there will be no more delay." That's not it. [It's] "there will be no more Time" with a capital "T"; that is to say, there will be no more space, there will be no more time. One leaves the human dimension with cycles and destiny to rejoin eternity. So, I finally wrote this quartet dedicating it to this angel who declared the end of Time.[10]

In the title of Messiaen's *Quartet*, time, in fact, is the key word. "While there is no play on words with reference to the duration of our captivity," said Messiaen, "there is a play on words, perhaps, about which I have often reflected myself, with regard to beats of equal duration in classical music."[11] The dual meaning of the title, as the composer explained, rests not with the notion of the interminability of captivity, but with the composer's desire to eliminate conventional notions of musical time and of "past and future."[12] The notion of time, musical as well as philosophical, is central to a basic understanding of this quartet.

■

> When I was a prisoner, the absence of nourishment led me to dream in color: I saw the rainbow of the Angel, and strange whirling colors. But the choice of "the Angel who announces the end of Time" is based on much more serious factors. As a musician, I focused on rhythm. Rhythm is, in essence, alteration and division. To study alteration and division is to study Time. Time—measured, relative, physiological, psychological—is divided in a thousand ways, of which the most immediate for us is a perpetual conversion of the future into the past. In eternity, these things no longer exist. So many questions! I have posed these questions in my *Quartet for the End of Time*. But, in actual fact, they have guided all of my research in sound and rhythm for some forty years.[13]

Messiaen referred to himself as a *"compositeur et rythmicien"* (a composer and rhythmician),[14] which illustrates the centrality of rhythm to his musical philosophy. "I love time," said the composer, "because it's the starting-point of all creation."[15] The love of time guided all aspects of Messiaen's musical career—his theoretical studies, his musical compositions—and even his taste in performance (apparently, he detested *rubato*, claiming that it "kills rhythm").[16] But Messiaen was dissatisfied with the constraints of conventional rhythm and meter. So he invented a new rhythmic language, drawing upon a variety of sources: ancient Greek meters, Hindu rhythms, and western developments.

Messiaen's teachers at the Paris Conservatory, Marcel Dupré and Maurice Emmanuel, introduced him to ancient Greek meters, and subsequently Messiaen continued studying these on his own. Messiaen's principal source for Hindu rhythms was the thirteenth-century treatise *Samgitaratnâkara* by Çarnagadeva, which lists 120 *deçî-tâlas* (rhythms from the different provinces).[17] In the first movement of the *Quartet,*

"*Liturgie de Cristal*" (Crystal Liturgy), the rhythmic ostinato in the piano part is based upon three of these *deçî-tâlas: râgavardhana, candrakalâ*, and *lakskmîça*.[18]

By altering rhythms, through such techniques as augmentation, diminution, and the "added value" ("a short value, added to any rhythm, whether by a sound, by a rest, or by a dot that prolongs one of the values"),[19] Messiaen created one of his trademarks: "nonretrogradable rhythms"—musical palindromes—"a grouping of values which read identically from left to right or from right to left, that is to say, which present exactly the same successive order of values, read in either direction."[20] The sixth movement of the *Quartet* employs nonretrogradable rhythms as well as augmentation, diminution, added values, and derivations of Greek rhythm and meter:

> This is, above all, a study in rhythm. The theme employs "added values" . . . and Greek feet: second *péon*, second *épitrite, amphimacre, antibacchius*. Toward the middle of the movement, an unexpected pianissimo casts "nonretrogradable rhythms" upon an independent ostinato. Then, the theme, in equal values in the violin and cello, struggles against the augmented and diminuted rhythms, introduced in the low register of the piano and the *chalumeau* register of the clarinet. These are augmentations and diminutions unknown to classical music, such as the addition of a quarter, the addition of a third, the addition of a double and a quadruple, subtraction of the dot and subtraction of ¾ of the value. Time accelerates; a furious stringendo followed by a long trill ushers in the conclusion on the fortissimo theme, which is altered by augmentation and changes of register.[21]

Messiaen described the *Quartet* as one of his "first rhythmically important works."[22] Indeed, the *Quartet for the End of Time* was one of the first works in which Messiaen channeled his research on rhythm into a synthesized form of musical expression. The section of the preface entitled "Brief Theory of My Rhythmic Language" represented, in fact, Messiaen's second important treatise on rhythm (the first being the preface to the 1935 work for organ, *La Nativité du Seigneur*), and as such prefigured his theoretical treatise *The Technique of My Musical Language*, published in 1944, in which the composer drew more examples from the *Quartet* than from any other work.[23]

The rhythmic language employed in the *Quartet*, particularly the use of nonretrogradable rhythms, is one of the technical means by which Messiaen realized the musical "cessation of time,"[24] a metaphor for the religious and philosophical idea of eternity: "The special rhythms, independent of the meter," the composer wrote in the preface, "powerfully contribute to the effect of banishing the temporal."[25]

Messiaen used other means to create the sensation of endlessness in the *Quartet*—most obviously, the length of the work itself (approximately fifty minutes)—but more important, the reliance on rhythmic duration rather than meter (movements 3, 5, and 6), and the use of extremely slow tempi (movements 3, 5, and 8). The overall form of the work also contributes to the idea of interminableness. The fact that there are two finales of notable similarity—two paeans, one "to Jesus's Eternity," the other "to Jesus's Immortality"—both slow solos for string instrument with piano accompaniment, both with the key signature of E major, and both with origins in earlier pieces—the cello movement from *Fête des belles eaux* (1937) and the violin movement from *Diptyque* (1930)—further complicates the sense of normal progression. "Once one knows how the work is going to end . . . the cello movement comes to seem like a finale, with all the rest taking place after the work is over. Alternatively, the potential remains for more movements and more finales, since the work has demonstrated that an apparent conclusion need not in fact be the end."[26]

Finally, the number of movements is in itself symbolic of eternity. As the composer wrote, "This *Quartet* comprises eight movements. Why? Seven is the perfect number, the Creation in six days sanctified by the divine Sabbath; the seventh day of this repose extends into eternity and becomes the eighth day of eternal light, of unalterable peace."[27]

For Messiaen, time was "the starting point of all creation."[28] Certainly, it was the starting point for the creation of the *Quartet*. By overcoming conventional expectations of rhythm and meter, Messiaen in fact "banish[ed] the temporal,"[29] unleashing a musical apocalypse in which one of the central foundations of the compositional universe—time—was no more.

■

Whenever I hear music, I see corresponding colours. Whenever I read music (hearing it in my mind), I see corresponding colours. . . . The colours are wonderful, inexpressible, extraordinarily varied. As the sounds stir, change, move about, these colours move with them through perpetual changes.[30]

The concept of sound-color, the relationship between hearing and seeing, is a fundamental feature of Messiaen's style. For Messiaen, the phenomenon of harmonics was analogous to that of complementary colors, in the sense that the former acts upon the ear, the latter upon the eye.[31] When listening closely to a note struck on the piano, for example, one hears not only that fundamental note, but also, in decreasing intensity, the numerous harmonics emanating from it. A similar phenomenon called "simultaneous contrast" occurs with colors. For example, if one stares at the color red placed alongside a white area, eventually one will see a pale green flashing intermittently upon the white zone, as green is the complementary color of red.[32]

Central to Messiaen's harmonic language are the "modes of limited transposition," a compositional technique in which modes may be transposed by a semitone a certain number of times, after which the original set of notes reappears.[33] As the composer explained, these modes are linked to precise colors that, heard in the same position, always produce the same combinations of hues, but, in their transposed form, yield a different spectrum:

> The first transposition of Mode 2 is defined like this: "blue-violet
> rocks speckled with little gray cubes, cobalt blue, deep Prussian blue,
> highlighted by a bit of violet-purple, gold, red, ruby, and stars of
> mauve, black, and white. Blue violet is dominant." The same mode
> in its second transposition is totally different: "gold and silver spirals
> against a background of brown and ruby-red vertical stripes. Gold
> and brown are dominant." And here's the third transposition: "light
> green and prairie-green foliage, with specks of blue, silver, and red-
> dish orange. Dominant is green."[34]

The second movement of the *Quartet* provides some examples of these colors: "In the piano: gentle cascades of chords blue and mauve, gold and green, violet-red, blue-orange—all dominated by steel grays."[35]

To what can Messiaen's extraordinary sensitivity to color be attributed? Messiaen acknowledged that he was not the first composer to associate colors with sounds. As he pointed out, from Mozart to Chopin to Debussy to Wagner, composers have employed certain chords to deliberately create or evoke images of color.[36] Scriabin, notably, created a novel harmonic and scientific system based on the relationship between sound and color. Like Debussy, Messiaen used timbre as a structural device, elevating it to an importance equal to that of pitch and duration.[37] However, for Messiaen, color had an even more particular function, and the shades that he associated with his sounds were staggeringly specific, as is evident from his description of the transpositions of Mode 2 (above).

The composer cited as one influence his discovery of the paintings and tapestries in "simultaneous contrast" by Robert Delaunay (1885–1941).[38] Messiaen also spoke at length about his meeting with the "painter of sounds"—Charles Blanc-Gatti—who suffered from synopsia, a disorder of the optic and auditory nerves that permitted him to see colors as he heard sounds.[39]

Messiaen traced his first colored emotion, however, to his childhood, when he viewed the stained-glass windows of Sainte Chapelle in Paris for the first time. "For me, that was a shining revelation, which I've never forgotten, and this first impression as a child—I was 10 years old at the time—became a key experience for my later musical thinking."[40] The composer also recalled how, when reading his beloved Shakespeare as a child, he recreated a theater set "that was linked with [his] love for stained glass":

> As a backcloth I used cellophane which I found in sweet-boxes or in cake containers and I would brush it with Chinese ink or just watercolours; then I placed my décors in front of a window-pane and the sun passing through the coloured cellophane would produce luminous and coloured projections on the floor of my little theatre as well as on the *dramatis personae*. Thus I managed to transform my décors just as an electrician controls lighting in a theatre.[41]

One of the greatest inspirations for Messiaen's research into the sound-color relationship was the Revelation of Saint John the Divine. He explained how his feeling of being overwhelmed by the rose windows of the Saint Chapelle, Chartres, Notre Dame, and Bourges cathedrals "became deepened by reading the Apocalypse with its dazzling, fairy-tale colors, which are so much a symbol of the Divine Light":[42]

> The Celestial City is built of many colorful precious stones, of violet amethysts, red rubies, blue sapphires, etc. One thing touched me especially: where it says that One is seated on the throne and His appearance is like fire or like jasper—and fire and jasper are red. And round about Him is a rainbow like an emerald, which is green: two complementary colors, then.[43]

The *Quartet* is unique among Messiaen's compositions in that its "sound-painting" stems not merely from the composer's lifelong fascination with color, but from his physical deprivation as a prisoner in Stalag VIII A. In his commentary on the seventh movement in the preface, Messiaen recalled in dazzling poetic prose the colored dreams that inspired him to reread Revelation:

> In my dreams, I hear and see classified chords and melodies, common colors and forms; then, after this transitory stage, I pass into unreality and lose myself in a rapture to a whirling, a gyrating fusion of superhuman sound and color. These swords of fire, these pools of blue-orange lava, these shooting stars: this is the tangled skein, these are the rainbows![44]

In later compositions, the brush worked hand in hand with the pencil, serving as one of Messiaen's principal guiding instruments.

■

"All the world knows that I'm an ornithologist and what an enormously important place the songs of birds occupy in my work," said Messiaen.[45] From the age of fifteen, when he began notating birdsong in the Aube countryside,[46] Messiaen's love of birds had a profound effect upon his musical compositions. The composer once proclaimed: "It's probable that in the artistic hierarchy, birds are the greatest musicians on our planet."[47]

Though his first reference to birdsong was in *La Nativité du Seigneur* (1935), the *Quartet for the End of Time* was the first composition in which Messiaen made systematic use of birdsong,[48] that is, in which he attempted to depict a particular species.[49] Birdsong would reappear in his subsequent works and function as the principal generating material for the series of compositions written in the 1950s.[50]

Messiaen was not the first composer to take an interest in birdsong, but he was "the first composer of any nationality to take it seriously as an extensive source of musical material."[51] Although numerous compositions throughout the history of Western music, from Couperin's *Rossignol en amour* to Beethoven's *Pastoral* Symphony, have included imitations of birdsong, in most of these works birdsong has been based on a stock repertoire of sounds consisting of staccato arpeggios, trills, and general ornamentation. As Messiaen stated: "All of these bear very little resemblance to real-life bird songs, except for the cuckoo because it's so easy to imitate!" Messiaen was unique in that he attempted to transcribe the exact musical patterns of birds without resorting to formulaic onomatopoeia. Indeed, Messiaen claimed: "I'm the first to have made truly scientific and, I hope, accurate notations of bird songs."[52] An amateur ornithologist, the composer could recognize "by ear and without hesitation the songs of fifty species of birds in France," and, with the aid of a manual, binoculars, and supplementary information, could identify some 550 other species living in France and Europe.[53] Traveling all over the world, including the United States, Asia, and New Caledonia, carrying pencils, manuscript paper, an identification manual, binoculars, and occasionally a tape recorder, Messiaen transcribed birdsong as though taking musical dictation.[54]

In attempting to transcribe birdsong and incorporate it into his musical compositions, Messiaen inevitably encountered complications. Music and bird calls share certain characteristics, including "pitched" and "unpitched" sounds; the repetition of melodic phrases; the repetition of rhythmic units; the use of crescendo and diminuendo, accelerando and ritardando; and the balance between sound and silence.[55] However, birdsong is different from music in several respects, mainly in its higher tessitura and speed. "Birds have extraordinary virtuosity that no tenor or coloratura soprano could ever equal," stressed Messiaen, "for they possess a peculiar vocal organ, a 'syrinx' which allows them to execute rolls and very small intervals and to sing extremely fast."[56] As a result, the composer had to adapt his transcriptions to accommodate the limitations of human beings:

> A bird, being much smaller than we are, with a heart that beats
> faster and nervous reactions that are much quicker, sings in ex-
> tremely swift tempos, absolutely impossible for our instruments. I'm
> therefore obliged to transcribe the song into a slower tempo. More-
> over, this rapidity is combined with an extreme shrillness, for birds
> are able to sing in extremely high registers that cannot be reproduced
> on our instruments; so I write one, two, or three octaves lower. And
> that's not the only adjustment: for the same reasons I'm obliged to
> eliminate any tiny intervals that our instruments cannot execute. I
> replace those intervals, which are on the order of one or two com-
> mas, by semitones, but I respect the scale of values between the
> different intervals, which is to say that if a few commas correspond
> to a semitone, a whole tone or a third will correspond to the real
> semitone; all are enlarged, but the proportions remain identical, and
> as a result, what I restore is nevertheless exact. It's a transposition of
> what I heard, but on a more human scale.[57]

In the *Quartet for the End of Time*, Messiaen had not yet achieved the level of accuracy that would govern his use of birdsong in his works from 1953 onward. But the *Quartet* contains the composer's first attempts at depicting particular species, namely the blackbird and the nightingale, which Messiaen encountered in the regions of France where he lived and vacationed.[58] The birds appear in the clarinet and violin parts of the first movement of the *Quartet*, "Crystal Liturgy." In the preface to the score, the composer described the birds celebrating the arrival of dawn: "Between 3 and 4 o'clock in the morning, the birds awaken: a solo blackbird or nightingale improvises, surrounded by dust-whirls of sound, by a halo of harmonics lost high up in the trees. Transpose this onto a religious plane: you have the harmonious silence of heaven."[59]

In the score itself, the composer did not identify which bird is depicted by which instrument, but indicated simply *"comme un oiseau"* [like a bird] in the clarinet and violin parts.[60] Robert Sherlaw Johnson, a Messiaen scholar, points out, however, that the qualities of these melodies are sufficiently distinct as to make it obvious that, throughout the movement, the violin plays the song of the nightingale and the clarinet the song of the blackbird.[61]

In the preface, Messiaen did not name the particular species of birds alluded to in the other movements. By comparison with the first movement, however, it is possible to identify blackbirds in the second and third movements, writes Johnson.[62] In the second movement, the trills and sixteenth-note triplets in the clarinet part beginning in the second and seventh measures of B, for example, are clearly derived from the clarinet's opening motive in the first movement. The middle section of the third movement contains these same trills and sixteenth-note triplets, this time notated as grace notes (second measure of *Presque vif*). In his later commentary, Messiaen, in fact, identified these motives: "The birdsongs are written in the whimsical and cheerful style of the blackbird."[63]

In the first movement, birds celebrating the arrival of dawn represent "the harmonious silence of heaven." In the third movement, they hold an even greater symbolic importance. As the composer wrote in the preface: "The abyss is Time, with its weariness and gloom. The birds are the opposite of Time: they represent our longing for light, for stars, for rainbows, and for jubilant song!"[64]

The third movement is in an ABA form, the slow A sections clearly suggestive of the abyss, probably a reference to John's prophecy in Revelation 11:7, "the beast that comes up from the abyss will wage war,"[65] and the lively B section representative of the birds. "Notice the immense sustained swelling sounds: pianissimo, crescendo molto, to the most excruciating fortissimo," wrote Messiaen. These fermati, believes Michel Arrignon, professor of clarinet at the Paris Conservatory who made a recording of the *Quartet* under the composer's supervision,[66] represent eternity in its negative sense, that is, the eternity of the abyss: "I never spoke to him about these passages . . . but the longer they lasted, the more satisfied he was. I always held them for as long as I possibly could. In my opinion, these notes are symbolic of eternity, but eternity in all of its horror—in the abyss."[67]

Far above the horror of the abyss fly birds in joyous freedom. To Messiaen, birds symbolized our longing for light, but also our desire for flight:

> It is in a spirit of no confidence in myself, or I mean in the human race, that I have taken birdsongs as a model. If you want symbols, let us go on to say that the bird is the symbol of freedom. We walk, he flies. We make war, he sings. . . . I doubt that one can find in any human music, however inspired, melodies and rhythms that have the sovereign freedom of birdsong.[68]

Musicologist Trevor Hold sees birds as representative of Messiaen's desire to free himself of self-imposed restrictions. Certainly, birdsong worked along with other central elements of Messiaen's musical language—rhythm, sound-color, and Catholic doctrine—to create a music that was uniquely his. Given the symbolic importance of birds to Messiaen, it also makes sense that the *Quartet for the End of Time* was one of the first works in which birdsong was prominently featured, for it was written in a setting in which the thought of freedom must have been the constant and overwhelming obsession.

The *Quartet* stands as Messiaen's triumph over time. In the abysmal prison of Stalag VIII A, "in a spirit of no confidence in . . . the human race," the composer took "birdsongs as his model,"[69] taking flight in his inner song. On 15 January 1941, Messiaen realized his dream of the bird. Where all around him men were making war, Messiaen, like a bird, was making music.

CHAPTER 5

The Premiere

Rehearsals for the *Quartet for the End of Time* continued for a couple of months until, one day, the finishing touches were complete. The camp commandant, who had all along been sympathetic to the composer's cause, agreed to hold the premiere on 15 January 1941, during the regularly scheduled time for classical concerts—six o'clock in the evening. While the usual concerts on Saturdays were followed by comedies and variety shows, the premiere of Messiaen's *Quartet*, held on a Wednesday, was accorded the entire evening.[1]

This was a special occasion indeed, and the camp commandant ensured that it would be remembered as such. He ordered programs to be printed listing the name of the camp, the title of the composition, the name of the composer, the date of the premiere, the names of the performers, and the camp's official stamp, *"Stalag VIII A geprüft"* (Stalag VIII A approved). Designed by one of the prisoners, Henri Breton, *"avec des moyens de fortune"* (making do with what was available),[2] these programs also served as invitations to the historic event (see figs. 1 and 22).[3]

Pasquier and his fellow musicians distributed the programs to the other prisoners, urging them to come to the premiere.[4] When word spread that a work by a famous composer was going to be premiered in Stalag VIII A, requests for tickets inundated the German officers. The demand was so great that, against his better judgment, the camp commandant issued a special authorization permitting the prisoners in the quarantine to come to the concert, recalled Pasquier:

> It's quite a story. In the camp, there were people who were to be
> repatriated because of their age or their health and sent back to
> France. So, for two weeks, we were not allowed to have contact with
> them; they were in an area surrounded by barbed wire. Naturally,
> among those who were going to return to France, some had been

very well acquainted with Messiaen's work before they had been quarantined. So, they sent a letter to the commandant of the camp asking for permission to come. It is normally not allowed to leave the quarantine. At first the officer refused, but finally he agreed. The whole quarantine came! It was an official authorization![5]

Prisoners from certain outlying commandos were granted permission to attend as well.[6]

Although we know that the four musicians played to a packed house on 15 January 1941, just how many prisoners were there that evening has long remained uncertain. Both the composer and his wife gave estimates in the thousands.[7] Numerous witnesses, however, including Pasquier and Le Boulaire, have affirmed that, because the premiere took place in an enclosed military barrack, no more than a few hundred spectators could possibly have attended. In one interview, Pasquier estimated that there were about two hundred listeners, in another interview he guessed four hundred.[8] Le Boulaire wrote: "Given the size of the barracks that were at our disposal, there could not have been more than 300–350 spectators, the German officers included."[9] In any case, affirmed Pasquier, "The barrack was full."[10] Even disregarding the testimony of these witnesses, Messiaen's estimate seems highly unlikely: What sort of hall in a prison camp could have accommodated an audience of 5,000? Certainly there was no such place at Görlitz, and the possibility that the premiere could have taken place outdoors in the middle of winter seems totally inconceivable.

In fact, all the witnesses confirm that the premiere was held in the theater barrack where rehearsals, concerts, and variety shows regularly took place. "The theater barrack was packed," writes Lauerwald. "The prisoners pushed into the maximum 400 available seats; more were not accommodated."[11] Abbé Brossard, the French priest who had heard Messiaen's lecture on "Colors and Numbers in the Apocalypse," was at the premiere together with most of the clergy, who had been encouraged to attend by the camp chaplain, Dr. Scholz, and his assistant, Father Avril. "In the first row sat those responsible for the camp, officers from the German armed forces," recalled Brossard. "The lighting was low, as was the temperature, for it was mid-winter and adequate heating was not available. It was also difficult because snow from one barrack blew right into the other."[12] Indeed, these were the most adverse conditions in which to hold any kind of a public event (see fig. 23). Winter temperatures routinely dipped below -13 degrees Fahrenheit in Upper

Silesia.[13] "The earth and the roof were covered with 40–50 centimeters [16–20 inches] of snow, and the windowpanes were frosted," writes Lauerwald.[14] Only the body heat of the prisoners kept the barrack warm, recalled Pasquier.[15]

Under such trying conditions, several hundred men, including wounded prisoners who had been brought from the hospital block and lay on stretchers at the front of the audience,[16] awaited an event that would eventually be regarded as one of the great premieres of the twentieth century. When the musicians finally entered the stage area to perform, they must have made a strange sight. Messiaen recalled that he was "dressed in the oddest way . . . wearing a bottle-green suit of a Czech soldier, completely tattered, and wooden clogs large enough for the blood to circulate despite the snow underfoot."[17] Pasquier laughingly recalled his vision of himself and his eccentrically dressed comrades: "I had a jacket from Czechoslovakia with pockets everywhere. We wore wooden clogs that made our feet hurt, but that was all there was. But the wood kept us warm. Messiaen had a jacket that was all patched up. He was very badly dressed, thanks to me [he laughed]. I'm the one who helped him find clothes."[18] Le Boulaire concurred: "I can only confirm from beginning to end what Messiaen said. He mentioned clogs, but I didn't complain at all about the clogs because my feet weren't cold. If all I had had were my poor shoes, I would have died of frostbite. We fought each other for those clogs!"[19]

Although Messiaen exaggerated the size of the audience, he accurately recalled the heterogeneity of that evening's crowd: "The most diverse classes of society were mingled: farmers, factory workers, intellectuals, professional servicemen, doctors, and priests."[20] Many of them were hearing chamber music for the first time in their lives, and none had ever heard anything like the music performed that evening. Understandably, the musicians had difficulty quieting the motley crowd, which was nearly as diverse in nationality as in social class. As Le Boulaire recalled:

You know, these shows in the prison camp, they were hurried, they were slapped together. There was noise. The great problem, above all, was to obtain silence. That was one of the hardest things to do [he laughed]. We managed to do it, but it wasn't easy! Olivier Messiaen's *Quartet* was a totally French thing at that time. So it didn't interest the Poles much, although many Polish musicians were there . . . but on this musical level, we were all a bit lost.[21]

When the crowd had been quieted, Messiaen arose. "Emboldened" by his preceding lecture on "Colors and Numbers in the Apocalypse" given before the prisoner-priests, who, the composer claimed, "approved of his commentaries," Messiaen made what he called his "first presentation of a musical composition":

> I told them first of all that this quartet was written for the end of time, without any play on words on the length of captivity, but for the end of the notion of past and future, that is to say, for the beginning of eternity, and that the work is based on the magnificent text of the Apocalypse in which Saint John says: "And I saw another mighty angel coming down from heaven, wrapped in a cloud, with a rainbow on its head. . . . His face was like the sun, and his legs like pillars of fire. Setting his right foot on the sea and his left foot on the land, and standing on the sea and on the land, he raised his hand toward heaven and swore by He who lives forever and ever, saying: 'there will be no more time.' "[22]

How did the audience react to this lecture? In an article published in *Le Figaro* in 1942, Marcel Haedrich, one of the prisoners in the audience, colorfully depicted the atmosphere:

> How distant he seems all of a sudden, the comrade of every day, different from himself, at ease in a world in which it will be difficult to follow him. One hardly recognizes him: he, so unassuming, almost shy, is now filled with uncommon self-confidence. All full of his composition, he would like to share with everyone the joy he feels at being able to hold its premiere tonight in the camp . . .
>
> The faces are marked with anxiety. What is he getting at? We listen with a little suspicion when, offering a few explanations of the originality of his quartet, he says: "The modes, realizing melodically and harmonically a sort of tonal ubiquity, bring the listener closer to infinity, to eternity in space. The special rhythms, independent of the meter, powerfully contribute to the effect of banishing the temporal."
>
> The musicians, next to the young master, are bent over their instruments. Etienne Pasquier, in a tender gesture, caresses his cello. Jean Le Boulaire prepares his violin, and Henri Akoka, his clarinet resting on his knees, looks around the room and smiles at his comrades. He already knows that when he returns to his barrack his friends will mock him for a long time, because Olivier Messiaen has just stated that the clarinet constitutes *"l'élément pittoresque"* [the

colorful element] of the quartet . . . Perhaps a new nickname will stay with him after this premiere, "*Monsieur Pitto*."[23]

Then the music began. What was the performance like? The practical obstacles reportedly encountered by the musicians at the premiere have been mentioned repeatedly by scholars as well as by the composer himself:

> I was given a piano, but my God, what a piano! It was an upright piano with keys that stuck. So, when I played a trill it would stop and I had to pull the keys back up again in order to be able to go on. The violin was more or less standard, but the cello, alas, had only three strings. Fortunately, I think that there was the E-string [sic][24] and there was the low C. So, we could play, but it was missing the second or third string, I don't know which one. But in the end, because he was so terrific, he managed wonderfully nevertheless. And the clarinet. Another catastrophe. You know that there are side-keys on the clarinet. One of the keys had been put near a heating-stove and had melted. The poor clarinetist. But in the end, we played on these horrible instruments, and I assure you that no one felt like laughing. We were all so unhappy that it seemed fantastic to us in spite of it all.[25]

Messiaen's description of the pathetic instruments on which he and his comrades played on 15 January 1941 has become legendary. Like his claim that 5,000 prisoners were in the audience, however, his description of the difficulties encountered by the musicians at the premiere is somewhat exaggerated. No doubt, the piano was sorely inadequate. The claim that one of Akoka's keys was partially melted by the paraffin stove that the German officials had provided is implausible, however, for the clarinet itself would have ignited if the heat had been intense enough to melt the keys.

Finally, the three-stringed cello story is sheer myth. Contrary to Messiaen, Pasquier repeatedly insisted that the instrument on which he played in Stalag VIII A at the rehearsals as well as at the premiere possessed all four strings. "I told him that I played on *four* strings," said Pasquier. "I kept telling him: 'I had four strings, and you know it.' I had gone to a dealer in Görlitz, where I bought a bow—with four strings, obviously. You can't play without strings! If Messiaen had played the cello, he would have known that you couldn't play that piece on three strings [he laughed]."[26] But Messiaen would continue to tell journalists that Pasquier played on three strings, despite the cellist's protests.[27]

Why would Messiaen deliberately falsify history? Because "it amused him to say that!" laughed Pasquier. "Whenever I saw him after the war, I would say: 'You know I had four strings.' Because it was impossible to play that piece on three strings. And that would make him laugh. But he would continue to say that I played on three strings."[28] In a subsequent interview, Pasquier speculated that Messiaen's persistent repetition of this story stemmed from his desire to illustrate the hardships the musicians faced in performing the piece.[29] The intentionally misreported details thus served to enhance the legend of the *Quartet* and to ensure that its premiere would forever be remembered as a triumph over all obstacles.

In his perpetuation of the three-stringed cello myth, then, a different aspect of Messiaen emerges. To Messiaen the composer and Messiaen the devout Catholic is added Messiaen the dramatist, one who misreported history not for the sake of a little personal amusement, as it would appear, but for an entirely different reason. In perpetuating the legend of the three-stringed cello, Messiaen imbued his story with an even greater aura of the miraculous, with an image of birds flying over the abyss, a quartet of musicians rising above the Apocalypse, redeeming the earth through music. In tattered clothing, in bitter cold, and on broken instruments, and at a time in which a real-life Apocalypse must have seemed imminent to many, these four men sang of resurrection, leading their audience in a musical prayer. Though Pasquier played on a cello with all four strings intact, and though there were several hundred, not several thousand, people in the audience, it can be certain, to use Lauerwald's words, "that in Messiaen's memory, a *messianic* vision of thousands of fellow prisoners stayed alive."[30]

Leslie Sprout, author of a paper titled "Messiaen's *Quatuor pour la fin du Temps:* Modernism, Representation, and a Soldier's Wartime Tale," has offered another theory. She reasons that Messiaen's exaggerations were rooted in his emotional attachment to the piece and to his subsequent "frustration with postwar criticism and neglect" of the *Quartet,* which "may have led him to provide the piece with a compelling subtext in the emotionally charged circumstances of the war.[31]

Whatever the reasons for Messiaen's misreportings, however, it can be certain that on 15 January 1941 an hour's worth of music made an unforgettable impression on the listeners. According to Loriod, the prisoners "trembled from emotion.[32] Among them was a Polish architect,

Aleksander Lyczewski, whose experience has been movingly recalled by the British musicologist Charles Bodman Rae. Rae, a specialist in Polish music, was a lodger in the Lyczewski home in the fall of 1981. Unaware of Lyczewski's internment in Stalag VIII A, the musicologist was rehearsing for a performance of the *Quartet* at the time, when, all of a sudden, Lyczewski "burst into the room with a mixed expression of confusion and distress on his face":

> He said he recognized the piece I was playing and wanted to know who had composed it. He sat down and I explained about Messiaen and the circumstances under which the *Quatuor* had been written and first performed. He then recounted to me his experience as a prisoner of war in the same camp at Görlitz in Silesia. Aleksander was in a very emotional state while he was recalling these events. There were tears in his eyes and it took some time for him to regain his composure. He had been present at the first performance and vividly recalled the atmosphere in the large freezing hut where hundreds of prisoners (many Poles, other central Europeans, and some French) assembled to hear the piece. He remembers his fellow-prisoners remaining in complete silence for the hour or so that it took to perform the piece. He himself had been deeply moved by the experience.[33]

Charles Jourdanet, another prisoner in the audience, eloquently depicted the experience in an article published in the French newspaper *Nice-matin* on the sixtieth anniversary of the premiere:

> A cello solo, then a grand violin solo with a long ascent toward the high register: these are the final notes that resonate throughout the "concert hall" as well as through the hearts of the listeners. There is silence . . . then applause. Members of the audience . . . approach the composer on stage. Outside, it is minus twenty degrees [Celsius]. Inside, despite several primitive heaters, winter military apparel (hoods, helmets, and mufflers) is everywhere. The temperature cannot be more than five degrees. . . . On this memorable day for the several hundred spectators so honored to witness not just a musical premiere but a world premiere, it was daily life as usual. At six o'clock: distribution of ersatz. From eight o'clock to noon: the prisoners attend to their assigned duties. At noon: cabbage soup for all. From one to four o'clock: various chores. At five o'clock: more ersatz is distributed, along with a fifth of a loaf of black bread with a little *fromage blanc* and quite a bit of grease. . . . Finally, at six o'clock: the

concert—in barrack 27—which, for several months, has served as
"the theater." . . . On this cold night in January 1941, seated on
benches in barrack 27, we listened, some moved by the unexpected
fervor, others agitated by rhythms and sonorities to which they were
unaccustomed—to the creation of what Messiaen called a "great act
of faith." . . . The concert was over, but for several of us, a beautiful
moment remained in which the awesome young master was surrounded by friends and admirers.[34]

As Jourdanet implied, some of the members of the audience admitted, understandably, to being somewhat perplexed by this avant-garde
composition. Lucien Akoka was correct when he surmised that "people
must have been very amazed at the premiere of the *Quartet*. For people
who listen to nothing but Mozart, Beethoven, and other works of that
kind, it must have been a little like listening to Stravinsky, at the premiere of *The Rite of Spring*."[35]

Yet the premieres themselves could not have been more different.
The first performance of *The Rite of Spring* was held under ideal conditions on 29 May 1913 at the Théâtre des Champs-Elysées in Paris and
provoked one of the most notorious scandals in musical history.[36] By
contrast, the audience at Görlitz listened to Messiaen's *Quartet* in re-
spectful silence. Brossard, one of the French priests present at the premiere, declared: "Of course, I listened religiously, without being, I confess, very inspired by music which was beyond my grasp."[37] Le Boulaire
recalled:

> The audience, as far as I remember, was overwhelmed at the time.
> They wondered what had happened. Everyone. We too. We asked our-
> selves: "What are we doing? What are we playing?" Even the prison-
> ers who weren't all highly educated—factory workers, electricians—
> could have screamed and shouted. But there was a long silence. And
> then, afterward, lots of unresolved discussions, discussions about
> this thing that no one had understood. Even the German officers,
> who probably were more educated, were a little lost.[38]

Other prisoners were confused as well. Apparently, the discord provoked by Messiaen's introductory lecture intensified when the music
began. "Henri Akoka's friends elbowed one another. 'It's awfully clever,
what he does, but why is it called "Abyss of the Birds"?'" wrote
Haedrich. "The audience is divided between passionate approval and in-
comprehension. 'What are these blocks of purple fury?' [referring to

Messiaen's introductory remarks on the sixth movement] We read this question on more than one face."[39]

Clearly, Messiaen's memorable statement to Goléa, "Never before have I been listened to with such attention and understanding,"[40] was a reference to the prisoners' emotional state, not their intellectual comprehension. In a later interview, he made this distinction more clear: "There was an enormous audience . . . [with] people from all classes of society. . . . But we were all brothers because we were all in the same situation. . . . And they listened with a religious silence. Never before had I been listened to like that. . . . Even if these people knew nothing about music, they readily understood that this was something special."[41]

Interestingly, while Messiaen emphasized the prisoners' diverse social backgrounds, Haedrich was unimpressed by this diversity. "What delighted him was the way social divisions helped recreate the contentious atmosphere of an important Parisian premiere in the most unlikely of places," observes Leslie Sprout. "In other words, the *Quartet* represented the normalcy of Parisian musical life to people trapped in the miserable atmosphere of the German prison camp, not the other way around."[42]

Like Messiaen, Pasquier was struck by the transfiguring power of the moment—how music transformed the banality of Stalag VIII A into something sublime. Echoing the religious theme in the *Quartet*, he described the premiere as a miracle that transcended not only place and time but differences in nationality and social class:

> Everyone listened reverently, with an almost religious respect, including those who perhaps were hearing chamber music for the first time. It was "miraculous."[43]
>
> These people, who had never before heard such music, remained *silent*. These people, who were completely musically ignorant, sensed that this was something exceptional. They sat perfectly still, in awe. Not one person stirred. No doubt, these people reassumed their original personalities afterward, but there they were subject to a miracle: the miracle of the performance of this music.[44]

After the performance, wrote Haedrich, "an awkward silence prolong[ed] the echo of the last notes, then the applause [began], hesitantly in places. Often, it is a sign of greatness for a work to have provoked a controversy at its premiere, but what should we think about this music so different from the kind we love? . . . The entire piece is filled with faith, and, for those who listen, it is like an act of revenge against captivity, against the miserable ambience of the camp."[45]

From anticipation to anxiety, from bewilderment to awe—for a brief musical moment the prisoners were free. When the performance was over, those from the quarantine were sent back, returning to Paris shortly thereafter.[46] The other prisoners, as well as the officers who had been in the audience, resumed their daily routines, though all would be profoundly affected by what they had heard and witnessed on that night. The most lasting impression, however, was no doubt made on the performers themselves. On the back of one of the printed programs to the premiere, Messiaen asked his colleagues write him a dedication in memory of the creation of the *Quartet* (see fig. 24):

> The camp of Görlitz . . . Barrack 27B, our theater. . . . Outside, night, snow, misery. . . . Here, a miracle. . . . The quartet "for the end of time" transports us to a wonderful Paradise, lifts us from this abominable earth. Thank you immensely, dear Olivier Messiaen, poet of Eternal Purity.
>   With deepest affection
>   E.T. Pasquier

> To Olivier Messiaen, who revealed Music to me. I try in vain by these few words to prove to him my gratitude but I doubt that I will ever be able to do so.
>   H. Akoka

> To Olivier Messiaen, my great friend, who with the quartet [for] "the end of time" made me take a grand and magnificent voyage to a wonderful world. A thousand thanks as well as my great admiration and friendship,
>   J. Le Boulaire[47]

CHAPTER 6

The Quartet Free

The premiere of the *Quartet for the End of Time* on 15 January 1941 marked the culmination of a musical and personal relationship and a turning point in the lives of Messiaen, Pasquier, Akoka, and Le Boulaire. For Messiaen and Pasquier, the premiere not only solidified their fame; it led to their liberation from captivity and their performance in both the *Quartet*'s Paris premiere and first recording. Akoka and Le Boulaire were driven down different paths, as the forces of war, displacement, and historical accident combined to edge them out of the musical sphere of their colleagues. For them, 15 January 1941 became a moment frozen in time, to be remembered but never repeated. But while Akoka and Le Boulaire never relived "the end of time," they continued to make history in their own extraordinary ways.

■

Confusion has surrounded the date of and reason for Messiaen's liberation. His biographer, Alain Périer, for example, wrote, "The world is delivered to the insanity of the Third Reich, but the good fairies watch over Messiaen: he is repatriated in 1942, with the sanitation service to which he had been assigned, and immediately appointed Professor of Harmony at the Paris Conservatory."[1]

Messiaen, in fact, was liberated from Stalag VIII A less than one month after the Stalag premiere, and began teaching harmony at the Paris Conservatory in May 1941.[2] According to Loriod, it was Marcel Dupré, Messiaen's former teacher at the Conservatory, who used his influence to get the composer liberated.[3] Abbé Brossard speculated that the composer was in one of the first liberating convoys, "very likely because of his personality and renown."[4] Echoing Brossard, Lauerwald wrote that Messiaen was repatriated because he belonged to "one of the intellectual professions," among those who, in addition to World War I veterans, fathers of large families, farmers, and others, were granted liberation under a Vichy law.[5] According to Sprout, the German army had captured over a million French soldiers in the 1940 invasion, and they were "determined to detain them as long as possible as hostages to French collaboration. Unable to obtain full repatriation, Vichy bargained for the release of prominent artists whose return they could celebrate as symbols of progress in their otherwise futile negotiations with the Third Reich."[6] "One thing, good or bad, leads to another," mused Pasquier:

> Because I was retained in the Val-de-Grâce Hospital, I was able to go to Verdun, where I met Messiaen. And it's thanks to him that I was able to return after less than a year.[7] . . . The commandant of the camp had us return to France because we were musicians, very well-known musicians. I had publicity papers in German containing the German critique of the Trio Pasquier.[8] It's music that saved me, time after time. Music was my good fairy. Without it, I probably would have been in the camp for five years.[9]

Although both Pasquier and Messiaen were well-known musicians, Pasquier claimed that he was liberated because of the particular concern that the camp authorities showed for Messiaen, and that Messiaen simply "took [him] along":

> During our rehearsals for the *Quartet for the End of Time*, we were often visited by some German officers, who would sit in the front of the hall and listen. . . . One day, one of them who spoke a very good French [Brüll] said to Messiaen: "Monsieur Messiaen, I have something to tell you. In a few weeks, there will be a return of prisoners to Paris. Don't miss the train."[10]

There was only one problem, however. The camp authorities thought that Messiaen and Pasquier were *soldats musiciens* (musician/soldiers); that is, men who had been drafted to serve in the armed forces as musicians, like Akoka, who was sent to play in the military orchestra in Verdun and who on principle did not carry arms. Apparently, musicians were regarded not as fighting men but as artists. Pasquier insisted, however, that he was a corporal of music, not a *soldat musicien*. "I myself had a rifle when I was caught," he said.[11] "I was a soldier like all others."[12]

Thus Messiaen and Pasquier shared a dilemma. They had been told that they would be liberated as *soldats musiciens*, but they had no papers to prove it. Then Pasquier got an idea. Word had spread that those who worked in the medical services, such as nurses, stretcher-bearers, and orderlies, who, like the *soldats musiciens,* were unarmed, would be among the first to be liberated. "Having been told that the medical personnel were going to be liberated immediately," wrote Le Boulaire, "as if by magic, everyone became an orderly!"[13]

And so Pasquier took action:

When the German officer came to tell Messiaen: "There's going to be a return. Don't miss the train," Messiaen looked at me and said: "How can I return?" The officer said: "Because you're *soldats musiciens.* You're unarmed." But it wasn't true. So, when the Germans left, I said to Messiaen: "Give me your papers." I wrote "ORDERLY." I handwrote it like that, with the permission of one officer [Brüll] who was an accomplice [he laughed]. It's he who wanted us to return. I also fiddled with my own papers. I put "orderly soldier."[14] . . . I cheated! I made everything up. I wrote "orderly" on the repatriation form, encouraged by what this German officer had told us. We left thanks to the commandant of the camp [Bielas].[15]

Thus, Périer was partially right when he wrote that Messiaen was repatriated with the sanitation service. It's just that his papers were forged. As for the "good fairies" who were said to "watch over Messiaen," they were actually the same mortals in uniform who provided the composer with manuscript paper and pencil, and the musicians with instruments: Hauptmann Karl-Albert Brüll and Commandant Alois Bielas. Had Pasquier not forged their papers, perhaps he and Messiaen would have been liberated anyway, but the cellist thought it best not to leave it to chance.

■

In February 1941, the much-awaited day finally arrived. Messiaen, Pasquier, and the actor René Charles were about to board the convoy.[16] Alongside them stood Akoka, who, as a *soldat musicien,* had the proper papers.[17] For some unknown reason, Jean Le Boulaire was excluded from this group, perhaps because he had neither the musical renown of Pasquier or Messiaen nor the *soldat musicien* status of Akoka.

Pasquier, Messiaen, and Charles boarded the convoy. Akoka was just about to do so when he was stopped by a German officer, recalled his sister, Yvonne Dran: "At the moment of boarding, a German officer told Henri to get off. When Henri asked him why, he responded, '*Jude*' [Jew]." Anyone else would have trembled with fear, but not Henri, said his sister. In his typically disarming humor, said Dran, Akoka motioned to pull down his pants in order to prove to the officer that he was mistaken:

> Henri said, "No," and gestured to pull down his pants, because his circumcision had not been well done and he thought that he could pass for a gentile.[18] But the officer arrested him and brought him back to the camp, while the others returned to France. I remember perfectly—Etienne Pasquier must have told you—it was he who said that when the convoy took off, they were filled with remorse. Because Henri had had to stay.[19]

While Akoka was sent back to the camp, Pasquier, Messiaen, and Charles headed back to France. The clarinetist did not let this incident discourage him, however, for he was accustomed to overcoming obstacles. "Henri was never demoralized," said his brother Lucien. "He was a fearless man who never flinched before any difficulty, whatever it might be. As soon as he got caught [on his first escape attempt in 1940], he would think about escaping again and would gather provisions for his next attempt."[20]

When the German officer arrested him on that day in February 1941, Henri Akoka was again unshaken, for he knew that he would find another way out. "Henri had a leitmotif," said his sister Yvonne. "He always said, 'Un prisonnier, c'est fait pour s'évader' " (a prisoner is made to escape).[21]

∎

Messiaen, Pasquier, and Charles were sent with the other repatriated prisoners of Stalag VIII A to Constance, Switzerland. From there they were driven through French territory to a barrack in Lyons where they waited to be liberated. Just as Pasquier had worked in the kitchen in Stalag VIII A, he was assigned to cook for the prisoners in the barrack in Lyons.

Pasquier, Messiaen, and their comrades remained in Lyons for three weeks. Upon their liberation, they returned to Paris by train, Pasquier to his house in the suburbs and Messiaen to his apartment in Paris.[22]

Both musicians had become dangerously thin as a result of their captivity. Pasquier lost twenty pounds. A painting by a Belgian artist upon

Pasquier's return to Paris depicts the cellist with sunken cheeks. Pasquier decided to spend several weeks at his in-laws' home in the country near Fontainebleau, where he could be cared for until he was strong enough to resume his post as assistant principal cellist of the Paris Opera Orchestra.[23] Messiaen went for a few weeks to a farm of two paternal aunts in the Aube, near Champagne, where he too was nursed to health and could then resume his organ post at the Trinity Cathedral.[24] Soon after, he went to Neussargues in the department of Cantal, where he wrote two sections of what would remain an unfinished work, *Chœurs pour une Jeanne d'Arc*, and in May 1941 he began teaching harmony at the Paris Conservatory (see figs. 25–26).[25]

Messiaen's appointment to the Paris Conservatory came about as a consequence of the Vichy government's anti-Semitic policies, mandated by the German occupation. On 3 October 1940 the Vichy government passed its infamous *Statut des juifs* [Statute on the Jews], which barred Jews from holding positions that influenced public opinion, such as education, the press, radio, film, and theater.[26] The Paris Conservatory thus faced a sudden demand for new teachers to replace a number of Jews who were dismissed, among them André Bloch, professor of harmony, whom Messiaen replaced. Yvonne Loriod, who was in Messiaen's first class, recalled the students' shock at the sight of their new professor's chilblains (swollen fingers) and their reverence for this man who analyzed before them Debussy's *Prelude to the Afternoon of a Faun* "with such intelligence, from the formal and harmonic points of view, that we left the room full of admiration for this master who had descended to us from heaven":[27]

> At the first class the pupils were absolutely astonished, because here was a man who was quite young and whose fingers were swollen on account of the privations which he had suffered during his time in captivity in Silesia. He brought out the miniature score of Debussy's *Prélude à l'après-midi d'un faune*, placed it on the piano and played it for us. We were absolutely astonished to discover that one could read and play from an orchestral score—we were very young!—and there he was, playing the piano with such beautiful sounds in spite of the deformity of his hands. We were absolutely captivated; the whole class adored him straight away.[28]

For the composer, said Loriod, it was a difficult period. In addition to the physical hardships he endured as a result of his captivity and the food rationing under the Germans in occupied France, Messiaen suffered emotionally. Since his first wife, Claire Delbos, was extremely ill and had to be sent to a rest home in the Unoccupied Zone, the composer had to raise his son, Pascal, alone while simultaneously working as an organist at the Trinity Cathedral, as a professor of harmony at the Paris Conservatory, and as a composer at home. Loriod explained:

> Messiaen suffered a lot in captivity. Like other prisoners, he lost his hair and his teeth. When he returned, he had swollen fingers, chilblains, because he hadn't eaten. The physical state of all of the prisoners—though not as serious as that of those who were deported—was terrible. So afterward, obviously, what saved him a little, were these aunts who had a farm in the Aube (near Champagne). He had these aunts on his father's side who had taken him in at this time to give him eggs, milk, etc., to make him eat a little, because at this time, we had food tickets. It was the *war*. We ate very badly.
>   When he returned, he was reunited with his first wife and his little boy. (His little boy was born in 1937. When little Pascal was just two years old, Messiaen had had to leave for war.) But his first wife had become sick. She had lost her memory and was put in an institution in the Free Zone. So it was Messiaen who raised this little boy all by himself in Paris. He didn't have anyone to help him. He heated the stove in the basement of the house all alone and he went to restaurants to eat with his son. They ate very badly, obviously. He worked all the time, all the time. He had to earn a living, so he was professor at the Conservatory, organist at the Trinity; but he still didn't have a lot of money. He would always say: "I'm going to economize. I'm going to walk to work instead of taking the metro. Because, then, I'll be able to eat." It was like that until the Liberation. Afterwards, he regained his health, but it was always difficult.[29]

■

While Messiaen and Pasquier were gradually regaining their health and resuming their musical careers in Paris, Henri Akoka and Jean Le Boulaire remained imprisoned in Germany. Determined to get out immediately after his comrades were liberated in February 1941, Akoka devised a plan.

Under a new order decreed by the Geneva Convention, French soldiers in the German prison camps who had been recruited from France's African colonies were given special consideration. According to Henri's sister, Yvonne, this order, which forced the Germans to transfer African-born soldiers to areas with milder climates, was established in response to a charge made by the Red Cross that prisoners accustomed to the Saharan climate could not tolerate Siberian winters. Thanks to his dark skin and Semitic features, Henri, born in Algeria, was able to pass as an Arab, and in March 1941 was transferred along with other Algerian-born prisoners to Dinan, a town in the French province of Brittany. There, Yvonne visited him, bringing some clarinet etudes that he had requested.[30]

Henri's brother, Lucien, told a different story. "The Mufti of Jerusalem was a great friend of Hitler's. At a certain point, he was able to get a lot of Arabs liberated." Apparently, although letters between prisoners and civilians were scrupulously censored, letters between prisoners at the different POW camps were not, so Henri was able to write to Lucien in Stalag IX A in Ziegenhain, urging him to pass himself off as an Arab so that he, too, could be transferred. " 'There's a convoy of Arabs,' he wrote me. 'If there's a convoy in your camp too, take it, because the Arabs are returning to France to be liberated.' "[31] Unfortunately, the Algerian prisoners transferred to Dinan in March 1941 were not liberated.

In April 1941, when the Germans reassembled the prisoners to send them back to Stalag VIII A, said Yvonne Dran, Henri resolved to escape.[32] Herding their prisoners into lead-sealed cattle cars on a train headed for Silesia, the Germans designated one prisoner per convoy as chief. If anyone escaped, the chief would immediately be shot. As he was planning to escape, Henri volunteered to be chief, for he did not want to endanger his fellow prisoners.[33] Dran recalled her brother's dramatic leap from the train, as he recounted it to her:

> As the train passed through the French village of Saint-Julien-du-Sault, Henri asked his comrades to tie their belts together to form a rope. They opened a little overhead plank, hoisted him up on this make-shift rope, and slid him through the hole. And there, in the middle of the night, while the train was still rolling, he jumped. And what is extraordinary is that he jumped with his clarinet under his arm! The clarinet never left him [she laughed].[34]

Henri's son, Philippe, concurred. "What is surprising is that during these escape attempts, the clarinet went with him all the time. The clarinet never left him." Philippe also recalled his father telling him how he tried in vain to persuade his fellow prisoners to leap from the wagon with him: " 'You have nothing to fear. I am the chief. I am the one who is responsible, so it's me whom they're going to kill if we jump. Follow me.' "[35] Fearful of the consequences, no one followed.

On leaping from the train, Henri fell onto a riverbank, fainting from the shock of the fall and injuring his hand as well. Two railway switchmen discovered him lying unconscious on the riverbank and brought him to a doctor to bandage his wounds. In order to placate the switchmen, who realized that Henri was an escaped prisoner, the doctor assured them that he would turn Henri over to the German authorities the next day. In fact, the doctor had no such plans. Recounting the story that Henri later told him, Pasquier claimed that when the switchmen left, the doctor said to Henri: " 'You must think I'm crazy. . . . I'm going to hide you.' So, he hid him in his home, restored him to health, and succeeded in getting him to the Free Zone. It's an extraordinary story."[36] The selfless doctor assisted Akoka "with total devotion, at the risk of his own life, for over a month."[37]

Before going into the Free Zone, Henri went to Bedouin, near Avignon, to the home of a Monsieur Coutelin, a clarinetist whom he knew from his years at the Paris Conservatory. His friend proceeded to contact a vicar in Bedouin who agreed to write Henri a false certificate of baptism.[38] From there Henri went to Paris to visit his family. Yvonne Dran vividly remembered the day her brother arrived. It was her birthday, 16 May 1941:

> With his clarinet still under his arm, Henri went to the home of our dear friend Julie Bailly, who lived on Bellefond Street. . . . He still had a very swollen hand. I believe it was eight o'clock in the morning when Julie came to tell us: "Madame Akoka, don't panic. Henri arrived at my home yesterday. He thinks that he is being followed. So he can't come to your house but would like to know where he might be able to meet Papa, Maman and the rest of the family in secret." So, we went to Bellefond Street, and spent the day together. . . . Papa was very worried. He was afraid that Henri's disappearance had already been broadcast.[39]

As it turned out, after 16 May 1941 Henri Akoka never saw his father again. The next day the clarinetist managed to pass the Line of Demarcation illegally and to reach the city of Marseilles in the Free Zone, where the Paris-based Orchestre National de la Radio, in which he had been playing immediately prior to his mobilization, had relocated due to the German Occupation.[40] Henri rejoined his orchestra in the Free

Zone, where he managed to live in relative tranquility until 1943, at which time life for Jews and for those active in the French Resistance became precarious.

■

In Paris, meanwhile, Messiaen was planning for the publication and French premiere of his *Quartet for the End of Time*. On 17 May 1941, the same day that Akoka reached the Free Zone, Durand received the manuscript.[41] That document is an interesting testimony to the composer's captivity. Written on German manuscript paper, *Beethoven Papier, Nr. 33 (16 Linien)*, the document is signed by the composer on the upper right-hand corner of every page, and it is stamped *"Stalag VIII A 49 geprüft"* [Stalag VIII A 49 approved] on the first pages of movements 2, 6, and 7. It also records the revisions that the composer made either before or after the premiere in Stalag VIII A.

Save for the change to the titles of the sixth and eighth movements (see fig. 24), the preface shows little evidence of major revision. However, many tempo markings in the music were crossed out and replaced with slower or faster indications. Both overall tempi and tempo relationships within movements were changed to produce a more extreme effect: in most cases, slow tempi were made slower and fast tempi faster. The inner tempi of the second and third movements were changed—the slow sections made slower and the fast sections faster—to produce a greater contrast of tempo within the movements themselves.[42] It is possible that, after hearing the work at rehearsals and at the premiere in Stalag VIII A, Messiaen thought that the piece needed starker differences in tempo, or that challenging the performers with more formidable demands might better ensure their achieving the truly desired tempo. Few clarinetists, cellists, and violinists, for example, actually play the third, fifth, and eighth movements, respectively, as slow as the indicated tempo, so difficult are they for breath and bow control. No doubt, if Messiaen had retained the faster tempo markings, performers would fall even shorter of his desired goal of "banishing the temporal."

■

The Paris premiere of the *Quartet* was held just over a month after Durand received the manuscript. It took place at a concert celebrating the composer's return to France, on Tuesday, 24 June 1941, at five o'clock in the evening, in the Théâtre des Mathurins, in the eighth *arrondissement* near the Madeleine. This concert, dedicated to Messiaen's chamber works, most notably, the Paris premiere of the *Quartet*, included *Thème et variations* (1932) for violin and piano, as well as four songs for soprano and piano: *"Le sourire"* from *Trois mélodies* (1930), *Vocalise* (1935), and *"Minuit pale et face"* and *"Résurrection"* from *Chants de terre et de ciel* (1938).[43] Soprano Marcelle Bunlet, whom Messiaen later cited along with Pasquier in his preface to *The Technique of My Musical Language* as one of his "most devoted interpreters,"[44] performed the vocal works, with Messiaen at the piano. Messiaen, of course, played the piano for this performance of the *Quartet for the End of Time* as well, and introduced and commented on all of his works, said Yvonne Loriod, who turned the pages for him. Pasquier returned as cellist, and his brother, Jean, from the Trio Pasquier, performed as violinist in the *Quartet* and in *Thème et variations*. André Vacellier, assistant principal clarinetist of the Opéra Comique in Paris, played the clarinet part.[45]

Where were Henri Akoka and Jean Le Boulaire? Obviously, Akoka was unable to participate. Not only was he an escaped prisoner of war, but a Jew. He would have put himself at great risk had he attempted to leave the safety of the Free Zone and cross the Line of Demarcation. Le Boulaire, of course, was still imprisoned in Stalag VIII A.

The concert was not recorded, said Loriod, for the Théâtre des Mathurins was not a concert hall. This concert actually took place during an afternoon break, when for a few unscheduled hours the theater rented out its facilities.[46] The concert was reviewed, however, in three important French newspapers: *Les Nouveaux temps* (Marcel Delannoy, "Depuis le mysticisme jusqu'au sport"), *Comoedia* (Serge Moreux, "Théâtre des Mathurins: Oeuvres de Messiaen"), and *L'information musicale* (Arthur Honegger, "Olivier Messiaen"). As was typical in wartime Paris, these reviews were delayed for several weeks, appearing in mid-July. Interestingly, as Sprout has observed, in spite of the presence of two recently repatriated prisoners of war and the politically charged date—the day before the first anniversary of France's armistice with Germany—the reviews scarcely mention Messiaen and Pasquier's captivity. Delannoy only briefly alluded to the Stalag premiere; Honegger and Moreux did not mention the captivity at all, such that French readers who were unfamiliar with the piece's background might have no idea that the piece was composed in a German prison camp. And yet, just one day after the Paris premiere, Messiaen was featured in a nationally publicized radio show honoring composers who had been killed or captured in the invasion. The show, hosted by Daniel Lesur, was broadcast on Wednesday, 25 June 1941, in commemoration of the first anniversary of the armistice. Featured were previous recordings of two of Messiaen's *Preludes* for piano (1928–1929), as well as music by Maurice Thiriet, who had been imprisoned in Lucien Akoka's camp, Stalag IX A, and Maurice Jaubert, who died in combat.[47]

In general, reviewers of the *Quartet*'s Paris premiere, though awed by the music itself, seemed to be, like the audience at the Stalag premiere, somewhat bewildered by the unusual musical language as well as by the intense mysticism and religious texts surrounding the work. The religious texts in particular angered at least two critics and alienated some members of the audience.

Moreux's short review is by far the most laudatory. In a bold opening statement, he declared the *Quartet* to be "the most striking piece of chamber music that we have heard since the performance in Paris of the last quartet of Schoenberg." Continuing, he explained:

> Why? Because, thanks to an original melodic and rhythmic language
> based on meditations on ancient Greek rhythms and Hindu modes,
> meditations imposed upon him in his artistic development, Olivier
> Messiaen invites us, yet a little farther this time, into the enchanted
> jungle within himself. There, he delights us with the joy of pure
> music. Shimmering harmony, the weight of slow lines intense in
> their sacredness, fanciful and noble dances of rhythmic values ex-
> traordinarily original in their inventiveness: everything in this major
> work works to stupefy and captivate, the most stubborn members of
> the audience readily admitted upon leaving.[48]

In conclusion, however, Moreux criticized "the prayer-like tone of the lecture that preceded the performance of each of the eight movements," (commentary that Messiaen excerpted from his own preface), which, he wrote, "besides destroying the musical continuity of the piece, surprised some and angered many by its apologetic [religious] tone. We expected a lecture of a more technical nature, especially since the usual public for these concerts is comprised of the musical elite of Paris."[49]

Perhaps as a friend and supporter of Messiaen's and member of the prominent group of French composers *Les Six*,[50] Honegger declined to pass judgement on either the musical or extramusical content of the *Quartet*, devoting most of his review to explaining the composer's style. Referring to Messiaen's religious inspiration and unique musical language, Honegger stated diplomatically:

> In principle, I have little faith in the pre-established theories but I admit all research on order of faith when the performance gives me the impression that these theories are an integral part of the musical conception and have not been added superfluously. This is the case here . . . Some may find that there is too much literature surrounding this music and will regret it. That is possible, but one feels such a strong conviction from the composer, and his strictly musical invention is of such a noble quality, that I won't allow myself to discuss it. The quartet for the end of time [sic] is a moving work, containing great beauty and denoting a musician of elevated aspirations.[51]

Honegger concluded his review by praising Messiaen's appointment to the Paris Conservatory: "I am certain that the influence of such an upright artist will be an excellent thing and that his students will draw upon his teaching a taste for art that will not conform to the usual expectations."[52]

The harshest critique came from Marcel Delannoy. Though he acknowledged Messiaen's sincerity, Delannoy, like Moreux, objected to the commentary accompanying the work, directly challenging the composer's assertions that: "such an act of faith must be expressed by resolutely revolutionary and superhuman musical means. The modes realizing melodically and harmonically a sort of tonal ubiquity, *bring the listener closer to eternity*. The special rhythms, independent of the meter, *powerfully contribute to the effect of banishing the temporal*." In response, exclaimed Delannoy: "These are grandiose intentions, unquestionably sincere! They disarm the critic in advance, as they assume the problem solved: the *ethereal* written black on white, the *superhuman* means; eternity comes closer, while the temporal moves away, due to the unraveling itself of the composition that should then be analyzed from the perspective of a mystical process, which, I confess, is beyond my capabilities." Then, following a digression into the philosophies of mysticism and art, Delannoy censured the composer: "For me, an artist who humbly seeks perfection has no need to *describe* God in order to come close to Him . . . In regard to Messiaen, [there is] a fanatical *subjectivism*, a quasi-Luciferian arrogance in wanting to describe light. What is more, he seeks to create in his music the force of a personal miracle and then calmly announces that he has succeeded!"[53]

As for the music itself, Delannoy was somewhat ambivalent: "The

Stalag VIII A
Görlitz

PREMIÈRE
AVDITION
DV

QVATVOR
POVR LA FIN DV TEMPS

D'
OLIVIER
MESSIAEN

15 Janvier 41

exécuté par
Olivier Messian - Etienne Pasquier
Jean Le Boulaire - Henri Akoka

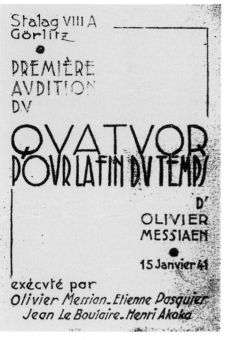

FIG. 1. Invitation to the premiere, first version. Courtesy Etienne Pasquier.

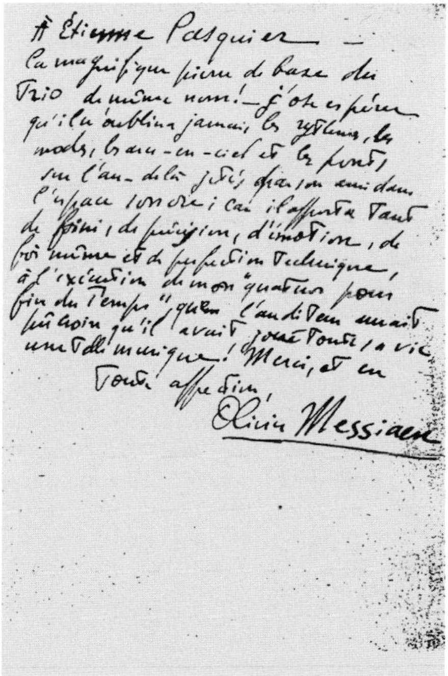

À Etienne Pasquier —
la magnifique pierre de base du
Trio du même nom! — J'ose espérer
qu'il n'oubliera jamais les rythmes, les
modes, les arcs-en-ciel et les fonds,
sur l'au-delà joués par son ami dans
l'espace sonore; car il apporta tant
de finesse, de précision, d'émotion, de
foi même et de perfection technique,
à l'exécution de mon "quatuor pour la
fin du Temps" que l'auditeur avait
l'impression qu'il avait joué toute sa vie
une telle musique! Merci, et en
toute affection,
Olivier Messiaen

FIG. 2. Dedication from Messiaen to Pasquier on the back of the invitation. Courtesy Etienne Pasquier. (See p. 2.)

FIG. 3. Olivier Messiaen at the organ in the Trinity Cathedral in Paris, 1931. Reprinted from Peter Hill's *The Messiaen Companion* with permission of Yvonne Loriod.

FIG. 4. Olivier Messiaen as a soldier on the eastern front of France in 1940. Reprinted from Catherine Massip's *Portraits d'Olivier Messiaen* with permission of Yvonne Loriod.

FIG. 5. Trio Pasquier, the early years.
Left to right: Etienne, Jean, and Pierre.
Courtesy Etienne Pasquier.

FIG. 6. Trio Pasquier, publicity photo.
Left to right: Pierre, Etienne, and Jean.
Courtesy Etienne Pasquier.

FIG. 7. Henri Akoka, age sixteen.
Courtesy Yvonne Dran.

FIG. 8. Henri Akoka, age twenty-five
Courtesy Lucien Akoka.

FIG. 9. Stalag VIII A, winter 1939–40.
Courtesy Hannalore Lauerwald.

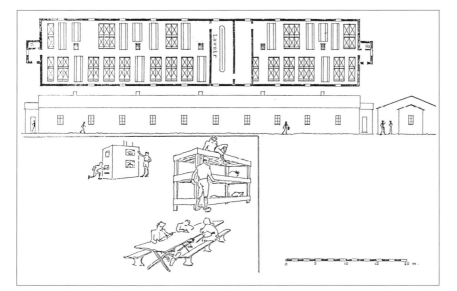

FIG. 10. Reconstruction of a barrack in Stalag VIII A. Each barrack held approximately 126 beds, with capacity for another 96 by removing the tables and benches. The washing area can be seen in the middle, and earthen stoves line the corridor. Courtesy Hannalore Lauerwald.

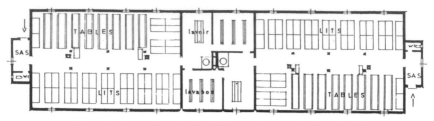

FIG. 11. Plan of a barrack in Stalag VIII A, showing beds and tables to the right and left of the washing areas in the middle. Courtesy Hannalore Lauerwald.

FIG. 12. The chaplain of Stalag VIII A. Courtesy Hannalore Lauerwald.

FIG. 13. The chapel at Stalag VIII A. Courtesy Hannalore Lauerwald.

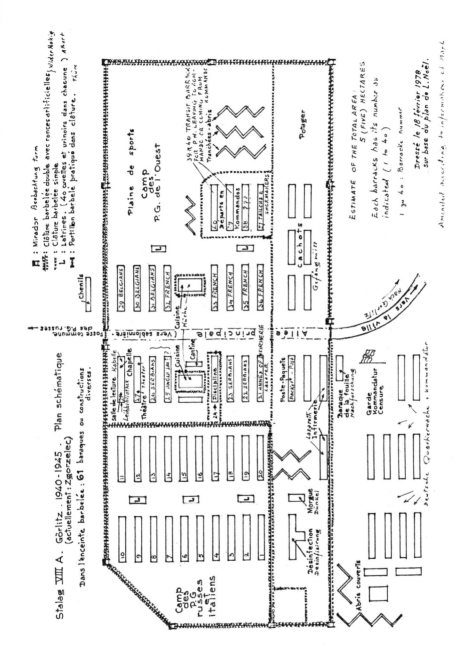

FIG. 14. Plan of Stalag VIII A. ("Clôture barbelée" is barbed wire.) Courtesy Hannalore Lauerwald.

FIG. 15. Ferdinand Caren, the orchestra conductor in Stalag VIII A, and his orchestra. Courtesy Hannalore Lauerwald.

NUMÉRO 20 · JUILLET 1942

13

le lumignon

journal mensuel du STALAG VIII A

AMI LECTEUR,

Voici ton journal réadapté, vivifié, ragaillardi. J'en ai accepté le parrainage; j'assume dès lors la responsabilité de le conduire dans la voie du succès.

Au Conseil d'Administration qui m'a choisi, j'adresse mes remerciements cordiaux. Soyez sûrs que je suis sensible à cette marque de confiance. Que ne puis-je souhaiter de plus que de m'en montrer digne, et de conserver la collaboration précieuse qui me permettra d'accomplir ma tâche.

Ami, je connais tes griefs. Notre modeste feuille ne répondait pas à tes besoins, à tes désirs. Elle ne t'amusait ni ne t'instruisait. Tu l'ignorais sim-

NOTRE ÉQUIPE

Directeur: B. SINELLE
Rédacteur en chef: G. HENNUY
Gérant responsable: R. GERBAUX
et nos Collaborateurs

Souvenir du Pays

Nous avons tenu à célébrer dignement notre fête nationale avec les moyens du bord! Nous y avons apporté tout notre cœur et toute notre âme! Il nous a donc

FIG. 16. The Stalag VIII A newspaper, *Le lumignon* (The Light), July 1942. Courtesy Hannalore Lauerwald.

LE TRIO PASQUIER

DISQUES Pathé

INTRAN STUDIO

Quelques Exraits de Presse

PARIS

On sait que le Trio PASQUIER réunit trois frères : Jean, Étienne et Pierre. C'est donc un vœu de la nature qui a rassemblé trois musiciens sérieux, dans une collaboration renforcée par l'intimité familiale et par un ensemble de goûts communs développés dès l'enfance. Voilà évidemment les conditions exceptionnellement favorables pour obtenir une cohésion et une unité parfaites.

Émile VUILLERMOZ (juillet 1934).

LONDON

Marvellous Ensemble

The PASQUIER Trio, which gave its first London concert last night, makes a speciality of finesse. Those very delicate shades of tone and colour, those exceedingly elastic rhythms are characteristic of the modern style.

If in this Jean, Pierre and Étienne Pasquier resemble other combinations of chamber-music players, their ensemble is unique rather than rare. One had the impression that they thought alike, locked at music from the same standpoint, and that the marvellous unanimity of their interpretation of Beethoven, Schubert, and Jean Cras was not the result of arrangements and adjustments, but the natural and inevitable consequence of absolutely similar temperaments.

It follows, as a matter of course, that their playing gave great pleasure. In Beethoven's C minor trio, in particular, they brought to light the inherent greatness of the music in a way that surprised those who believe that the real Beethoven is to be found only in the quartets and symphonies.

Daily Telegraph (May 3rd, 1934).

WIEN

Die Darbietungen des PASQUIER Trios verrieten ein tiefes Verständnis der deutschen Musik in den Werken von Beethoven, Reger und Mozart; ferner zeigte das Trio romantisches Temperament

PRAHA

„České Slovo", 7. března 1936:

Trio Pasquier je sensačně zajímavé již tím, že je tvoří tři bratři: houslista Jean, violista Pierre a violoncelista Etienne. Jeden jako druhý ovládá svrchovaně svůj nástroj a společně vytvořili apartní těleso komorní, jehož souhra je po všech stránkách mistrovská.

Dr. Pála.

„Lidové Noviny", 5. března 1936:

Umění bratří Pasquierů má vynikající kvality jak v jednotlivcích, kteří ovládají mistrovsky svoje nástroje, tak v

„Prager Tagblatt", 6. března 1936:

Die Trio-Vereinigung der Brüder Pasquier, die die Kammerwerke interpretierte, zählt zu den besten Europas. An jedem Pult ein Virtuose, die Ebenmässigkeit des Zusammenspiels ist klassisch zu nennen.

Dr. Steinhardt.

BRUXELLES

Le Trio Pasquier nous a donné beaucoup plus encore qu'une mise au point parfaite. L'aisance, la virtuosité de chacun des frères Pasquier leur permettraient de briller comme solistes, mais tout cela cependant est mis avec la plus grande simplicité au seul service de la musique et se décèle dans la qualité de la sonorité, des accentuations, des nuances. Enfin, le style de leurs interprétations est parfait, empreint de vraie grandeur et d'une noblesse sans emphase.

und Klangfülle. Es war ein Genuss, dem ausgeglichenen Zusammenspiel und der zarten Klangfarbe der drei Musiker zu lauschen.

Neues Wiener Tagblatt (7. Juli 1932).

ROMA

In un' audizione al Liceo, i fratelli PASQUIER si son rivelati dei concertisti di grande valore. Hanno costituito un Trio che, per la sua omogeneità, la sua grazia e la sua eleganza, raccolse suffragi ed elogi.

L'insieme dei tre esecutori non lascia nulla a desiderare e le sue interpretazioni si impongono per i loro brillanti colori e per il loro ardore comunicativo.

La Tribuna (1º Marzo 1933).

AMSTERDAM

In de tweede uitvoering van de serie der Concertgebouw-Kammermuziekavonden traden Jean, Pierre en Étienne Pasquier — het fameuze « Trio Pasquier » — op met een programma van werken van Beethoven, Mozart en Max Reger.

Ze zijn in korte jaren goede vrienden van het Amsterdamsch muziekpubliek geworden, deze drie brillante strijkers. Goede en bijzonder hoog-geachte vrienden, wier prestaties men taxeert als hors concours: verfijnde musici die het geheim van een verrukkende ensemble-kunst bezitten en die een mate van bekoring meester zijn, waarop slechts uiterst weinig combinaties zich beroemen kunnen.

Groote virtuozen in hun genre. En groote virtuozen in het allerbesten zin des woods : begaafd met sterke instrumentalistische talenten, bekeerschend een volmaakte, allerluiverste techniek, en kunstenaars. Vertolkers die een partituur van Reger even juist verstaan — wat wèl curieus is bij hun Franschen aard — als Mozart, en die beide uitersten van muzikale kunst herscheppen met een even groote kracht, een even groote warmte en een even grooten stijl.

L. M. G. ARNTZENIUS, De Telegraaf.

von Beethoven in klassischerer Weise, mit schönere Klangfülle und höherem Ebenmass gespielt werden könnte.

Der Bund (Dezember 1930).

MADRID

En este concierto participaba el Tercelo francés PASQUIER, joven grupo cuyo prestigio se confirma cada vez más. Jean, Pierre y Etienne Pasquier son tres artistas excelentes que unen, a su entusiasmo, la técnica más pura. Los tres hermanos interpretaron a la perfección tres obras de Beethoven, Schubert y Jean Cras y fueron aplaudidos caluros amente.

Joaquín TURINA, El Debate (8 de Octubre de 1932).

BERLIN

Zur grossen Überraschung wird der Abend des PASQUIER-Trios aus Paris. Da peart sich die Kultur eines staunen swert spitzan, tonschönen Strichs mit der geistigen Konzentration, die zum Zeichen der ersten Leistungsklasse gehört. Dieses Triumvirat schenkt sich nichts. So erleben wir Beethoven und Reger in erregender Vollendung. Starker begeisterter Beifall grüsst die Gäste aus dem Nachbarland.

D. Z. am Mittag (10-0-1900).

NEW-YORK

One can recall little chamber music playing of this season that matched the expertness and musicality of the performance by the Pasquiers.

Irving KOLODIN, « The Sun » 1938.

FIG. 17. Trio Pasquier press release. Courtesy Etienne Pasquier.

FIG. 18. Jean Le Boulaire, age fifty. Courtesy Jean Lanier.

FIG. 19. Theater production at Stalag VIII A. Courtesy Hannalore Lauerwald.

FIG. 20. The piano on which Messiaen premiered his *Quartet for the End of Time*. Courtesy Hannalore Lauerwald.

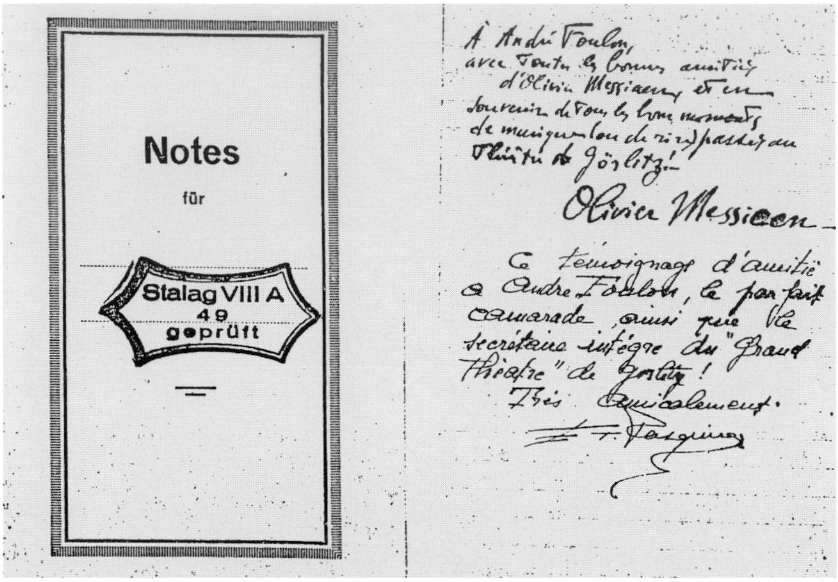

FIG. 21. Dedication. "To André Foulon, with best wishes from Olivier Messiaen, in memory of all the good moments of music (and laughter) shared in the Görlitz Theater! Olivier Messiaen." "This token of friendship to André Foulon, the perfect friend as well as the faithful secretary of the 'Grand Theater' of Görlitz! Fondly, E. T. Pasquier." Courtesy Yvonne Loriod.

FIG. 22. Invitation to the premiere, second version. Courtesy Yvonne Loriod.

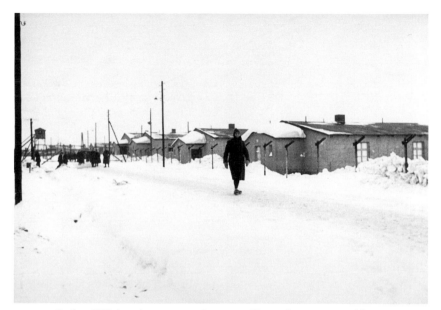

FIG. 23. Stalag VIII A, winter 1942. Courtesy Hannalore Lauerwald.

Le camp de Gorlitz . . . Baraque 27B, notre théâtre . . . Dehors, la nuit, la neige, la misère . . . Ici, un miracle . . . Le "quatuor" Pour la fin du temps" nous transporte dans un Paradis merveilleux; nous soulève de cette terre abominable. Merci infiniment a notre cher Olivier Messiaen, poète de la Pureté Eternelle . . .

En toute et grande affection.

T. Pasquier

A Olivier Messiaen, qui m'a révélé la Musique. J'essaie vainement par ces quelques mots de lui prouver ma reconnaissance mais je doute d'y parvenir un jour

H. Akoka

a Olivier Messiaen mon grand ami, qui avec le quatuor "La fin du Temps" me fit faire un grand et magnifique voyage dans un monde merveilleux. Merci mon ami que ma grande admiration et toute ma sympathie

J. le Boulaire

1° Liturgie de cristal
2° Vocalise pour l'Ange qui annonce la fin du temps
3° Abîme des oiseaux
4° Intermède
5° Louange a l'Eternité de Jésus
6° Fanfare
7° Fouillis d'Arcs en ciel pour l'Ange qui annonce la fin du temps
8° Second Louanges a l'Eternité de Jésus

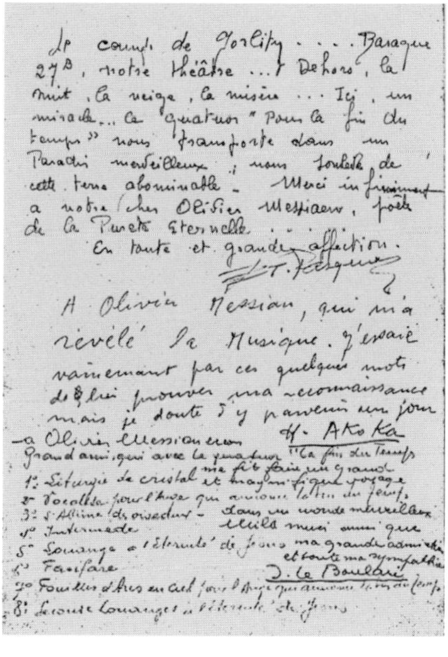

FIG. 24. Dedications from Akoka, Le Boulaire, and Pasquier to Messiaen on the back of the invitation. The titles of the movements (lower left) were handwritten by Messiaen. Note the original titles of movements 6 and 8: "Fanfare" and "*Sécond Louange à l'Eternité de Jésus,*" which Messiaen later changed to the more descriptive "*Danse de la fureur, pour les sept trompettes*" and "*Louange à l'Immortalité de Jésus.*" Courtesy Yvonne Loriod. (See p. 70.)

FIG. 25. Olivier Messiaen at the Paris Conservatory, 1952. Reprinted from Hill's *The Messiaen Companion* with permission of Yvonne Loriod.

FIG. 26. Olivier Messian and Yvonne Loriod at the piano at the Paris Conservatory, 1952. Reprinted from Hill's *The Messiaen Companion* with permission of Yvonne Loriod.

FIG. 27. Dedication from Messiaen to André Vacellier on the clarinet part of the *Quartet for the End of Time*. The date is written incorrectly, it should be 1941. Courtesy Guy Deplus and Yvonne Loriod. (See p. 93–94.)

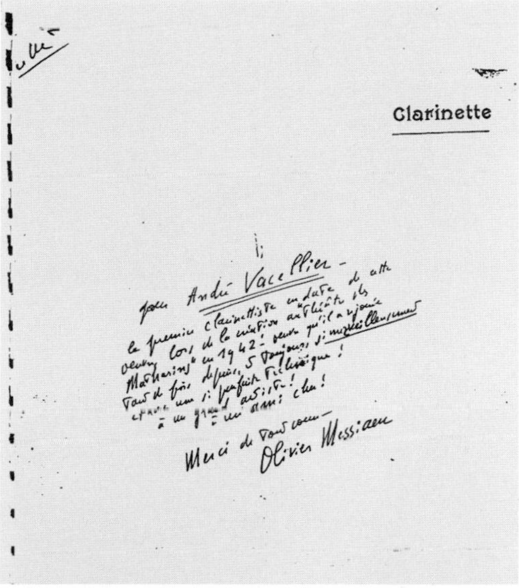

FIG. 28. Karl-Albert Brüll, age eighty. Courtesy David Gorouben and Hannalore Lauerwald.

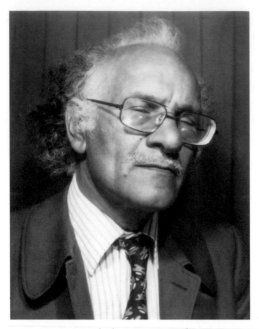

FIG. 29. Henri Akoka, age sixty-three. Courtesy Yvonne Dran.

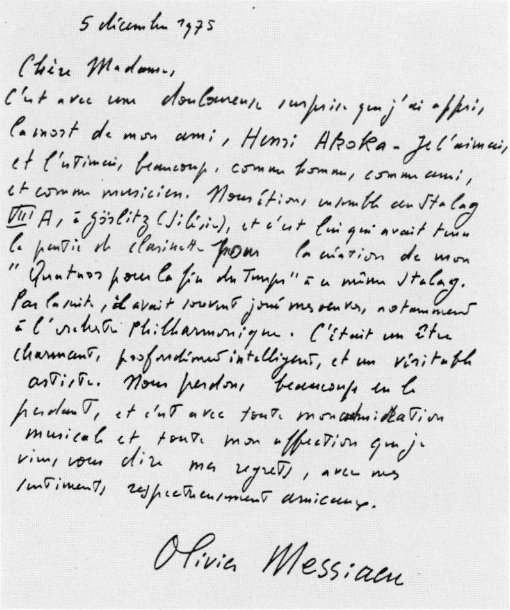

5 décembre 1975

Chère Madame,

C'est avec une douloureuse surprise que j'ai appris la mort de mon ami, Henri Akoka. Je l'aimais, et l'estimais, beaucoup, comme homme, comme ami, et comme musicien. Nous étions ensemble au Stalag VIII A, à Görlitz (Silésie), et c'est lui qui avait tenu la partie de clarinette pour la création de mon "Quatuor pour la fin du Temps" à ce même Stalag. Par la suite, il avait souvent joué mes œuvres, notamment à l'orchestre Philharmonique. C'était un être charmant, profondément intelligent, et un véritable artiste. Nous perdons beaucoup en le perdant, et c'est avec toute mon admiration musicale et toute mon affection que je viens vous dire mes regrets, avec mes sentiments respectueusement amicaux.

Olivier Messiaen

FIG. 30. Letter of condolence from Messiaen to Jeannette Akoka on the occasion of the death of Henri Akoka, 5 December 1975. Courtesy Jeannette and Lucien Akoka. (See p. 97.)

Fig. 31. Messiaen and Loriod in Petichet, summer 1991. Courtesy Yvonne Loriod.

FIG. 32. Stalag VIII A today. The sign at the main entrance reads: "Prison Camp for Non-Commissioned Officers of Enlisted Rank. Stalag VIIIA Görlitz, founded on 7 September 1939. Liberated on 8 May 1945. In September 1939 more than 10,000 Polish soldiers were imprisoned here. More than 120,000 prisoners passed through here: Americans, Britons, Italians, French, Yugoslavians, Russians and Poles. The high death rate was caused by hunger, cold, illnesses, and brutal murders committed by the staff of the camp." Trans. Jan Jakub Bokun.

FIG. 33. The plaque on the memorial to prisoners at Stalag VIII A. (See p. 100.)

FIG. 34. Trio Pasquier, with composer Florent Schmitt (seated). Standing, left to right, Etienne, Jean, and Pierre Pasquier. Courtesy Etienne Pasquier.

FIG. 35. Etienne Pasquier in rehearsal. Courtesy Etienne Pasquier.

FIG. 36. Etienne Pasquier at home in Paris, 6 June 1994. A portrait by Louise Larrut of his wife, Suzanne Gouts, hangs on the wall.

FIG. 37. Jean Lanier (ca. 1965).
Courtesy Jean Lanier.

FIG. 38. Jean Lanier, left, curtain call following *Mozartement vôtre* (ca. 1975).
Courtesy Jean Lanier and Marée-Breyer.

FIG. 39. Jean Lanier giving a violin lesson. Courtesy Jean Lanier.

FIG. 40. Jean and Yvette Lanier, at home in Paris, 3 March 1995.

FIG. 41. Lucien and Dominique Akoka, at home in Paris, 27 April 1995.

FIG. 42. Philippe Akoka, Paris, 16th arrondissement, 15 July 2002.

FIG. 43. Jeannette Akoka (left) and Yvonne Dran, La Coste, France, 14 July 2002.

FIG. 44. Henri Akoka, age thirty-
five. Courtesy Lucien Akoka.

FIG. 45. Yvonne Loriod.

FIG. 46. Olivier Messiaen, 1988.
Courtesy Yvonne Loriod.

instrumental texture is sometimes unrewarding," he wrote. In particular, he objected to the clarinet, which, in the third movement, he wrote, "did not seem to be equal to the occasion." He then added: "But this movement belongs to the whole, which is broad. It constitutes an excellent solo by itself." Delannoy also noted the poor quality of the piano at the Théâtre des Mathurins and criticized the sixth movement: "It is obvious that we never will have thought about seven trumpets of fury (and about the orchestra they call) without the "*petitio principii*" stated by the composer." By contrast, Delannoy extolled the "melodic design . . . of great beauty" of the fifth and eighth movements.[54]

In spite of these mixed reviews, and perhaps due to the very faith that his critics derided, Messiaen was apparently undeterred. Though the *Quartet for the End of Time* was not actually published until a year later, in May 1942—in a print run by Durand limited by chronic paper shortages to only one hundred copies—for many months the piece was on the composer's mind.[55] In the summer of 1941, Messiaen sent his favorite cellist a special souvenir from their experience in captivity—a copy of the invitation to the premiere of the *Quartet for the End of Time*, with a personal dedication on the back. One year later, in Neussargues, in the summer of 1942, Messiaen began writing *The Technique of My Musical Language* (published in 1944), in which he drew more examples from the *Quartet* than from any other composition.[56]

■

For the privileged few like Messiaen and Pasquier, life during the war, though difficult, went on. The Akoka family, by contrast, was less fortunate. As a World War I veteran, Henri's father, Abraham Akoka, like other Jewish veterans, was supposedly exempt from Vichy's anti-Semitic legislation.[57] Although a law of 27 September 1940 required Jews in the Occupied Zone to register and have their identity cards stamped with the word "*juif*" or "*juive*,"[58] Jews were not yet being regularly rounded up for deportation. Members of the French Resistance, however, were being pursued with a vengeance.[59] Sometimes, even those completely uninvolved in the Resistance, both Jews and non-Jews, were also being arrested in retaliation for merely living in an area in which an act of resistance had occurred or for being related to someone suspected of resisting. On 13 December 1941 the French police arrested Abraham Akoka in his bed. Ironically, it was not because he was Jewish.[60]

The police had been looking for Abraham's fourth son, Georges, who was active in the French Resistance under the assumed name of Manouret. Unable to find Georges, the police arrested Abraham instead.[61] His war veteran status was flagrantly ignored, wrote his daughter-in-law Antoinette in her book, *"C'est sûrement un juif," dit Papa*:

> This decent Frenchman, who had fought alongside other Frenchmen in World War I, who was a decorated soldier and proud of it, did not want to hide as others advised him, believing himself invulnerable. He was proud to be French, to have defended his country, to have transmitted his sense of patriotism to his children, of whom three were prisoners of war [Henri, Lucien, and Joseph]. He has nothing to fear! Alas! The Germans mock him—what he did, what he thought, and what he stood for. Brutally, barely giving him time to embrace his wife, who does not understand what is happening, they push him out of the apartment, with a rifle at his back.[62]

The arrest of Abraham Akoka followed a round-up the day before of 643 French Jews, arrested apparently in retaliation for a series of anti-German attacks by the French Resistance. The action was timed to follow the American entry into the war after the Japanese attack on Pearl Harbor on 7 December.[63] Yvonne Dran recounted below the painful story of her father's arrest:

> My father was arrested following the rebellion at the Rex movie theater. And it wasn't he whom they had come for; it was my brother Georges. And so, for a very long time, we received no news. And every time that there was an act of resistance, the police would crack down even harder.
>
> My father spent a few months in Compiègne, then in Drancy, then in Pithiviers. He was very proud to be a war veteran, very very proud. I used to say to him: "What difference does it make that you're a war veteran? It proves merely that you fought against *them* [the Germans]." He was very loyal and so he made my mother register as Jewish. I myself refused. I never registered.
>
> When my father was in Drancy, he wrote us saying: "Finally we're being recognized as former combatants and as Frenchmen. I'm leaving the camp of Drancy for Pithiviers, and it's only a question of days before I come home." But he never returned.[64]

The Akoka family learned exactly what happened to their father in a book published in French in 1978, Serge Klarsfeld's *Le mémorial de la déportation des juifs de France*. Using materials obtained from the Centre de Documentation Juive Contemporaine, Klarsfeld's study meticulously documents every convoy of Jews deported from France, listing the name, date of birth, and place of arrest of each deportee. On the list for convoy number 35 appears the name of Abraham Akoka. This convoy of one thousand French Jews left the camp of Pithiviers on 21 September 1942, wrote Klarsfeld, arriving on 23 September in Auschwitz: "Before the arrival of the deportees, over 150 men were selected in Kosel to depart for work camps. . . . In Auschwitz itself, 65 men were retained for work and were assigned numbers from 65356 to 65420. There were also 144 women, who were given numbers from 20566 to 20709. The rest of the convoy was immediately gassed."[65] Among them was Abraham Akoka.

■

While Messiaen and Pasquier resumed their musical careers in Paris, and Henri Akoka returned to his clarinet post in the Orchestre National de la Radio, in the Free Zone of Marseilles where he could escape the horrors that were ravaging Jews all over Europe, the violinist Jean Le Boulaire remained imprisoned in Stalag VIII A. "Condemned to die of boredom,"[66] as he ironically put it, he was now bereft not only of Messiaen and Pasquier but also of his best friend, Akoka, with whom he had enacted one of the most memorable events of his life. Like many other prisoners, Le Boulaire was anxious to flee.[67] In October 1941 he and two other prisoners attempted to escape, but unfortunately were recaptured after three days and taken back to the camp at Görlitz.[68]

A few months later, near the end of 1941, Le Boulaire got a lucky break. Aided again by Hauptmann Brüll, Le Boulaire managed to escape in the same way as his comrades Messiaen and Pasquier—thanks to papers forged by Brüll that claimed he was an orderly: "It was like something out of a comic strip. Brüll forged papers for us, using fake stamps made out of potatoes. He allowed us to cheat. And so, that's how we left. We passed ourselves off as orderlies."[69]

Arriving in Paris at the beginning of 1942, Le Boulaire was "extremely disoriented," and felt that his "career as a violinist was over." Military service had consumed almost seven years of his life in the most critical period in the career of an aspiring musician. These years of lost technique, Le Boulaire felt, were irretrievable:

Given my military obligations—dating from 1934—I basically gave up the violin until 1942 [excepting his performance of the Messiaen Quartet]. Practicing was out of the question. I thought that, in the meantime, others had made it, and that I would never catch up with them. My life was in shambles. I wanted to scrap everything. With a little will, maybe I could have made it. I thought, at the moment, of forming a trio or a quartet, but then it all turned to chaos. I did not want to be a little orchestral musician, but a soloist, and, if possible, to become a conductor. So, from 1934 to 1942, without hearing music, without practicing a single hour, I considered that it was pointless. Right or wrong, that's the way it was.[70]

Though liberated, Le Boulaire felt trapped, until a friend from the Paris Conservatory "threw [him] a life jacket." Pointing to his beautiful speaking voice, this friend, an actress herself, suggested that Le Boulaire read with her at an upcoming audition for the director Charles Dullin at the Sarah-Bernhardt Theater in Paris. "Figuring that I had nothing to lose, I agreed. I arrived at the theater with the script. She read the cues. And I was hired! So that was the beginning of my new career."[71]

Taken with Le Boulaire, but finding his name too long for the stage, Dullin suggested a shorter name beginning with the same letter: Lanier. And so in August 1942, Jean Le Boulaire became Jean Lanier.[72] He learned his first role, that of the trainer in J. Sarment's play *Mamouret*, in only twenty-four hours. His next role as the Duke of Buckingham in Shakespeare's *Richard III* was much more substantial, as he modestly admitted: "Note well that I was a little surprised that Dullin would pick me, who had never before uttered a word in the theater, for the role of the Duke of Buckingham, a big part. I plunged into it like a lunatic without realizing what I was doing."[73]

Following *Richard III*, Le Boulaire starred as Oreste in the premiere of Jean-Paul Sartre's important play *Les mouches*. Many more roles followed, not only in theater, but in film and television as well. "One thing that really surprised Dullin was that I played the violin. Yes, it really amused him. Moreover, he made use of it," laughed the violinist-turned-actor.[74] Whenever there was a script calling for a violinist, Jean Le Boulaire, alias Jean Lanier, was the first to be invited. It seemed that he had found his calling.

CHAPTER 7

After the Quartet

As the years passed, the musicians of the Stalag premiere of the *Quartet for the End of Time* went their separate ways. Olivier Messiaen became one of France's most celebrated composers and pedagogues, and Etienne Pasquier's Trio Pasquier became one of the country's premier chamber ensembles. Henri Akoka realized a successful career as an orchestral clarinetist, and Jean Le Boulaire, alias Jean Lanier, gained artistic renown in the theater and on film and television. Though they eventually lost contact, occasionally their paths crossed after the *Quartet*'s premiere, for Messiaen, Pasquier, and Akoka traveled in the same professional circles. However much the careers of these four men diverged, their intersection in the *Quartet for the End of Time* would forever be remembered.

■

Once out of Stalag VIII A, the musicians of the *Quartet* suddenly realized that they faced circumstances replete with new hazards. Until the end of the war, life in France, though obviously far better than it had been in Stalag VIII A, was extremely difficult. Food was scarce and artistic freedom was restricted. All the inhabitants of France lived under daily surveillance by the German and Vichy authorities, and some lived in constant fear.

Life became even more difficult following the landing of the Allied forces in French North Africa in early November 1942, when Hitler ordered the total occupation of France. On 11 November, German troops crossed the Line of Demarcation without opposition. All of France was now occupied.[1]

For Messiaen, Pasquier, and Le Boulaire, who had been living in the Occupied Zone all along, the suppression of the Line of Demarcation made little difference. For Akoka, however, the new order had far-reaching implications. Paris-based orchestras that had fled to the Free

Zone after France's surrender were forced to return to Paris. Henri had been living with his sister, Yvonne, and his brother, Pierre, in Marseilles, where he had been playing in the Orchestre National de Radio. While in Marseilles, Yvonne, fearing that her Jewish identity would be discovered, assumed the name *Angéli*, the maiden name of her sister-in-law Antoinette, who was not Jewish. Antoinette-"angel" Akoka lent Yvonne her identification card.[2] When the orchestra moved back to Paris, Henri and Pierre assumed false identities as well, under the name Auriole. With unexpected good humor, Yvonne explained the complicated process:

> When the orchestra returned to Paris, we all changed our names. Oh là là [she laughed], did we ever devise schemes to get identification cards. I myself had the valid identity papers of my sister-in-law. But the other papers were false.[3] . . . And so we "married" our mother to a Mr. Auriole so that she could have Henri, then "divorced" him so that she could wed Mr. Angéli and give birth to me, and then we had her "redivorced" in order to "remarry" Mr. Auriole so that she could have my brother Pierre. It was quite a scheme.[4]

After staying with friends in Paris, the three siblings under their assumed names rented an apartment at 237 rue Saint Charles, across from the Citroën factory, convincing the proprietor that they were refugees from Dunkerque. Every evening, recalled Yvonne, they would come home saying, "That's one more day won."[5] The three Akokas continued to live in Paris under false names until the Liberation. In the orchestra, Henri actually retained his real name and went unreported, "no doubt due to his [charming] personality," claimed his sister-in-law Antoinette.[6] Other Jewish musicians in the orchestra were less fortunate.[7]

The Occupation also made it difficult for the other three members of the original quartet to pursue their careers. Although the demand for new actors declined as France sank deeper into economic crisis, Lanier managed to establish himself in the theater, starring in Sarment's *Mamouret* (1942), Shakespeare's *Richard III* (1942), Sartre's *Les mouches* (1943), Giraudeux's *Sodome et Gomorrhe* (1943), and Priestly's *Virages dangereux* (1944).

Before the war, Pasquier already was a celebrated cellist. The Trio Pasquier had made an impressive list of recordings and commissioned works by Jean Françaix (1934), Bohuslav Martinu (1935), and André Jolivet (1938).[8] The war, obviously, put an abrupt end to the trio's touring schedule. From the time of his return to Paris in 1941 until the Liberation, Pasquier's musical activity was limited to his performances with the Paris Opera Orchestra and an occasional concert with the Trio Pasquier in France.[9]

While compositionally prolific at this time, Messiaen's pedagogical freedom at the Paris Conservatory was somewhat inhibited by the apparent Nazi censure of "modernist" composers such as Stravinsky and Berg, as well as by the fact that he was still a professor of harmony rather than of composition. In 1943, however, at the invitation of his friend Guy-Bernard Delapierre, the Egyptologist whom Messiaen had met en route from Nancy to Stalag VIII A, the composer began giving private composition courses at Delapierre's grand apartment on Visconti street, which at one time had belonged to the great seventeenth-century dramatist Jean Racine and which had two excellent grand pianos.[10] Among the first works to be analyzed were the "modernist" *Rite of Spring* and the *Quartet for the End of Time*.[11] As had his comrades in captivity, the students in these classes, which included Serge Nigg, Claude Prior, Françoise Aubut, Maurice Le Roux, Yvonne Loriod, Yvette Grimaud, Jean-Louis Martinet, and Pierre Boulez, worshipped the composer, endowing him with a kind of "Messiaenic" power. Messiaen referred to them as his "attentive and affectionate disciples."[12] Drawing on the symbolism in his name, they nicknamed themselves *"flèches"* (arrows), explained Loriod: "We were known as the 'flèches' because, like all young people, we imagined that we were going to revolutionize the world and we were shooting these arrows in every sense; and then we also thought that the arrows represented the letter M, M for Messiaen, and that the O of Olivier Messiaen represented the circle of his disciples."[13]

Surely Messiaen's contact with this group of admiring and talented students must have encouraged his writing of *Technique of My Musical Language* (1944), which he dedicated to Delapierre, and what Griffiths describes as "a decade of rapid growth in his art, a creative burst associated very much with the musicianship, and one may guess also with the person, of Yvonne Loriod."[14] A number of works in this period, including *Visions de l'Amen* (1943) and *Vingt regards sur l'Enfant-Jésus* (1944), were dedicated to and premiered by Loriod, who, three years after the death of Claire Delbos in 1959, became Messiaen's second wife.[15]

Obtaining performance opportunities for new compositions in Vichy France was difficult, however. According to Nigel Simeone, author of the article, "Messiaen and the Concerts de la Pléiade: A Kind of Clandestine Revenge against the Occupation," by 1943 the Nazis had

banned the performance in concert halls of all unpublished works by
French composers. It was partly to circumvent this interdiction that the
Concerts de la Pléiade, a concert series open by invitation only to the
intellectual and cultural elite of Paris, was founded by Gaston Galli-
mard and Denise Tual: "to provide an important platform for several
leading French composers whose music would otherwise have remained largely unperformed during the Occupation." Two of Messiaen's most important works were commissioned for and premiered at
this series: Visions de l'Amen (1943) and Trois petites liturgies de la
Présence Divine (1945).[16]

Leslie Sprout has downplayed the importance of the Concerts de la
Pléiade however, and challenges the claim that "modernist" French
composers were persecuted during this period:

> Most scholars have assumed that . . . the ban on public performances
> of new French music in Germany was also in effect in occupied
> France; and that Nazi persecution of modernist composers at home
> would have rendered performances of Messiaen's latest compositions
> in occupied Paris politically unadvisable. Messiaen's close connec-
> tion to the Concerts de la Pléiade . . . has reinforced such assump-
> tions. Postwar rumors that the series was alone in programming the
> music of the avant-garde in wartime Paris, coupled with Tual's
> claims to have defied German prohibitions by specifically planning
> each concert to feature music banned by the Germans, have long
> been taken at face value. Yet no such ban on contemporary French
> music, or modernism in general, ever existed. Paris was an interna-
> tional showcase for the Third Reich, and the continuation of an ac-
> tive and diverse cultural life was invaluable propaganda for what a
> New Europe might look like under Nazi rule. German officials
> hoped that a permissive attitude toward French culture would also
> encourage collaboration. At the very least, diverse artistic activities,
> even—or especially—controversial ones, would distract the popula-
> tion from the hardships of the war.[17]

But Messiaen's relationship to the Vichy regime was more complicated. While many French composers received commissions from the
Vichy government, Messiaen did not. As Sprout explains, Messiaen's
appointment to the Paris Conservatory in 1941

> scandaliz[ed] many prominent older composers on the faculty. Messi-
> aen's intensely personal musical language and his innovative ap-
> proach to teaching tonal harmony as a creative act of composition

set him apart from nearly all his colleagues. Those in charge of Vichy's Administration of Fine Arts, fearing the implications of modernism for the future of a distinctly French aesthetic, excluded Messiaen from the recently expanded funding opportunities aimed at bolstering new French music against German propaganda.[18]

Even more surprising than Messiaen's exclusion from these government commissions is the way in which his *Quartet for the End of Time* "was passed over when concert organizers, encouraged by Vichy's Diplomatic Service for Prisoners of War, explicitly sought out music written in captivity."[19] One such concert, entitled "Composers in the Camp," presented by the Société des Concerts du Conservatoire on 11 January 1942, featured works by three recently liberated composers: Messiaen, Jean Martinon, and Maurice Thiriet. Both Martinon and Thiriet, who were prisoners in Lucien Akoka's camp, Stalag IX A, presented works that they had composed in captivity; Messiaen did not. Since this was an orchestral concert, the conductor, Charles Munch, chose *Les offrandes oubliées* (1930) rather than the *Quartet* to represent Messiaen's work.[20] Even Denise Tual ignored Messiaen's request that the *Quartet* be performed at the *Concerts de la Pléiade*.[21] Messiaen did present two private performances of the *Quartet* during this period: one expressly intended for his analysis students on 2 December 1942, in a salon on l'avenue du Président-Wilson; and another under the auspices of "Les Amis de la Jeune France" on 25 May 1945 at the home of Guy-Bernard Delapierre.[22] However, aside from an encore performance of the fifth movement one month after the Paris premiere, the *Quartet* was not heard in public again until after the war.[23]

Apparently, the neglect of the *Quartet* was not due entirely to its musical content, claims Sprout: "Critics and audiences in Paris readily accepted other modernist works as testimonials to the war, as long as they used music to confront, not escape, the harrowing current events."[24] Two examples are André Jolivet's song cycle *Laments of a Defeated Soldier*, which shared with Messiaen's *Quartet* many of the modernist features to which Vichy's traditionalists objected, but which received wide exposure during the war; and Martinon's *Chant des captifs* for chorus and orchestra, performed in June 1943 by the Société des Concerts du Conservatoire, which was awarded the Grand Prize of the City of Paris for the best new music composition of 1943.[25] Both of these compositions passionately expressed the plight of the defeated soldier; Messiaen's *Quartet*, by contrast, ignored the issue entirely. As the composer said in a later interview in which he denied that the apocalyptic allusions were a commentary on his captivity, ". . . I composed this quartet in order to escape from the snow, from the war, from captivity, and from myself. The greatest benefit I gained from it is that among three hundred thousand prisoners [sic], I was probably the only one who was free."[26]

And yet, eventually, it would be Messiaen's work, not the others, that would become so universally identified with the prisoner's experience. It would be the *Quartet* alone that would stand the test of time.

■

On 6 June 1944 the Allied forces landed in Normandy. As the Germans fell back and as local Resistance organizations began to assume control, General de Gaulle's provisional government sent delegates into the liberated areas to oversee the transfer of power. On 19 August Resistance forces in Paris rebelled against their German occupiers, and on 25 August, as German troops withdrew, Free French units entered the city under General Jacques Leclerc. The next day General de Gaulle headed a victory parade down the Champs-Elysées. The French were ecstatic; Paris was liberated. Great Britain, the United States, and the USSR formally recognized the French provisional government headed by General de Gaulle on 23 October.

On 27 January 1945, Auschwitz was liberated. The last prisoners of Stalag VIII A were liberated on 8 May 1945.[27]

Germany surrendered on 2 May 1945 and Japan on 14 August 1945. The most destructive war in history was finally over.

As the world was restored to order, the musicians of the *Quartet* began to resume normal lives. Henri Akoka, along with his siblings Pierre and Yvonne, shed his false identity and joined his brothers, all of whom had survived. Lucien and Joseph were both liberated from their respective prison camps in the spring of 1945 and Georges, who had been fighting in the Resistance under the name Manouret, had eluded both the Vichy and German authorities.[28] The joyful mood of the Akoka family reunion was dampened only by the absence of their parents, Abraham, who was gassed in Auschwitz in September 1942, and Rachel, who died "of grief" just a few months later in January 1943.[29]

In 1945, Henri Akoka met Jeannette Chevalier, a pharmaceutical student in Paris. She married him in 1947, giving birth to two children, Geneviève ("Gigi") in 1950, and Philippe in 1952.[30] In 1946, Henri won the post of assistant principal clarinet in the Orchestre Philharmonique de Radio France. Eleven years later, in 1957, his brother Lucien won the fourth trumpet position in the same orchestra, playing alongside the legendary principal trumpeter Maurice André. Lucien recalled how Henri and Messiaen visited with each other at the rehearsals for Messiaen's *Turangalîla-symphonie* (1948), a work the orchestra performed frequently. "During the breaks, Messiaen was always with Henri. He would not leave Henri. And the feeling was mutual, for Henri was fond of Messiaen as well."[31] Subsequently, Akoka and Messiaen saw each other less often. Although Messiaen and Pasquier met more frequently, they too, lost touch, due to their busy schedules.[32]

After the war, Pasquier played the *Quartet* again with the musicians from the Paris premiere—Messiaen, piano, his brother Jean, violin, and André Vacellier, clarinet—at the magnificent home of the Comte de Beaumont on rue Duroc near Les Invalides in Paris. In 1957, Messiaen, Vacellier, and Etienne and Jean Pasquier made the first recording of the *Quartet for the End of Time* at the Scola Cantorum in Paris.[33] Unfortunately, this recording has been out of print for more than twenty years, and the company that produced it, Club Français du Disque, is now defunct.[34] The LP is available for library use, however, at the discothèques of the Bibliothèque Nationale and of Radio France in Paris.[35] The only recording of the *Quartet* that Messiaen ever made, it was regarded by Pasquier as the authoritative reference for tempo and dynamics:

> There's one thing, in my opinion, that is very important, and it's this recording that we made in Paris, with Messiaen at the piano. For those who want to play the piece, they can listen to this recording for the *tempi*, the dynamics, those kinds of things. Because Messiaen himself was at the piano, and he was very demanding. And we did exactly what he requested. It's authentic.[36]

Sometime after this recording was made, Messiaen wrote a dedication to André Vacellier on the cover of his clarinet part of the *Quartet* (see fig. 27):

For André Vacellier—
The premier clarinetist of this work on the occasion of its premiere at the Mathurins Theater in 1942 [*sic*]: a composition that he has played many times since, and always as wonderfully and with as perfect technique!
    To a great artist!

To a dear friend!
Thank you with all my heart,
Olivier Messiaen[37]

One of the last times Pasquier saw Messiaen was on the occasion of a ballet production of the *Turangalîla-symphonie* by the Paris Opera Orchestra, in which he was still playing cello. Recalling a comment that the composer had made at the first rehearsal, Pasquier pointed out a humorous side of Messiaen's personality rarely mentioned in biographies of the composer:

> One time, the Opera did a ballet set to the music of *Turangalîla*. I was still in the Opera as a cellist and I remember the first rehearsal [he laughed]. Messiaen was there. He had greatly expanded the orchestra, adding all sorts of equipment: there were *ondes Martenot* [a percussion instrument similar to the celeste], [additional] percussion, and a solo piano part with amplification, played by his wife, Yvonne Loriod. There was other equipment that was extremely loud. During the first half of the rehearsal, the equipment was badly adjusted and created a horrible racket. We all had broken eardrums. At intermission, I went into the lobby with Messiaen, and he said to me: "Boy, what a racket I'm making! That must be why they criticized Debussy. He didn't make enough noise." You see the wit that he had! He had a great sense of humor. He was an absolutely remarkable man.[38]

Having launched a full-scale acting career, Le Boulaire no longer had occasion to see the composer. However, Messiaen did correspond with another former prisoner, the Polish architect Aleksander Lyczewski, who had been present at the *Quartet*'s premiere. In December 1984, Lyczewski sent Messiaen a copy of a program from a Polish performance of the *Quartet* given to him by another former Stalag VIII A prisoner, Czeslaw Metrak, a professor of agriculture. The program is signed by Metrak and three other former prisoners from the camp: Cebrowski Konrad, Bohdan Samulski, and Zdzislaw Nardelli. Nardelli, recalled Lyczewski, a writer who was in charge of the Stalag library, apparently wrote a book in which he recalled the *Quartet*'s premiere and Messiaen's work on the piece in the library. Lyczewski wrote:

> I'm writing this letter listing [sic] to the sounds of the Quartet reproduced from the record given to me by Charles Rae. As an archi-

tect and unprofessional painter I rejoice at the construction of this composition as well as its colouring and the whole spirit.

Thank you once again for your letter and for the spiritual experiences rousing [sic] especially by Abyss of the Birds.[39]

One more associate from Stalag VIII A sought out Messiaen's company after the war—Hauptmann Karl-Albert Brüll (see fig. 28). After the war, Brüll resumed his law career in Görlitz in newly established East Germany. Following a failed insurrection in 1948, he was condemned to three years of forced labor. After his liberation, he went to West Berlin to work for the West German government.

Messiaen had apparently written a dedication to Brüll in which he thanked him for having secured his liberation. Brüll showed this dedication to David Gorouben, one of the Jewish prisoners in Stalag VIII A whom Brüll had befriended and with whom he had kept in touch after the war.[40] In 1968 Gorouben wrote a letter to Messiaen on Brüll's behalf asking if the composer would be available to meet him sometime in Paris:

I am a former prisoner of Stalag VIII A, and it was there that I met Mr. Brüll. At first, in 1940, I was an interpreter in the infirmary. Then, being a leather craftsman by profession, I was sent to work in the commando. It is for this reason that I never met you. . . .

The sole purpose of this introduction is to tell you that I saw Mr. Brüll again. I think it unnecessary for me to tell you about him, as he showed me a notebook of autographs in which you wrote some moving lines.

It is Mr. Brüll, a German officer and attorney by profession who, I believe, secured your liberation.

Should you want to see him again one day, we can meet on one of my trips to Paris where I go every month . . . [and] I can arrange a meeting for you wherever you would like.

Please accept, Monsieur and dear friend, my most distinguished regards. I look forward to your reply.[41]

As it turned out, a meeting between Messiaen and Brüll never occurred. Gorouben obtained Messiaen's address and took Brüll to visit him. But, claims Gorouben, the concierge said that Messiaen did not wish to receive them. Brüll "was very upset, and did not want to insist."[42] Loriod, however, wrote that sometime later, the composer made several unsuccessful attempts to seek out the former German officer, but Brüll may have already died by that time.[43] According to Gorouben, Brüll was hit by a car. The exact date of his death is unavailable.

■

After the premiere in Stalag VIII A, Henri Akoka never played the *Quartet for the End of Time* again, apparently because the Orchestre Philharmonique demanded musical exclusivity of its members.[44] In 1971 he retired from the orchestra and began working with his wife at her pharmacy in Paris.[45] Then, in 1975, he was diagnosed with cancer.[46]

Akoka died on 22 November 1975 at the age of sixty-three (see fig. 29). Remembered for his captivating personality as well as his beautiful playing, he was called "the Kreisler of the clarinet" by his colleagues in the Orchestre Philharmonique. "When he played his clarinet," said his brother Lucien, "he would reach a truly remarkable level of sensitivity."[47] His unflagging optimism was inseparable from his lovable sense of humor, said his son Philippe: "What I myself remember is that he was someone who always saw the positive side of life. He always spoke to us with joy about this period, even though it was a very difficult time in his life. He would recount his escapes with a lot of humor."[48]

Though he lacked a formal education, Akoka was an extremely well read and erudite man, said his brother Lucien, and his intellect and wit affected everyone with whom he came in contact. In her book *C'est sûrement un juif," dit Papa*, Antoinette Angéli-Akoka eloquently captured the essence of Henri's charm:

> Self-taught, he has a burning desire to know everything: all subjects interest him. Shorter than Georges and Pierre, very thin, always shabbily dressed, he is incredibly absent-minded and yet can devote total attention to a subject that interests him. One could not call him handsome, with his frizzy hair, his large nose, his small, deep-set eyes, his sunken cheeks. One searches in vain for a complimentary trait. He has a swarthy complexion that makes his brothers nickname him "the negro." But he doesn't care, because, in spite of his unattractive appearance, he knows that he has a sort of indefinable personal charm: a gaiety that nothing can change, a sense of humor that enables him to capture the tiniest shred of beauty or comfort in the most hopeless situation. He could make a stone laugh, and when one laughs, however unhappy one may be, one is virtually redeemed.[49]

For Olivier Messiaen, Akoka's death was also a great loss. On 5 December 1975 Messiaen wrote a letter of condolence to Jeannette Akoka (see fig. 30):

> I was stunned and grief-stricken to learn of the death of my friend, Henri Akoka. I loved him and respected him very much, as a man, as a friend, and as a musician. We were together in Stalag VIII A in Görlitz (Silesia), and it is he who played the clarinet at the premiere of my *Quartet for the End of Time* in the very same Stalag. Subsequently, he often played my works, notably in the Orchestre Philharmonique [de Radio France]. He was a charming, profoundly intelligent human being, and a genuine artist. We lose a lot in losing him, and it is with my complete musical admiration and all of my affection that I offer you my condolences.
>   With my respectful and fond regards,
>   Olivier Messiaen[50]

■

After the war, commissions, teaching appointments, honors, and prizes confirmed Messiaen's greatness. His *Quartet for the End of Time* eventually became one of his most famous and most frequently performed compositions throughout the world. In France, his reputation as an outstanding teacher was crowned by his appointment in 1947 to an analysis class at the Paris Conservatory especially created for him by the director, Claude Delvincourt. Here, for almost twenty years, Messiaen went beyond the traditional conservatory courses to analyze Greek meters, Hindu rhythms, and birdsong alongside Debussy's *Pelléas et Mélisande* and the serial works of the Second Viennese School. That class became world famous as a "super-composition" class, unique in its musical approach.[51] In 1966, Messiaen was appointed professor of composition at the Paris Conservatory, where he remained until his retirement in 1978.[52] The roster of famous students who either enrolled in or audited these harmony, analysis, and composition courses between the years 1941 and 1978 is a grand testament to the composer's sterling pedagogical reputation. Alongside such aforementioned luminaries as Pierre Boulez, Serge Nigg, and Yvonne Loriod appear the names Karlheinz Stockhausen, Iannis Xenakis, Betsy Jolas, Gilbert Amy, Tristan Murail, Gérard Grisey, Gerald Levinson, William Bolcom, and George Benjamin.[53]

Messiaen's reputation as a composer soared in these years, bringing him a series of major commissions of orchestral compositions, including the *Turangalîla-symphonie* (1949), *Réveil des oiseaux* (1953), *Oiseaux exotiques* (1956), *Couleurs de la cité céleste* (1964), *Et exspecto resurrectionem mortuorum* (1965), *Des canyons aux étoiles* (1974), and *Eclairs sur l'au-delà* (1992), as well as the opera *Saint François d'Assise* (1983). During the last years of his life, huge festivals of Messiaen's music took place all across Europe, testifying to his international renown. Among the homages paid to the composer in France included one on the occasion of his seventieth birthday, sponsored by the Ministry of Culture and Communication, Radio France, and the city of Paris; one on the occasion of his eightieth birthday, sponsored by the Paris, Conservatory; and another in 1996, sponsored by the Bibliothèque Nationale. In 1986 he was awarded France's highest medal of distinction, the Grand-Croix de la Légion d'honneur.[54]

Soon after his eightieth birthday, Messiaen's health began to decline. Many tributes were subsequently paid to the composer and countless concerts featuring his music were given—more than he could possibly attend. On 15 January 1991, a concert honoring the fiftieth anniversary of the premiere of the *Quartet for the End of Time* was held in the crypt of St. Peter's church in Görlitz, Germany. In addition to the *Quartet*, the program featured Messiaen's *Diptyque* for organ and *Le Merle noir* for flute and piano. Messiaen did not attend this concert; his agent, Maurice Werner, claimed that the city aroused "too many painful memories" for the composer and that he had "to curtail his traveling" due to his recent illness.[55] Two years earlier, however, he had sent a generous contribution to Amicale Nationale des Anciens Prisonniers de Guerre des Oflags et Stalags VIII, a national organization founded in 1965 to reestablish and maintain contact among former prisoners of war of the Oflag and Stalag VIII camps.[56] In a letter to Yvonne Loriod thanking Messiaen for his large donation, the national president of the organization, Paul Dorne, wrote:

> The very generous check that you had the kindness to address to the Friends of VIII on behalf of our more needy comrades and as a token of remembrance of the days spent in captivity will move, I'm sure, all of our friends. In their name, I want to wish you all our gratitude for this admirable gesture, which touches our hearts.
>
> I read and reread, with passion I will say, the magnificent profession of faith in music which comes straight from the heart of our

master Olivier Messiaen. It is with honor and fervor that I will read, to my comrades, this eloquent message upon our gathering in Nîmes at the end of May.

When on May 23, at 6:00 PM in the *Sainte Perpétue* church the recording of the *Quartet for the End of Time* resounds for us alone, all the thoughts of our comrades—and their prayers—will turn toward our very dear master Olivier Messiaen.[57]

In 1992 the comrades' prayers again turned toward the devout composer. In the St. Pierre Church in the city of Chalon-sur-Saône in Burgundy, the Amicale Nationale des Anciens Prisonniers de Guerre des Oflags et Stalags VIII held a religious service commemorating those former prisoners who died in that year. Among them was Olivier Messiaen,[58] who, in the wee hours of the morning of 28 April 1992, at the age of 83, passed away in the Beaujon hospital in Paris after two operations and "many months of suffering."[59]

Messiaen's last orchestral work, *Eclairs sur l'au-delà*, was completed only two weeks earlier with Yvonne Loriod who, after consulting with the composer, added the tempo markings. With the guidance of George Benjamin, Loriod also completed the final movement of *Concert à quatre*, which, at the time of Messiaen's death, was only partially orchestrated.[60]

His final work, left unfinished, promised to be monumental, the composer's most definitive treatise on composition and analysis since his 1944 *Technique of My Musical Language*. This *Treatise on Rhythm, Color, and Ornithology* would represent forty years of teaching at the Paris Conservatory and would comprise seven volumes, each running over three hundred pages.[61] For the ten years following Messiaen's death, from 1992–2002, Loriod worked tirelessly with the publisher Alphonse Leduc to complete this massive enterprise.[62] She predicted that, like *The Technique of My Musical Language*, it would be translated into numerous languages in order to reach the vast public interested in the music of Olivier Messiaen.[63]

In 1994, under the auspices of the Fondation de France, the Fondation Olivier Messiaen was established. Directed by Loriod, the foundation seeks to oversee activities related to the dissemination of Messiaen's works, the encouragement of young musicians and scholars, the conservation of Messiaen's manuscripts, and the preservation of his house and garden at Petichet, as the composer had wished. It was in Petichet, in the Dauphiné area on Lake Laffrey, where he retreated to compose almost every summer, from 1936 until his death (see fig. 31). His workroom, preserved in the state in which he left it in the fall of 1991, with its table, grand piano, and libraries, has become the "Messiaen Museum." Most of his manuscripts have been placed in the Bibliothèque Nationale in Paris.[64]

Another type of memorial can be found at the site of Stalag VIII A. After the war, the city of Görlitz was equally divided between Germany and Poland. The grounds of the prison camp today lie covered with weeds in the Polish town of Zgorzelec, near the German border. The barracks no longer exist, but at the main entrance stands a sign in Polish summarizing the history of Stalag VIII A; alongside it, there is a memorial containing a plaque in French and Polish commemorating the grounds made world famous by a quartet of French prisoners. The plaque reads simply: "In this camp lived and suffered tens of thousands of prisoners of war" (see figs. 32–33).

So the memory of Stalag VIII A and its prisoners recedes into history, for history is a time-bound perspective. But Messiaen saw beyond the boundaries of time. "Messiaen was always struck by Time," said Loriod.

> My husband considered Time to be a creature of God. Because Time is a creature of God, one day, at the end of the world, Time will be over and it will rejoin Eternity. And it's very hard to imagine that when someone dies, he is no longer subject to time anymore. He is in Eternity. This is the subject of the *Quartet*: at the end of Time, when the universe is no more, it will drift into Eternity. And this is the riddle that fascinated my husband.[65]

In rejoining eternity, the composer lives on.

CHAPTER 8

Into Eternity

This *Quartet* comprises eight movements. Why? Seven is the
perfect number, the Creation in six days sanctified by the divine
Sabbath; the seventh day of this repose extends into eternity and
becomes the eighth day of eternal light, of unalterable peace.[1]

This book comprises eight chapters. Why? Seven is the
perfect number, the creation of a quartet for the end of a
time unfolding over the collapse of an imperfect world;
the seventh chapter extends into eternity and becomes an eighth relived.
Why this eighth chapter? It addresses the second aspect of the creation of the *Quartet for the End of Time*: the history that continues to
be made after the passing of Messiaen and Akoka; the lives of those
who outlived them, Étienne Pasquier and Jean Le Boulaire, their impressions and those of the relatives of Messiaen and Akoka; and the effect upon them all of a terrible past resurrected through music. It continues the conversation retold here in the opening pages of the
"Invitation." It represents an era that has been brought back to life
through conversations with surviving witnesses. It represents the
Quartet in this time, immortalized on paper.

■

At our first meeting at Étienne Pasquier's apartment on rue du
Faubourg St. Honoré in the eighth *arrondissement*, a lovely neighbor-
hood just a ten-minute walk from the Arc de Triomphe and the avenue
des Champs-Elysées, I was cheerfully greeted by a thin, elderly man
whose proper coat and tie hung on his frail frame. He had remarkable
energy, I thought, and a charming sense of humor that instantly calmed
my initial fear of intimidation by the celebrated cellist, whose trio had
given some 3,000 concerts all over the world.[2]

During our first interview, as he began to recount in precise detail the events leading up to his captivity, his friendship with Messiaen, Akoka, and Le Boulaire, his life in Stalag VIII A, the premiere of the *Quartet for the End of Time*, his career with the Trio Pasquier and his association with nearly every major French composer since Debussy, it immediately became clear that in spite of his advanced years, the cellist had remarkable powers of recall. Here was a musician with wide contacts in the musical world who could recount his experiences with amazing precision and charm. Reminiscing over a bottle of Port and a plate of crackers, he took out a trunk full of trio scores signed by Milhaud, Dohnányi, Villa-Lobos, Roussel, Hindemith, and Pierné, while speaking of Pablo Casals, Georges Enesco, and Maurice Ravel, whose lives had intersected his own (see fig. 34).

When asked to describe his experience of forty-seven years as a member of the Trio Pasquier, the cellist remembered only good times: "It was amazing to see three brothers gifted more or less in the same way, and with a fraternal bond. Never did the slightest thing come between us. We would argue a little, but as soon as we began to play music, those little things didn't seem to matter anymore."[3]

Pasquier spoke with adoration about his late wife, Suzanne Gouts (see fig. 36). Describing not only her musicianship, her beauty, and her devotion, he also gave examples of her kindness and bravery during the war. Apparently, on more than one occasion, she risked her life to help her Jewish friends:

> My wife and I had a friend at the *Comédie Française*, an actor named Le Courtois, who was my military chief, one of my non-commissioned officers. Before his imprisonment, he had married a young Jewish woman. When he came back from the camp, he and his wife of course had to hide. So, my wife helped them as much as she could. She even gave this woman her identity card, changing the photo, to enable her to get to the Free Zone. Another friend who was threatened phoned my wife: "I have a suitcase of documents that must be removed from my home," he said. "If the Germans find it, I'll be arrested." Their house was very close to ours, and it had a back staircase. My wife went up that back staircase, got the suitcase, and brought it here. If she had been caught, it's she who would have been sent to a concentration camp. Oh, she was greatly self-sacrificing.[4]

But it was when questioned about the origins of the *Quartet for the End of Time* that the cellist wholeheartedly shared his enduring memories: the myth of the three-stringed cello and the "thousands" at the premiere; the composition and first readings of "Abyss of the Birds;" and the extraordinary escape of Henri Akoka. And when asked if he had ever imagined that the *Quartet* would become so famous, Pasquier remarked: "No, naturally not. I couldn't imagine that it would arouse so much interest. It deserved it, of course, as it was totally exceptional."[5]

In recalling his past with Messiaen, Pasquier did not simply offer dates and names, but narrated in precise detail. In recreating the atmosphere of the war years, Pasquier not only filled in historical gaps, but told an endearing story. Listening to his marvelous account of his bird-watching expeditions with Messiaen in Verdun, I felt as if I could actually hear birds chirping.

What was even more remarkable about Pasquier's testimony was that, in recalling the events of the war period, he managed to find humor in tragic situations. As he recounted with indignation the meager portions of food served to the prisoners in Stalag VIII A, his tone suddenly lightened: "I remember noticing a French prisoner, a big guy, a Norman, tall and hefty—fat. After two weeks, we saw him literally deflate. Finally, he was transparent, this guy. Then the [Red Cross] packages arrived, and he reinflated [he laughed]. He went back to his original size."[6]

In recalling a time notorious for its barbarism, Pasquier remembered instead the people who made small gestures of humanity. "War is a lesson in humanity," he said:

> I was sent, for a short period of time, to what we call a *commando*. I was sent about 100 kilometers from the camp to Strigau, to work for an individual, a gentleman who owned a granite quarry. We were twenty-eight in a room which was built for about ten. We were one on top of the other. And the cooking was done by German women, whose husbands were working in the granite industry with us. We would get up and arrive there around six in the morning to start work. And at 11 o'clock, we got something to drink . . . not to eat. It was just ersatz. But the German men were served by their wives, who would get all sorts of cans of meat, potatoes, things that we ourselves didn't have! Bread, above all. They had a half an hour to eat. It was thirty minutes, hop, then a cigarette. We had to go back to work. But when these men passed us, being careful not to be seen by the German guards, they would give us half of their bread . . . which proves . . . the absurdity of war.

Boasting good-humoredly about the superiority of French cooking, the cellist, laughing, added, "Everything we ate in that *commando* was boiled. So one time, one of my friends said to me: 'I bet these German women don't know how to fry.' So we taught them how to make fried potatoes. They must have thought: 'These Frenchmen are geniuses.' "[7]

At times during these conversations, the cellist employed his art as a raconteur to delight his American guest. Recalling the period following his liberation from Stalag VIII A when he was still under German supervision, Pasquier was sent to work as a cook, no less, in Lyons. Acting as the representative of a country famous for its cuisine, he once again mocked the cooking of the Germans. Their cleanliness and efficiency, he claimed, did little to enhance their tasteless food. "I am going to entertain you a little," he said:

> I had been a cook in Germany. And when I returned, I was put in a French barrack in Lyons. I was assigned to the soup. So, the first day, we were told: "Soup is at six o'clock. Here are the utensils to serve it, etc." The ladle that they gave us wasn't very clean. But the soup was really good. It tasted much better than the soup we made in Germany, where everything was always so neat and tidy [he laughed]. In France, it wasn't very clean, but it was very good.[8]

Pasquier spoke about Messiaen with reverence, not only about his brilliance, but about his magnanimity and respect for others, recalling how Messiaen encouraged young composers seeking new forms of musical expression:

> Messiaen was extraordinarily tolerant. On all issues. It was only people who weren't good, people who weren't decent, whom he didn't like. Otherwise, everyone had the right to live. He was a remarkable man, and he was especially fair to the composers who preceded him. He had an *absolute respect* for the old masters. One time I criticized Massenet. I said to him, "Massenet always tried to win over with the public. In fact, he courted the public. He did cartwheels to get public approval." And Messiaen replied, "Maybe that's a tendency, but in any case, he knew how to compose admirably well. Moreover, Massenet was Debussy's teacher, and Debussy received the *Prix de Rome* for *Cantate de l'enfant prodige,* which resembles Massenet from a melodic point of view." So you see how fair he was. And he was always encouraging of young people who were trying to find new formulas.[9]

But Pasquier's most fervent words came when he spoke about the effect of music on his comrades in the prison camp. The prisoners had donated money so that he could buy a bow, rosin, and a cello with *four* strings, he laughed (alluding to Messiaen's erroneous claim that his cello at the premiere had only three strings). When he returned to the camp, he said, gesturing animatedly, the prisoners "cried for joy."[10] Echoing this same sentiment, Pasquier described the premiere of the *Quartet for the End of Time* as a "miracle" in which these same musically uneducated people sat perfectly still.

In describing some of the events of this terrible period, seldom did the cellist exhibit anger or bitterness. Admittedly, as a renowned musician and the friend and colleague of Messiaen, Pasquier had had some good luck, which is perhaps why he was able to maintain such a positive attitude. "Just think," he said, "there were people who stayed in those camps for five years! I had incredible luck to be with Messiaen. It's due to Messiaen that I returned."[11]

In view of the special treatment he received in Stalag VIII A, it is therefore less surprising that the cellist claimed that he was never demoralized in captivity. "I never doubted that we would throw the Germans out the door," he said. "I was sure that they would lose. . . . I was about thirty-five years old. I still had my strength. . . . I never lost hope."[12]

Only once during our five meetings, upon recalling the loss of his childhood faith when witnessing his father return from World War I "completely transformed," and how soon World War I was followed by World War II, did the cellist's tone shift to anger. "I had many illusions when I was little. I was optimistic when I was young," he said:

> In the First World War, I was nine years old, and I saw my father
> leave for the war and come back completely transformed. My
> mother had been anxious about her husband. He could have been
> killed. It was horrible. A child remembers that. At the end of the
> war, we said: "That's it. There will never be another one like that."
> It's impossible. Twenty years later, we did it again! [He stomped his
> foot.] Unbelievable.[13]

"Wartime is an injustice," he concluded at a subsequent meeting. "Yet I never tried to dodge my responsibilities. I could have avoided the draft. But I said to myself that I would take the place of someone else. So I never tried to avoid being a prisoner. Neither did Messiaen, for that matter."[14]

Pasquier also shared with me his views on more personal subjects.

Questioned about Messiaen's religiosity, he segued into an explanation of his own agnosticism:

> My brother Jean was traditional and would go to church every Sunday. My brother Pierre didn't. Neither did I. I found it hypocritical. I gave it up. . . . One time, I was curious. I looked up the word "agnostic" in the *Grand Robert* to see what it meant. The definition pleased me. It said this: can we imagine what happens when we pass away? Either everything is possible or nothing is possible. We don't know. Agnostic means that we are incapable of knowing. That's my position. Not at all atheist! Why atheist? One can find God in nature, in music . . . the music of Schubert is divine. But we've created a sort of character with a long beard and his son. . . . All that is contrived.

He showed me a couple of paintings that he made, including a still life of tulips that hung in his living room. Finally, he shared with me a poem dedicated to the glory of childhood that he had written just a few days before in the Monceau Park in Paris. "The older I get," he said, "the more I love children. Because they haven't yet been corrupted by everything."

PARK MONCEAU

There, in this superb garden,
in full spring bloom,
I was moved, captivated.
My young little neighbor
was amusing herself
feeding crumbs to the pigeons.
She was grace itself,
her hair, cascading spun gold,
her eyes the most beautiful
to be found in the child's kingdom,
of which she seemed to be the little queen.
Wondrous childhood
that has not yet known the corruption of the soul.[15]

In reciting his poem, Pasquier recalled a famous aphorism of Jean-Jacques Rousseau: " 'A child is born good. It's society that corrupts him.' I will interpret this in my own way. A child is born neither good nor bad. He does not yet know what is good or what is bad . . . it is up to him to determine."[16]

At the time we met, Etienne Pasquier no longer played the cello; his fingers had stiffened from Dupuytren's disease, but as one of the last living witnesses to nearly a century of French chamber music, he was in great demand as a speaker. On 31 May 1992, one month after Messiaen's death, the Théâtre Impérial in Compiègne hosted a memorial concert featuring Messiaen's *Quartet for the End of Time* and *Theme and variations* for violin and piano. It was Etienne, then eighty-seven years of age, who provided the pre-concert commentary, and his nephew Régis who played the violin.[17] In the spring of 1995, a festival dedicated to Messiaen's complete works for organ was held in the Trinity Cathedral in Paris where the composer had been the titular organist for over sixty years. One of nine featured speakers, Pasquier spoke about the "miraculous" premiere in Stalag VIII A and the *"très grand"* composer at the center of it all.

A childless widower and the longest living member of the Trio Pasquier, Etienne Pasquier resided alone with his memories in Paris for over thirteen years after the death of his wife. Every Sunday he would visit his nephews Régis and Bruno of the Nouveau Trio Pasquier and his nieces, grand nephews, and grand nieces at the home of his sister-in-law Nelly.[18]

Etienne Pasquier passed away on 14 December 1997 at the age of ninety-two in a convalescence home in the Parisian suburb of Neuilly-sur-Seine.[19] But in Neuilly, where Nelly teaches music to her fourteen grandchildren, the "music box" atmosphere of Etienne's early childhood in Tours lives on.

■

Although I had been told by Etienne Pasquier that Jean Le Boulaire had become an actor under the name Jean Lanier, I had had few expectations of locating him, let alone meeting with him in his home. Knowing how protective American actors were of their private lives, I assumed that French actors would be equally so. With such expectations, I looked up his name in a directory of French actors in the Centre Pompidou public library in Paris. There I found the name of his agent, who, after hearing the reason for my inquiry, kindly gave me his home address. I sent him a letter asking if he was indeed the same Jean Le Boulaire who had premiered Messiaen's *Quartet for the End of Time* in Stalag VIII A, and if he would consent to meet with me. He replied in a note: "It is not without emotion that I relive this moment now far gone. The best thing I believe is for us to meet in person so that we can talk leisurely. Please be assured, Madame, of my sincerest regards."[20]

At our first and only meeting at his apartment on rue de la Cavalerie in the fifteenth *arrondissement*, his wife, Yvette, a pleasantly garrulous woman in her late sixties, greeted me at the door.[21] Admonishing me for bringing flowers, she immediately proceeded to arrange them in a vase in the kitchen. Amid the clatter of dishes and running water, she continued to chatter to her husband who was still out of view, while I arranged my materials on the dining room table. The clatter suddenly stopped when he entered (see figs. 37, 40). A tall, sturdy man with thinning white hair, dressed casually in gray slacks and a flannel shirt, he appeared completely unintimidating—until he spoke.

Jean Lanier had a deeply resonant voice, one that seemed to melt the walls around him regardless of the topic of conversation. At first he wanted to catch up on the past. Surprised when I told him that Pasquier was still alive, he said: "Since we parted at the end of the war, we never saw each other again. Oh, Pasquier, I don't know why I assumed that he was dead. I heard about his brothers, but I never heard anything more about him." I asked why he had not kept in touch with him.

> Our friendship in the prison camp was very amicable. But afterwards, everyone resumes his life. It's somewhat the liability of professionalization, whether one is a violinist, a clarinetist, or an actor. We vow, when we work together, that our friendship will be eternal. When we part, we say, "We'll phone each other." But we never phone. This was the same kind of thing. The Pasquiers—I say the Pasquiers because Etienne was not alone—this was a very elite little group in Paris. It was a family of musicians. It was the Pasquiers, plural. So, I didn't want to bother them. I saw Akoka again, we joked around . . . but unfortunately, he died very early.

Then the actor turned on his charm: "What would amuse me a lot is to see you with your clarinet," he said. "You know, it was one of the favorite instruments of the man himself [Messiaen]. Yes, the clarinet is the instrument of love for Messiaen." When I asked him why, he exclaimed, "Oh là là! I would like to tell you something. Every time he gave us a cue for these birdcalls that he loved [Lanier sang the theme from the first movement of the *Quartet*], he would hum, he would imitate the very sweet sound of a clarinet. He had a lot of fun with that."

When the conversation shifted to the subject of Lanier's captivity and to his subsequent career change, however, the charming exterior gave way to reveal a deeply unhappy man. "I was very, very distraught at this end of captivity," he said. "I changed professions, I had lost my dreams about being a violinist and about music." He had difficulty recalling many details of the war, he said, because he had deliberately repressed them from his memory: "The memories are a little worn. Many of them have faded, except for a few specific moments that I've deliberately tried to forget. It's been fifty years. Apart from the music, I don't wish to remember anything. This war, my God, I'm not the only one who went through it, but it was a very bad time in my life."

As the interview went on, it became clear that Lanier had deliberately lost touch with some of his comrades from captivity because they reminded him of a chapter in his life that he preferred to keep closed:

> I may horrify you when I say this, but you probably should hear it anyway. I detest the military. Moreover, I detest myself as a former member of the military. Everything I saw in the war and everything in which I participated disgusts me. So, thank God that I had this little musical awakening that helped me remain optimistic because at the end of the war, and even at the end of my captivity. . . . In sum . . . the only memory of the war that I wish to keep is the memory of the *Quartet for the End of Time*. It's this musical moment in my life. Everything else I'd prefer to forget. So no, I have no friends from the military. Often I meet people who retained ties with their superior officers, but I myself, no. I effaced all that and I don't want to hear about it anymore. I've disassociated myself from it completely.

When asked to recount the events leading up to his captivity, Lanier recounted the Battle of Dunkerque and the subsequent struggle to return to Paris. "It's then that we were taken prisoner in conditions that were so ugly that I don't even want to talk about them." Not wanting to press him to recall this painful event, I asked about his experience in captivity. He replied, "My God, it was very banal." It was "a world so cosmopolitan and yet so alien to all . . . that singled me out."

It was Lanier who first identified Brüll as the officer who had provided the musicians with instruments and forged their liberation papers. And it was due to Messiaen and Brüll, said Lanier, that he was able to find relief from the "infernal monotony" of that camp.

Though the former violinist did not suffer much physically as a result of his captivity, he was completely altered psychologically:

I remained pessimistic for a very long time, a very long time, for a thousand reasons, very personal reasons . . . upheavals in my romantic life. I admit that there was an absolutely dreadful disorder that lasted many years. It took me a good ten or twelve years to get back on my feet. But physically speaking, I didn't do too badly. Did I benefit from earlier good health? Perhaps.

"As for the food," he added, "I don't even want to talk about it. It was vile." Recalling how musicians were treated "with total propriety," but that some prisoners were executed for "stealing three potatoes," he reiterated, "in short, that's why I prefer not to talk about it."

But when Lanier spoke about Messiaen, his eyes suddenly brightened. The pessimism momentarily disappeared and the discourse turned reflective, as he recounted how, when deeply depressed in the prison camp, Messiaen often quieted his weeping, even bringing him close to a conversion experience.

Asked for his impressions of the eighth movement, the glorious solo for violin, the former violinist replied: "The eighth movement is something that is mine only. . . . I am delighted to talk about it with you today, I speak about it with friends, but it's a jewel that's mine and that will never belong to anyone else. Musically speaking, it's probably one of the most beautiful things that I've ever experienced in my life."

The remainder of the interview focused on Le Boulaire's acting career. I asked if he had been interested in drama before his initial audition.

I had never before thought about a career in acting. And I'll even tell you something else: I didn't like it very much. I only began to like the profession from the moment at which I began to have fun with it. I worked with great people—Dullin, Rouleau—who knew how to entertain. We went through hell. They also went through hell, but we had fun all the same. You know, an actor is, above all, an imitator. He's a liar, an individual who delights in, who s'amuse (and I really think that's the right word), by convincing others. It's the art of amusement. One can do a lot with words—do them, undo them. It's this that I had fun with. It's not so much the fact of being a star, of getting applause. I don't care about applause. What was important for me was to amuse myself. When I returned from captivity, I was a little crazy. I did this silly thing, although it succeeded fairly well. Was I right or wrong to change careers? I don't know. In any case, I did it. I'm not complaining. It could have been worse.

During the course of this interview and over months of correspondence, I learned more about Lanier's acting career. After his initial stage roles in *Mamouret* (1942), *Richard III* (1942), *Les mouches* (1943), *Sodome et Gomorrhe* (1943), and *Virages dangereux* (1944, 1947, 1953, 1958), he continued to do a good deal of theater. His work in *Virages dangereux*, directed by Raymond Rouleau, spawned a twenty-five-year collaboration with the director that Lanier described as the happiest association of his career.[22] During this time, he premiered a number of important plays, including André Malraux's *La condition humaine* (6 December 1954). He also appeared in a number of films that would become classics of the French cinema, including *Les enfants du paradis* (1945) and *L'année dernière à Marienbad* (1961). He was in particularly high demand as a television star. Ironically, one of Lanier's last roles in the theater was that of the first violinist in a comedy about the trials and tribulations of a quartet in rehearsal. "Not Messiaen's quartet," laughed Lanier, "Mozart's," his quartet in B-flat major, K. 458, subtitled "The Hunt." Premiered at the Marais Festival in Paris in June 1975, Eric Westphal's *Mozartement vôtre* (Mozartly Yours) was then rebroadcast on television (see figs. 38–39). It was the last time Lanier played his violin. Soon afterward, he was stricken with arthritis.

As our conversation was coming to a close, I asked Lanier if he had anything to add about his experience in captivity or the *Quartet for the End of Time*. He replied:

> No, I think that one should tell things as they are. My life is ending. I'm an old man and my life is not going to continue for very much longer. I don't aspire to anything more than tranquility now. Will I have time to redo anything? No. I amuse myself by fiddling with violins, I make cabinets. It draws me close to wood again. My first loves.

Had he ever before been interviewed about the premiere of the *Quartet for the End of Time* and his experience with Messiaen, Pasquier, and Akoka in Stalag VIII A? Surprisingly not, he answered. And then, the actor turned charmer once more. "Now," he said gleaming, "it is I who will ask the questions."

Following the interview, I received four more letters from the former violinist in answer to further questions. What was striking was that although each letter differed in content, each bore very much the same tone—a mixture of sadness, bitterness, irony, and charm. In his first letter, he expressed his sadness about being passed over for a prize at the Paris Conservatory: "I point out immediately, in order to make you avoid an error, that in the course of our interview, auditory difficulties made me give a wrong answer to your question about my diploma at the Paris Conservatory. I did not get my first prize. This failure was very difficult to forget."[23]

In his second letter, in answer to my questions about his liberation, his second wife, Yvette, and his children by his first marriage, he wrote: "I don't know how this good and brave Brüll certified our papers but I can assure you that the stamps on them were perfectly illegible. . . . My wife's maiden name is Yvette de Cahagne. . . . My children are named Annick, Jean-Robert, and Françoise and it's been a long time since I've known their birth dates!" The concluding tone of the letter was strangely similar to that of his initial note to me: "It is not without emotion that I have stirred up these old memories, dear Rebecca, and I dare hope that they will be able to serve you in your enormous work."[24]

In his third letter, Lanier once again apologized for his inability to remember certain details of his captivity. Then, when recalling his childhood during World War I, his tone turned bitter. This was one of the last letters I received. In September 1996, I sent him another in which I asked him to clarify a minor detail about Henri Akoka's escape from Stalag VIII A. A few weeks later I received a message from his son saying that his father had suddenly become very ill and would not be able to answer.

While on vacation in France the following summer, I called his wife, who explained to me what had happened. Just two days after my letter arrived, on 2 October 1996, Lanier had a stroke, after which he remained in long-term hospital care in Paris. Though not paralyzed, he lost his reflexes, his sight, and, worst of all, his memory.[25] Fearful that my presence might evoke memories of the war, and indirectly trigger another stroke, his wife discouraged me from visiting him. In tears, she explained over the phone:

> My husband had always banished the war from his spirit. He never spoke about it, finding the memories too painful. You remember how difficult it was for him to retrieve his memories for you. But now that he has no control over his reflexes, all these terrible memories have come back. At times, he even hallucinates that the war is still going on. One time, I visited him, and he said to me: "How are you going to get home? It's dangerous." He was afraid that the Germans were following him and he told me that he had tried to escape by hiding in the cellar. "How did you find me?" he said. "I was hiding in the cellar. They were chasing me."

Since the stroke, she said, "we avoid even uttering the word 'war' in my husband's presence."[26]

I never saw Jean Lanier again. I did, however, visit his wife in Paris. Distraught not only by her husband's condition but by the sudden financial burden of hospital fees for long-term care, she wept as she explained her predicament. Then, wiping away the tears, she went over to the dining room table to fetch me an old program of *Fait divers* (News in Brief), an autobiographical drama by Aimé Declercq in which Lanier had starred. In the program was an article entitled *"Un café avec l'auteur (le faux) ou Qui est Jean Lanier?"* (Coffee with the Author (the Actor) or Who Is Jean Lanier?), which included the following description:

> He is very tall, and his voice envelops you. His eyes sparkle. A quiet flame. A stare into the distance, toward what dreams? Ravel? Molière? Mozart or Vivaldi? Jean Lanier, in any case, will transport you tonight into the realm of the author, whom he will portray. And then, he will return to his violin, and to his favorite pastime: weaving at a hand loom. For him, it is another way to dream. If I had to find a word to describe him, I would say: harmony. It must be wonderful to be his friend. As it is wonderful to see him on stage. *A tout de suite, Jean Lanier! Et merci.*[27]

So long, Jean Lanier. And thank you.

■

"We came to France in 1926. My father was a trumpeter, a remarkable musician. May I say a few words about my father?"[28]

This is how my interview with Lucien Akoka began. He was the only surviving brother of Henri Akoka, and I had obtained his name from Pierre Akoka, the son of Georges Akoka, a French Resistance fighter who, Pasquier told me, had subsequently become a physician in Paris. Pierre, who had been a piano student of Yvonne Loriod's at the Paris Conservatory, told me that his father had recently passed away, but that his uncle Lucien was still alive. As a former prisoner himself and as a musician in the same orchestra as Henri, Lucien, I was told, would be able to tell me everything I needed to know.

Arriving for dinner at his grand apartment with a view of the Eiffel Tower on avenue Charles Floquet, I was warmly greeted by a small, modest-looking man with gray hair and mustache who escorted me past several rooms into a large kitchen (see fig. 41). There, he assured me, we would not be bothered. I had told him that I had come to Paris to research the history of the *Quartet for the End of Time.* But Lucien wanted to talk about his father, Abraham Akoka. I did not interrupt him:

> My father was an exceptional musician. I am convinced that, if he had been in Paris during his youth, he would have become a rather remarkable musician. He was a trumpeter, but he also played the violin, the piano, and he learned music theory all by himself. When he was fourteen years old, a circus passed through his village. One of the trumpeters was sick and couldn't go on tour, so the conductor looked everywhere for a replacement. So, someone told him: "Go to the Akoka house. There's a young man who plays the trumpet really well." "How old is he?" "Fourteen." "You can't be serious." "Listen to him." He listened. My father sightread everything. It was perfect. He had exceptional technique. And so he was hired. His mother let him go on tour to Italy and to southern France on the condition that the director take good care of him.
>
> My father had a subscription to a magazine called *L'écho des concours.* He received it in Algeria. One day, in this *Echo,* there was a "help wanted" announcement for musicians to play in Ponthierry . . . in Seine-et-Marne, near Melun, fifteen kilometers from Fontainebleau. A wallpaper factory provided lodging and work in exchange for playing in the factory band. And this is how we arrived in Ponthierry in 1926. My brother Henri, who was already playing a little clarinet, was fourteen years old. I was twelve, and the youngest of my brothers was two. We were six children in all, five brothers and one sister: Joseph, Henri, Georges, Pierre, Yvonne, and myself.
>
> My father had wanted us all to become professional musicians and to get a good musical education. That's why he brought us to France. Of course, he was criticized by the rest of his family: "But you're not going to just pick up and move to France with six children, the youngest of whom is two years old!" But he did, and my mother followed him. And that's how we came to Marseilles, to Paris, and then to Ponthierry. Because my father would say: "In life, one must make music. One can not go through life without making music."

As the interview went on, the conversation shifted toward his brother Henri. Laughing, he recalled: "Before entering the Conservatory, Henri had begun to play in orchestras for silent films. He also worked in the wallpaper factory for a year. And so he would return in the evening all covered with little pieces of colored paper." Lucien then went on to speak about Henri, chronicling his musical career, his Trotskyist activities, his captivity, and his heroic escape from Stalag VIII A. He also told me about his own experience in captivity in Stalag IX A in Ziegenhain, Germany. With great pride Lucien recalled Henri's nickname, "the Kreisler of the clarinet," bestowed upon him by his colleagues in the orchestra; his determination ("Note well that he tried to escape twice before he finally succeeded"); his political radicalism; and his intelligence and personality. "Everyone with whom he came in contact was fascinated by what he knew, by what he said, and by his way of expressing himself," including, he claimed, Messiaen.

When asked about his own experience as a prisoner for five years in Stalag IX A, Lucien, again with pride, enumerated the famous musicians, artists, and future politicians, notably former president François Mitterrand, who were in his camp. He also confirmed that musicians in Stalag IX A, like those in Stalag VIII A, were given special treatment·

> I was taken prisoner in France, near Dijon, in Flers, to be more exact. But instead of going to Silesia like Henri, I was steered toward Kassel, near Frankfurt. I was a prisoner for five years. There I made music with some wonderful musicians. Jean Martinon, you've heard of him perhaps? He directed the Chicago Symphony. He also conducted the Orchestre National de France, and he was in my camp. There was also the composer Maurice Thiriet and the violinist Michel Warlop. There were also painters with us. There was someone with the *Grand Prix de Rome* for painting. There were actors from the *Comédie Française*. . . . Among the prisoners, all the professions were represented, but in my camp the artists were privileged. . . . We got a little more coal to keep warm. We had a lot of things that other prisoners didn't have. We were lodged in special barracks. That is why Mitterrand, who was a prisoner in our camp, was always with us, in the musicians' barracks. Because it was warmer in our barrack.

It was only then that Lucien's tone changed. With some bitterness he recalled how the Nazis' gentle treatment of musicians often functioned as a propaganda tool to convince the world that they were taking good care of their prisoners and to ensure France's continued collaboration. Then, recalling his father's arrest, he assailed the country that had chosen to collaborate:

My father had served in World War I when he had three little children at home. He spent four years in the Dardanelles. And he had the
croix de guerre and other medals. At the time of his arrest, he said:
"Don't worry. I'm a war veteran. I have the *croix de guerre.*" But he
was sent to Auschwitz. And it was the French police who arrested
my father, not the Germans, the French. France and Germany were
practically allies! France was the only country that collaborated with
its conquerors![29]

Toward the end of the interview, Lucien's spirit lifted again when recalling his brother's taste in art, leading him to speak proudly about
how Henri is remembered today:

Henri loved modern art. I'm going to show you the paintings he did.
He was a surrealist; and he was a friend of André Breton's. You've
heard of André Breton? Breton was the father of surrealism and he
was a friend of Henri's. In one of his books, André Breton speaks of
his friend "the clarinetist."[30] Henri was very curious about new
things. That's why he liked Messiaen's music so much. It was very
different from the usual classical works that we play. . . .

What one can surely say about Messiaen is that he wrote a composition that is known throughout the entire world. When my children play in orchestras abroad, people ask, "Akoka! You mean from
the *Quartet?*" "Yes, it was my uncle who premiered that." In Paris,
London, New York, Dallas, Moscow, everywhere, they speak of Henri
Akoka. So, I have to say, "Thank you, Messiaen. My brother is spo-
ken of around the world."

With this last remark, an evening of quiet conversation turned into
one of boisterous celebration. A total of nine guests, including Henri
Akoka's son and daughter, Philippe and Gigi, both in the film industry;
Lucien's wife, Dominique, a psychologist; and their children, Gilles, a
violinist, and Jerôme, a trumpeter like his father and grandfather, delighted in recalling the quirks and proclivities of the clarinetist from
the *Quartet for the End of Time*: how Henri bathed fully clothed so as
to "kill two birds with one stone"—to bathe himself while relieving
his wife of laundry duty; his habit of wrapping himself in a plastic sail
in order to maintain his body temperature when swimming in the
summer in the Mediterranean Sea; and his one-time attempt to eat an
entire French meal backward (coffee, dessert, cheese, main course, ap-
petizer) just to see what would happen (he got sick). The laughter became so contagious that, after dinner, Lucien, Philippe, and I had to

move to another room in order to discuss more serious subjects in quiet.

"My father was never demoralized for a moment in his life," said his son, Philippe (see fig. 42). Describing Henri's optimism, his escape attempts, and his eagerness to "get going," he explained that, although Messiaen refused Henri's appeals to escape, he responded to the clarinetist's calls to compose. Thus, Philippe claimed, Henri was directly responsible for the *Quartet's* creation. "My father had an enormous influence on everyone he met. He had such charisma, such personality, that no one could remain indifferent to anything he said," he concluded.[31] Confirming his nephew's statement, Lucien concluded by recalling one of Henri's students from the Conservatoire de Musique de Villeneuve-St. Georges, which Lucien founded and directed:

> Henri used to give clarinet lessons at the conservatory that I directed. The class lasted three hours. You would arrive sometime during that three-hour period, have your lesson, maybe listen to someone else, and then leave. People would come and go. That was the way it was everywhere in France. But there was this one student who was an engineer at SNCF, an amateur, about sixty years old, and a real enthusiast. He would stay for the entire class! The children would leave, but for three hours, this man would be there. He never missed a class. And I later learned why. He said to me: "Your brother is the most extraordinary man that I have ever met in my life. He's so fascinating that I arrive on time. I go to all of his classes, from beginning to end. Because with him, I don't just learn about the clarinet; I learn about life."[32]

■

Henri's widow, Jeannette, and his sister, Yvonne Dran, lived in Nice, on the French Riviera. We met at Jeannette's beautiful apartment overlooking the Mediterranean Sea. A lovely woman in her seventies, Jeannette remained quiet throughout most of the interview. Perhaps it was simply her temperament, but I could not help recalling her son Philippe's comment to me in private that his mother had been deeply shaken by her husband's death and that she "could not live without Henri," who had had such a strong personality. Yvonne, however, recounted in passionate detail the comedies and tragedies of her family history—Henri's studies at the Paris Conservatory, his escape from Stalag VIII A, their life under the Occupation, and their father's arrest. At times she spoke so quickly that it was difficult to follow. She had a lot to say, and she wanted all of it to be heard.

She began by speaking about Henri's frustration at having to spend five years at the Paris Conservatory to get his first prize (the usual time is three to four years):

> My parents came to France to work in a wallpaper factory. But my father had a subscription to a magazine in which they were asking for personnel in a band, and that's what really lured him. The music director was a Monsieur Briançon. Briançon saw that Henri was very gifted and he began to give him lessons. Later, he took him to audition at the Paris Conservatory. But there was a bitter antagonism, because Briançon and the professor at the Conservatory, [Auguste] Périer, were from the same area and were enormously jealous of one another. So, all of the students whom Briançon sent to the Conservatory were torn to shreds.
>
> So, Henri went through every stage, first a second honorable mention, then a first honorable mention, then a second prize, then, the fourth year, no prize, and finally, the last year, he got his first prize. And every single time he deserved it. My father had the sense to tell him: "It's very good that they didn't give it to you, because that's one more year that you get to study at the Paris Conservatory." Because my father was very—how shall we put it—practical. He also wanted, I think, to console Henri. When Henri finally got his first prize, my father said to him: "I predict that one day you'll be a member of the jury at the Conservatory." And it happened that one day, he received a letter from the Minister of Culture inviting him to be a member of the jury for the clarinet class. He was very proud. Later, when Mr. Périer became very ill, he telephoned Henri to apologize. Because there had been much injustice, and he wanted to make up for it.[33]

When asked about Henri's experience in Stalag VIII A, Yvonne recalled Henri's successful escape and how his clarinet miraculously made it through all his travails. Giggling, her face suddenly brightening, Jeannette added: "Henri would go from village to village with this clarinet. He would jump into ditches with it. That instrument must have been in quite a state!"

Having heard much about Henri's sense of humor and absent-mindedness from the rest of the Akoka family, I asked Jeannette to recollect some other comic anecdotes. The giggles turned into laughter:

One day at the beach Henri put on a diving suit—with a lot of difficulty, of course. Naturally, everyone was looking at him thinking that he was going to go scuba-diving or perform some other great feat. He went down to the seashore, put two or three toes in the water, and then came back and took off the diving suit! Another time he was invited to go on a fishing trip. It was an evening expedition. He had put on this famous diving suit again, and when it was time to take a break, he didn't want to take it off. So, dressed in this diving suit, he went with some friends to this woman's house for tea. Between the diving suit and the tea, he was dying of the heat, but he didn't want to refuse the tea, he said, because that wouldn't have been polite. It had not occurred to him to take off the diving suit![34]

Recalling another humorous incident from the war, Yvonne illustrated Henri's frustrating yet endearing lackadaisical side:

During the Occupation, there would be alerts, and the subway would stop running for fifteen minutes. I would get around by bicycle. One day Henri had a rehearsal near *les Halles*. There had been an alert and he was very late. My bicycle was sacred to me, but I consented to let him borrow it. I said: "Be careful, OK?" When he returned from the rehearsal, he plopped down on the couch and said: "Oh là là là, were there a lot of people in the subway." As it turned out, he had left my bicycle and come back by subway. He had forgotten the bicycle! Boy, was he spacey!

Both women agreed that Henri Akoka dwelled "in his own world."

After dinner, the conversation turned serious. Returning to the subject of Henri's escape, I asked whether the clarinetist had had any idea of how serious the consequences might have been had he been caught. Yvonne insisted that her brother made his escape because he was a prisoner of war, not because he was a Jew. Mass deportations of Jews from France had not yet begun at this time, she said, and no one imagined that there might be a "final solution" so unthinkable. "But from the moment my father was arrested, we began to have some doubts," she added. It was then that she recounted the painful story of his arrest. With anger and sadness, she lashed out against the world that allowed the Holocaust to happen, citing a note that her father had tossed out of the train from Pithiviers:

When they got on the train, they realized that they were not going to return. My father tossed out a little piece of paper that someone sent us—I don't know who it was—in which he said: "I'm leaving for an unknown destination."

The whole world knew that there were concentration and extermination camps and they did nothing. There were people who managed to make it known, who went to Churchill's office. But the British had other concerns. And the pope was pro-Hitler; he did not do a thing. In the United States, it was the same thing. People say sometimes that the Jews went like lambs to the slaughterhouse, without reacting, without doing anything at all. But one wonders why the Allies did not parachute us arms so that we could defend ourselves. Nothing was done.

But Yvonne also spoke about those who did help her and her brothers during the war. In particular, she spoke about Etienne Pasquier:

Upon his liberation, one of Pasquier's first visits was to my parents' house. He said that he was absolutely sorry that Henri could not have accompanied him. And he and his wife gave us all the details that I've given you. During the Occupation, these were people who were extremely supportive. And I think it was out of friendship for Henri. It's extraordinary, because Messiaen never came to the house. Whereas the Pasquiers, they had us over, and they were continually in contact with my mother.[35]

In answer to my further inquiries about how Pasquier and his wife helped them during the war, Yvonne recalled:

The Pasquiers were very kind. They had connections with people in the French police who were in the Resistance, and so they were well-informed about the round-ups. And every time they would hear about something, the two of them would come to the house.

One day, they said to my mother: "You know, Madame Akoka, this may be very painful for you, but if you do not want Georges and Pierre" (who were 20 and 16, respectively, and in the Resistance) "to be arrested" (our father had just been arrested), "send them to stay with Henri in Marseilles. The sooner the better. Don't worry. They will manage. You absolutely have to send Georges, Pierre, and even Yvonne to Marseilles. Reliable sources tell us that they're going after your children. Mrs. Akoka, let them go." When I came back from work, my mother told me about their visit: "The Pasquiers told me to send Pierre and Georges away, because there are going to be raids." I said: "I myself have nothing to fear. I'm not wearing the star,"[36] because I had not registered as Jewish. I considered registering an insult. But it was dangerous either way.

At that time we had many ways of passing the Line of Demarcation, and so Mama let her sons go. And I went with them. Papa had already disappeared.

Unexpectedly, Yvonne then spoke about Messiaen. After the arrest of her father in December 1941, she went to visit Messiaen one Sunday at the Trinity Cathedral, where he had resumed his post at the organ and was trying to make his way back into a tolerable daily existence as a teacher, composer, and organist. Trusting in Messiaen's stature in French culture, she hoped his name and reputation would secure the release of her father, a decorated World War I veteran. But Messiaen said that there was nothing he could do.[37] Yvonne is bitter to this day. Her feelings of betrayal are certainly ones with which anyone who has lost a family member to the Holocaust could identify. It may be, though, that there was indeed nothing that Messiaen could do. It may be that, like other civilians in occupied Europe, he was wary of becoming involved, given the possible consequences of his actions. No doubt many French committed small acts of resistance. Yvonne Loriod reportedly played encores of Mendelssohn at her recitals in occupied Paris, just to spite the Nazis.[38] Yet even these small acts of courage were fraught with great risk.

Like everyone else in December 1941, Messiaen could not have imagined the Holocaust. He probably assumed that, in the end, goodness would reign. Note that he refused Henri's pleas to escape from Stalag VIII A, claiming that "God willed" that he be a prisoner.

In contrast to the Trotskyist clarinetist, Messiaen was apolitical. Clearly, he felt more comfortable in his interior world of music and prayer than in the exterior world at large. In the camp, when hungry, cold, and anxious, Messiaen would listen to complete acts of Debussy's *Pelléas et Mélisande* in his mind in an effort to soothe and sustain himself. He transcended his experience in Stalag VIII A by transfiguring it into exalted musical language—the *Quartet for the End of Time*—rather than by confronting its everyday realities. "I composed this quartet in order to escape from the snow, from the war, from captivity, and from myself. The greatest benefit I gained from it is that among three hundred thousand prisoners [sic], I was probably the only one who was free."[39]

For many war veterans and former prisoners of war, like Jean Le Boulaire, their experiences were sometimes too dreadful to invite recall, and became effaced from memory. This, of course, partially accounts for Messiaen's decision not to attend the *Quartet*'s fortieth anniversary concert in Görlitz. Perhaps it also accounts for Messiaen's avoidance of a reunion with Hauptmann Brüll and his failure to mention what would appear to be key facts about his fellow musicians: most notably that Henri Akoka was Jewish; that he escaped from Stalag VIII A, and along with his brothers and sisters, managed to survive the Holocaust; and that "Abyss of the Birds" was the first of the *Quartet* movements to be composed, and one in which Akoka played a crucial role.

Though Yvonne Dran is still upset that Messiaen did not come to the aid of her father, she spoke reverently about the absolute kindness of Etienne Pasquier and his wife, Suzanne, who gave the Akokas the feeling that somebody cared. "I remember how humane he and his wife were with us. And it was out of love for Henri, I believe, that they were so kind." With tears in her eyes, she looked at me then and said: "Perhaps we didn't thank them enough. Perhaps we never said 'thank you' to the Pasquiers."

As I left, I thanked the women for the lovely dinner and for their generous help with my research. Yvonne replied, "It's we who should be thanking you. The other day, when you phoned me, oh là là, did it make me feel good. Because, whenever I talk to Philippe [Henri and Jeannette's son] about our family's experiences in the war, he says to me: 'Tata, you have to write that all that down.' But I'm lazy, and so I don't do it. It's a shame, because it's an unusual story."[40] Jeannette added, "Henri used to recount his memories to his musician friends every summer in the Vaucluse. He would tell them all about his captivity and his escape. And we regret that we did not record these memories, all these adventures, because it would have been fantastic. But we never thought about it."[41]

Surprisingly, Henri Akoka was never interviewed about the premiere of the *Quartet for the End of Time* and his experience with Messiaen, Pasquier, and Le Boulaire in Stalag VIII A. His family had never been approached before either.

A couple of years later, when I was vacationing in France, Jeannette and Yvonne invited me to dine with them and their friends and relatives at Jeannette's beautiful house in La Coste, in Provence (see fig. 43). There, once again around a huge table spread with wine, cheese, bread, and pastries, I sat among a dozen nieces, nephews, aunts, uncles, and grandmothers as they grieved and laughed about their remarkably tragicomic family history.

■

"My husband always said, '*Je suis né croyant*'" (I was born a believer), said Yvonne Loriod at our meeting in her lovely apartment on rue Marcadet, near Montmartre, famous as much for the many artists who frequented its quarters as for its breathtaking view of Paris from the steps of the Sacré-Cœur cathedral. A charming, petite lady then nearly seventy years of age, with thick gray hair piled up in a *chignon* (see fig. 45), Yvonne Loriod sat at a desk on top of which rested a framed photo of Pope John Paul II and a pile of papers about the *Quartet*, documents that she had only recently discovered. Among them was the original manuscript of the preface, with the Stalag stamp. She then went through the documents relating to the *Quartet*'s publication by Durand in 1942. "This music was very difficult to print. There are directions for the printer and directions to be printed in the score. Messiaen said that the preface and all the fingerings had to be included. He also told the printer to mind the page turns."[42]

Emphasizing the suffering that her husband underwent in the prison camp that had made musical history, Loriod described the atmosphere there as her husband had apparently recounted it to her: how he had arrived at the camp clutching a satchel of musical scores to his chest and how he struggled with one German officer who had tried to confiscate his scores; how Messiaen had had so little to eat that he and his comrades would recite menus and recipes in order to console each other; how, one morning, while on watch, the composer saw the northern lights; and how Brüll gave him pencil, manuscript paper, and extra pieces of bread and supposedly put him in the camp toilets to compose in peace. Loriod then described the famous premiere, a succession of miracles that had arisen in the unlikeliest of places. Though some of these details, I later discovered, were not given accurately, her words left me with a powerful impression of a man who had triumphed over time through music.

Loriod also emphasized how much Messiaen had suffered, both physically and emotionally, not only in captivity but before and afterward.[43] She reiterated that Messiaen had been brought up during the First World War by his mother and grandmother because his father had been drafted. When he was eighteen his mother died of tuberculosis. Around the same time, Messiaen himself became ill, and was then nursed back to health by his aunts who had a farm in the Aube. Following his imprisonment and liberation during World War II, he had to care for his son, Pascal, alone while eking out a living as an organist at the Trinity Cathedral, as a professor at the Paris Conservatory, and as a composer at home, for his wife had been institutionalized.[44]

I asked Loriod about an interview in which Messiaen had affirmed that the *Quartet* was a work due entirely to circumstance, and had declared that certain genres, notably the string quartet, were becoming outmoded: "Of course, there are a few modern masterpieces of this genre," he had said in the interview: "the six quartets of Bartok, the *Lyric Suite* of Alban Berg. But modern music has become too complex to be written in four voices, especially, four strings."[45] Was this why Messiaen had not written more chamber music? Loriod pointed out that Messiaen received a large number of commissions for other types of compositions after the war and simply did not have the time to write chamber works. It was not because he did not like chamber music, she emphasized, but because these commissions helped him both gain exposure and make ends meet.

The conversation then turned to the performance of Messiaen's works. Recalling a recording of the *Quartet* made on 21 November 1990 at the Notre-Dame du Liban Cathedral in Paris with Christoph Poppen, violin, Wolfgang Meyer, clarinet, Manuel Fischer-Dieskau, cello, and herself at the piano,[46] Loriod mentioned the composer's remarks to the performers:

> For this recording, he always took notes on his writing pad and would have us restart when something wasn't good. In general, I remember that he gave bowing advice in the "Louange" movements, so that the tempi would be slow enough. He would say, "Change the bow whenever you want, but it has to be very slow." He would demand that everything be in the exact tempo that he wanted. And sometimes, we would do several versions so that afterward he could choose the best sonority and the best dynamics. He was very demanding, but he always made his requests very kindly. He was always very nice. I think that this was a really good recording because, as Messiaen was present, the tempos and dynamics are exactly the ones he wanted.

Loriod commented on Messiaen's other performance preferences. Messiaen apparently "detested" rubato, she said, claiming that it "kills" rhythm. When asked if the composer objected to clarinetists, cellists, and violinists playing the solo movements ("Abyss of the Birds," "Praise to the Immortality of Jesus," and "Praise to the Eternity of Jesus") separately as organic compositions rather than as movements within a performance of the entire *Quartet*, Loriod replied,

> Absolutely. He would get very angry. Messiaen did not want these pieces to be played alone. For example, there is a piece for solo horn

in *Des canyons aux étoiles,* a piece based on his impressions of Bryce Canyon in Utah. (In the United States, in Parowan, Utah, they named a mountain after him! It's called Mount Messiaen!) Well, in *Des canyons aux étoiles,* there's a piece for unaccompanied horn. And as there is not an enormous repertoire for horn, all these hornists play it on their solo recitals. Messiaen did not want this. He wanted his works to be played integrally. But once his compositions are published, we can't prevent these things from happening.

"What Messiaen wanted," said Loriod, "was that we respect his works." This is why, she said, her husband asked that a Messiaen Foundation be established after his death, in order to oversee the proper dissemination of his works. That is also why Loriod worked faithfully on realizing her husband's other last wish—assembling and publishing the seven volumes of his *Treatise on Rhythm, Color, and Ornithology,* his last will and testament to forty years of teaching and a lifetime of composition. For Loriod, immersion in this massive project was cathartic, as she explained:

> I must tell you, that when my husband passed away, I had an enormous amount of grief, because, in short, I lost my husband, I lost my teacher, I lost my collaborator, and I lost my master. I lost four people in one. I had a terrible time regaining my strength but what saved me was working on the *Treatise* immediately. Before entering the hospital in December 1991, my husband told me to organize box by box everything concerning the *Treatise.* Every volume is organized in a box. Did he know that he wouldn't live to see the publication of this treatise, and that he wouldn't even finish it completely? It represents the work of forty years. Forty years of composition, of analysis from his class, and all of that makes up his personality. So, when he departed, in order to forget my sorrow, I immediately set out to finish the treatise. And believe me, it's been very long, and very hard. For the fifth volume, for example, I had to cut and paste pictures of birds to go along with the text. There were 1,350 pages on birds! So this is what I've been doing since May of 1992: I've been working on this treatise day and night.

Upon returning to the subject of the *Quartet,* the conversation shifted to religion. In 1964, the famous writer André Malraux, then the minister of culture, asked Messiaen to write a requiem commemorating the dead of the two world wars, said Loriod. Messiaen responded: "Why death? I believe in Resurrection."[47] Thus he entitled this work *Et exspecto resurrectionem mortuorum* (I await the resurrection of the dead), based on the Catholic Creed. (Although "Messiaen had an absolute horror of hatred, of war, and of wickedness," said Loriod in an interview with Peter Hill in 1993, "I think he had enough strength not to use these subjects in his works. . . . He was above that—even though he himself suffered.")[48] Did not Messiaen wonder, however, whether he would ever get out of that prison camp alive, whether the end of *his* time might be drawing near? I asked. Loriod again replied no, and went on to explain the reason for the Apocalypse in the *Quartet*. It was a work whose fairy-tale-like images had dazzled the composer as a child, and whose concepts of Time and Eternity had inspired him to search for new rhythms:

> My husband always said: "I was born a believer." And he was not from an especially Catholic family. His mother and father were married in the church, but he was a little boy who had always believed very strongly, who had never doubted. And he read everything: the Gospels, the Acts of the Apostles. He knew the Bible by heart. In the New Testament, the Apocalypse always struck him. When he was little, he read a lot of Shakespeare—of theater, of make-believe. But when he discovered the Apocalypse, he said that it was the most enchanting, the most awesome, and the most wonderful of fairy tales. Because all of it is true.
>
> My husband was always struck by Time. . . . He often read on the subject of Eternity in the *Summa Theologica* of Saint Thomas Aquinas, and he was always interested in rhythm and in time. In the Apocalypse there was this moment called Eternity in which the universe would be no more. So when Messiaen read the Apocalypse, he would get the desire to look for new rhythms. Precisely the nonretrogradable rhythms that you have in the *Quartet*. These nonretrogradable rhythms are quintessential Messiaen; if you read them from left to right or from right to left, you have the same order of note values. It was an extraordinary discovery because these rhythms were within time and yet had the possibility of independence. And in the *Quartet for the End of Time* (it's with a capital "T"), Messiaen imagined the moment in which there would be no more Time, in which Time would rejoin Eternity.

When asked why she thought the *Quartet* had become one of the most popular of Messiaen's compositions, she replied: "The *Quartet* is so famous because the music is so beautiful. It is also a revelation. Because there's the thought of a *believing* musician. It's with such emotion that Messiaen speaks about the eternity of Jesus that we feel He actually lived."

As our meeting drew to a close, Loriod pointed to the boxes of papers devoted to Messiaen's *Treatise,* apologizing for the "disorder." She kindly gave me a beautifully wrapped box of *Calissons d'Aix,* cookies from Aix-en-Provence, and led me on a brief tour of the apartment. It had originally been a hotel, she said, but they had had it sound-proofed. There was red carpeting everywhere. As we entered the study where her husband used to compose, Loriod pointed out that Messiaen's desk was just as he had left it, with pencils neatly lined up in a row, and his various pairs of eyeglasses for writing orchestral, chamber, piano, and vocal music. She then showed me one of Messiaen's six libraries. "This is a man who read a lot," she said, recalling his libraries for subjects as diverse as theology, rhythm, literature, music, and ornithology. "He read everything . . . and he never wrote anything that was not sincere."[49]

Subsequently, in between her own concerts, her work on Messiaen's *Treatise,* and the many other activities related to the dissemination of her husband's works, Loriod took the time to answer all my letters, in the process sending me several important documents that shed light on the history of the *Quartet.* The interviews with Pasquier, Le Boulaire, and the Akoka family soon followed, and little by little a story began to take shape.

And so, this is how this book came into being. As I chased down people, hunted down facts, and sorted out changes of identity and misreported information, I felt transformed into a sort of quasi-fictional detective searching for the solution to a musical mystery. It was then that I was reminded of something Etienne Pasquier had said.

Recounting the war, his fortuitous meetings with Messiaen, Akoka, and Le Boulaire, the actions of a kind German officer, the miraculous premiere, Akoka's heroic escape, Le Boulaire's later success as an actor, Messiaen's subsequent fame, and the heavenly music that united them all in a time notorious for unimaginable barbarism, Pasquier, then ninety years old, remarked: "C'est un roman policier. Mais, c'est vrai, cette histoire" (It's a detective novel. Only, it's a true story).[50]

■

Music is an abstract art, capable of being received without regard for its form, structure, style, or compositional history. Messiaen's *Quartet for the End of Time* can of course be appreciated for its musical beauty alone, and yet, at the same time, the work is inseparable from its time. No doubt, its apocalyptic and intensely Catholic message would not ring so painfully prophetic today had the piece been composed in a different place and time, and were it not for the horrifying events that unfolded following its premiere in 1941. And yet, one need not be Catholic to appreciate Messiaen's beautiful music, which speaks to all who suffered. Indeed, in retrospect, the *Quartet* resounds more powerfully with the passage of time, for in its compositional history, religious message, and technical and aesthetic innovations, it has become a paradigm for the horrors, the complexities, the ironies, and even the miracles of the twentieth century.

The Olivier Messiaen circle is diminishing. Eyewitnesses to the creation of the *Quartet* or to its relevant history are becoming fewer and will soon vanish. Most of the eyewitnesses interviewed for this book have since passed away. Others are well into their eighties. Two years after Etienne Pasquier died, Jean Le Boulaire passed away on 9 August 1999 after a prolonged coma. His wife Yvette died on 22 January 2002. Lucien Akoka passed away on 28 June 1998 following a series of terrible strokes.

At the very moment that this project was begun, it immediately became apparent that time was crucial. Yet while the months and years pass, the *Quartet* continues to stand the test of time, and the participants in its history live on through this retelling.

On 15 January 1941, in a German prison camp in Silesia, music triumphed over Time, breaking free of rhythm and liberating a quartet of French prisoners and their listeners from the horrors of their time. The *Quartet for the End of Time* has earned its place in the canon and history of Western music, but, more important, it has earned its place in our hearts. Its musical beauty, at once terrifying and sublime, exalts listeners and performers alike, and the story of its creators stands as a testament to the powers of music and human will to transcend the most terrible of times.

Appendix A

I. Subject of the Composition and Commentary on Each Movement

"And I saw another mighty angel coming down from heaven, wrapped in a cloud, with a rainbow on his head; his face was like the sun, and his legs like pillars of fire. . . . Setting his right foot on the sea and his left foot on the land . . . and, standing on the sea and on the land, he raised his right hand toward Heaven and swore by He who lives forever and ever . . . saying: 'There will be no more Time; but in the days when the seventh angel is to blow his trumpet, the mystery of God will be fulfilled.' "

Revelation of Saint John, chapter 10

Conceived and composed during my captivity, the *Quartet for the End of Time* was premiered in Stalag VIII A on 15 January 1941, by Jean Le Boulaire, violin; Henri Akoka, clarinet; Etienne Pasquier, cello; and myself at the piano. The piece was directly inspired by the above passage from Revelation.[1] Its musical language is essentially ethereal, spiritual, Catholic. The modes, realizing melodically and harmonically a sort of tonal ubiquity, bring the listener closer to infinity, to eternity in space. The special rhythms, independent of the meter, powerfully contribute to the effect of banishing the temporal. (But given the awesomeness of the subject, all of the above serves merely as inarticulate and tentative explanation!)

This *Quartet* comprises eight movements. Why? Seven is the perfect number, the Creation in six days sanctified by the divine Sabbath; the seventh day of this repose extends into eternity and becomes the eighth day of eternal light, of unalterable peace.

1. "Crystal Liturgy." Between 3 and 4 o'clock in the morning, the birds awaken: a solo blackbird or nightingale improvises, surrounded by dustwhirls of sound, by a halo of harmonics lost high up in the trees.[2]

Transpose this onto a religious plane: you have the harmonious silence of heaven.

2. "Vocalize, for the Angel Who Announces the End of Time." The first and third sections (both very brief) evoke the power of this mighty angel, crowned with a rainbow and clothed in a cloud, who places one foot on the sea and the other on the land. The "middle" [second section] evokes the impalpable harmonies of heaven. In the piano: gentle cascades of blue-orange chords, encircling with their distant carillon the plainchant-like song of the violin and cello.

3. "Abyss of the Birds." Unaccompanied clarinet. The abyss is Time, with its weariness and gloom. The birds are the opposite of Time; they represent our longing for light, for stars, for rainbows, and for jubilant song!

4. "Interlude." Scherzo, in a more outgoing character than the other movements, yet related to them nevertheless by melodic "recalls."

5. "Praise to the Eternity of Jesus." Here, Jesus is considered the Word of God. A long phrase in the cello, inexorably slow, glorifies, with adoration and reverence, the eternity of this mighty yet gentle Word, "of which the ages never tire." The melody unfolds majestically, as if from a regal yet soft-colored horizon. "In the beginning was the Word, and the Word was with God, and the Word was God."

6. "Dance of Fury, for the Seven Trumpets." Rhythmically, the most characteristic movement of this series. The four instruments in unison create the effect of gongs and trumpets (the first six trumpets of the Apocalypse followed by various calamities, the trumpet of the seventh angel announcing the fulfillment of the mystery of God). Use of added values, augmentation and diminution, and nonretrogradable rhythms. Music of stone, tremendous ringing granite; perpetual motion of steel, of enormous blocks of purple fury, of frozen intoxication. Listen, above all, to the terrifying fortissimo of the theme in augmentation and register alteration toward the end of the movement.

7. "Tangle of Rainbows, for the Angel Who Announces the End of Time." Certain passages here recall the second movement. The Angel full of might appears, and in particular the rainbow that crowns him (the rainbow, symbol of peace, of wisdom, and of every luminous sound

and vibration). In my dreams, I hear and see classified chords and melodies, common colors and forms; then, after this transitory stage, I pass into unreality and lose myself in a rapture to a whirling, a gyrating fusion of superhuman sound and color. These swords of fire, these pools of blue-orange lava, these shooting stars: this is the tangled skein, these are the rainbows!

8. "Praise to the Immortality of Jesus." Long solo for violin, the counterpart to the cello solo in the fifth movement. Why this second eulogy? It addresses more specifically the second aspect of Jesus: Jesus the Man, the Word made flesh, immortally resurrected, to impart us his life. This movement is pure love. The progressive ascent toward the extremely high register represents the ascension of man toward his Lord, of the son of God toward his Father, of deified Man toward Paradise.

—And I repeat again what I said earlier: "Given the awesomeness of the subject, all of the above serves merely as inarticulate and tentative explanation!"

II. Brief Theory of My Rhythmic Language

Here, as in my other compositions, I employ a special rhythmic language. In addition to my secret predilection for prime numbers (5, 7, 11, etc.), the notions of meter and tempo are replaced here by the feeling of a short note value (the sixteenth note, for example) and by its free multiplication; also by certain "rhythmic forms," such as: added values; augmentation and diminution; nonretrogradable rhythms; and rhythmic ostinato.

a) The added value. Short value, added to another rhythm, whether by a note, a rest, or a dot.

By a note:

By a rest:

By a dot:

Ordinarily, as in the examples above, the rhythm is almost always immediately followed by the added value, without having been heard previously in its simple form.

b) Augmentation or diminution. A rhythm may be immediately followed by its augmentation or diminution, following various forms; here are several examples (in each of which the first measure contains the normal rhythm, the second measure the augmentation or diminution):

Addition of a third of the value:

Subtraction of a quarter of the value:

Addition of a dot:

Subtraction of a dot:

Standard augmentation:

Standard diminution:

Addition of double the value:

Subtraction of two thirds of the value:

Addition of triple the value:

Subtraction of three fourths of the value:

Inexact augmentations and diminutions can also be employed.

Example:

This rhythm contains three eighth notes (standard diminution of three quarter notes), with a dot (added value), which results in an inexact diminution.

c) Nonretrogradable rhythms. Whether read from right to left or from left to right, the order of their values remains the same. This feature exists in all rhythms that can be divided into two groups of retrograde related to each other by a central "common" value.

Example: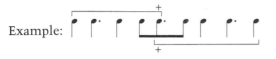

Succession of nonretrogradable rhythms (each measure containing one of these rhythms):

Employed in the sixth movement of the *Quartet*: "Dance of Fury, for the Seven Trumpets" (see letter F).

d) Rhythmic ostinato. Independent rhythm, which repeats unrelentingly, and functions autonomously of the rhythms that surround it.

The piano part in the first movement of the *Quartet*, "Crystal Liturgy," is based on the following rhythmic fragment:

Numerous repetitions of this fragment, independent of the rhythms of the violin, clarinet, and cello, constitute a "rhythmic ostinato."

III. Advice to the Performers

Read, first of all, the "Commentary" and the "Brief Theory" above. But do not become preoccupied with all of this in the performance: it will suffice to play the music, the notes, and the exact values, and to faithfully follow the dynamics indicated. In the nonmetered movements such as "Dance of Fury, for the Seven Trumpets," you can, to help yourselves, mentally count the sixteenth notes, but only at the beginning of your work: this process may encumber the public performance; you should, therefore, mentally retain the feeling of the rhythmic values, no more. Do not be afraid to exaggerate the dynamics, the accelerandos, the ritardandos, everything that renders an interpretation lively and sensitive. The middle of "Abyss of the Birds," in particular, should be full of imagination. Sustain implacably the two extremely slow movements, "Praise to the Eternity of Jesus" and "Praise" to his "Immortality."

OLIVIER MESSIAEN
translated by Rebecca Rischin

Appendix B
SELECT DISCOGRAPHY

The recordings of the *Quartet for the End of Time* listed here are currently available or of particular historical interest. They are listed alphabetically by the title of the ensemble or the last name of the violinist. The five recordings marked with an asterisk (*) were made under the artistic direction of Olivier Messiaen and can thus be considered historical references. All of the recordings, however, are highly recommended. Information was obtained from the recordings themselves, the *Schwann* and *Diapason* catalogues, and the *discothèque* at the Bibliothèque Nationale in Paris.

For a recording that has been reissued, only the most recent catalogue number is given. Unless otherwise specified, the number refers to the compact disc format. If available, the date of recording and/or copyright is listed as well as additional works included on the recording.

In allegiance to the composer, who preferred that the *Quartet* be performed in its integral form, only recordings of the complete work are listed. Moreover, the number of separate recordings of *"Abîme des oiseaux," "Louange à l'Eternité de Jésus,"* and *"Louange à l'Immortalité de Jésus"* is far too overwhelming to be included here. The length of this select discography further testifies to the popularity of the *Quartet*, by far the most frequently recorded composition by Olivier Messiaen.

■

Amici Chamber Ensemble: Scott St. John, violin; Joaquin Valdepeñas, clarinet; David Hetherington, cello; Patricia Parr, piano. Naxos 54824. Recorded in Ontario, Canada, December 15–16, 1999.

Amici Quartet: Shmuel Ashkenasi, violin; Joaquin Valdepeñas, clarinet; David Hetherington, cello; Patricia Parr, piano. Summit SMT

168. Copyright 1995. With Chan Ka Nin, *I Think that I Shall Never See*.

Joshua Bell, violin; Michael Collins, clarinet; Steven Isserlis, cello; Olli Mustonen, piano. Decca 452 899-2. Copyright 1997. With Shostakovitch, Piano Trio no. 2.

Vera Beths, violin; George Pieterson, clarinet; Anner Bijlsma, cello; Reinbert de Leeuw, piano. Philips 422 8342. Copyright 1980; remastered 1989. With Messiaen, *Et exspecto resurrectionem mortuorum*.

Chamber Music Northwest: Ik-Hwan Bae, violin; David Shifrin, clarinet; Warren Lash, cello; William Doppman, piano. Delos 3043. Recorded in Rutgers Presbyterian Church, New York City, March 24–29, 1986. Copyright 1986. With Bartók, *Contrasts*.

Per Enoksson, violin; Håkan Rosengren, clarinet; Mats Rondin, cello; Stefan Bojsten, piano. Caprice 21481. Copyright 1997. With Schoenberg, *Ein Stelldichein*, and Martinu, *Oboe Quartet*.

Ensemble Walter Boeykens: Marjeta Korosec, violin; Walter Boeykens, clarinet; Roel Dieltiens, cello; Robert Groslot, piano. Harmonia Mundi 7901348. Copyright 1990.

*Huguette Fernandez, violin; Guy Deplus, clarinet; Jacques Neilz, cello; Marie-Madeline Petit, piano. Erato 4509-91708-2. Recorded in Paris, 1963. Copyright 1963, 1968, 1995. With Messiaen, *Cinq Rechants*. Remastered.[1]

Saschko Gawriloff, violin; Hans Deinzer, clarinet; Siegfried Palm, cello; Aloys Kontarsky, piano. Angel CDCB 47463. With Messiaen, *Turangalîla-symphonie*.

Erich Gruenberg, violin; Gervase de Peyer, clarinet; William Pleeth, cello; Michel Beroff, piano. EMI Classics 7639472. Recorded in London, 1968, remastered 1991. With Messiaen, *Le merle noir*.

Emilie Haudenschild, violin; Fabio di Casola, clarinet; Emeric Kostyak, cello; Ricardo Castro, piano. Accord 201772 MU/750. Recorded 26–28 December 1990. Copyright 1990.

Houston Symphony Chamber Players: Eric Halen, violin; David Peck, clarinet; Desmond Hoebig, cello; Christoph Eschenbach, piano. Koch International Classics 7378. Copyright 1999.

Incanto Ensemble. Recorded July 1991. EBS 6024.

Oleg Kagan, violin; Eduard Brunner, clarinet; Natalia Gutman, cello; Vassily Lobanov, piano. Live Classics LC LCL 712. Recorded live at Kuhmo Festival, in Finland, 27 July 1984.

Kontraste Ensemble: Kathrin Rabus, violin; Reiner Wehle, clarinet; Christophe Marks, cello; Friederike Richter, piano. Thorofon CTH 2232. Recorded in Hannover, Germany, October 1993, June 1994.

Maryvonne Le Dizes, violin; Alain Damiens, clarinet; Pierre Strauch, cello; Pierre-Laurent Aimard, piano. ADDA 581.029. Recorded in Paris, 1–3 October 1986. Copyright 1986.

LINensemble: Christina Astrand, violin; Jens Schou, clarinet; John Ehde, cello; Erik Kaltoft, piano. Kontrapunkt KPT 32232. Copyright 1996.

Margaret Mitchell, violin; David Campbell, clarinet; Christopher van Kampen, cello; Joanna MacGregor, piano. Collins Classics 1393. With Zygmunt Krauze, *Quatuor pour la Naissance*.

Martin Mumelter, violin; Martin Schelling, clarinet; Walter Nothas, cello; Alfons Kontarsky, piano. Koch Schwann SCH 311882. Recorded in March 1991 at the Bayerischen Rundfunk, Munich. With Dünser: *Tage- und Nachtbücher*.

New York Philomusica Chamber Ensemble: A. Robert Johnson, director; Isidore Cohen, violin; Joseph Rabbai, clarinet; Timothy Eddy, cello; Robert Levin, piano. Candide CE 31050. Copyright 1972. With Messiaen, *Le merle noir*. 33⅓ LP.

*Jean Pasquier, violin; André Vacellier, clarinet; Etienne Pasquier, cello, Olivier Messiaen, piano. Club Français du Disque. Musidisc 34429. Recorded at the Scola Cantorum, Paris. Received at the Bibliothèque Nationale, Paris, 29 May 1957. 33⅓ LP.

Régis Pasquier, violin; Jacques di Donato, clarinet; Alain Meunier, cello; Claude Lavoix, piano. Arion ARN 38453. Recorded in 1978. 33⅓ LP.

*Christoph Poppen, violin; Wolfgang Meyer, clarinet; Manuel Fischer-Dieskau, cello; Yvonne Loriod, piano. EMI Classics CDC 54395. Recorded in the Eglise de Liban, Paris, 19–21 November 1991. Copyright 1991. With Messiaen, *Thème et variations*.

Gil Shaham, violin; Paul Meyer; clarinet; Jian Wang, cello; Myung-Whun Chung, piano. Deutsche Grammophon 289-469-052-2. Recorded at the Maison de la Radio, Studio 103 in Paris, June 1999. Copyright 2000.

*Quatuor Olivier Messiaen: Alain Moglia, violin; Michel Arrignon, clarinet; Réné Benedetti, cello; Jean-Claude Henriot, piano. Cybelia. Reissued by Pierre Verany 794012. Recorded May 1987. Copyright 1987, 1994.

Tashi: Ida Kavafian, violin; Richard Stoltzman, clarinet; Fred Sherry, cello; Peter Serkin, piano. RCA Gold Seal 7835-2-RG. Recorded in 1975. Copyright 1976, 1988. Remastered.

Trio Fontenay and Eduard Brunner, clarinet. Teldec 9031-73239-2. Copyright 1993.

*Luben Yordanoff, violin; Claude Desurmont, clarinet; Albert Tetard, cello; Daniel Barenboim, piano. Deutsche Grammophon (20th Century Classics) 23247. Recorded in Paris, April 1978. Copyright 1979.

Notes

INVITATION

1. Etienne Pasquier, interview, 6 June 1994.
2. "A Etienne Pasquier—la magnifique pierre de base du Trio de même nom!—J'ose espérer qu'il n'oubliera jamais les rythmes, les modes, les arcs-en ciel et les ponts sur l'au-delà jetés par son ami dans l'espace sonore; car il apporta tant de fini, de précision, d'émotion, de foi même et de perfection technique, à l'exécution de mon 'quatuor pour fin du Temps' que l'auditeur aurait pu croire qu'il avait joué toute sa vie une telle musique! Merci, et en Toute affection, Olivier Messiaen."
3. Claude Samuel, *Olivier Messiaen: Music and Color: Conversations with Claude Samuel*, trans. E. Thomas Glasow (Portland, Ore.: Amadeus Press, 1986), 26.
4. Ibid., 15.
5. Paul Griffiths, *Olivier Messiaen and the Music of Time* (Ithaca, N.Y.: Cornell University Press, 1985), 23.
6. Ibid., 25.
7. Messiaen, in Samuel, *Music and Color*, 23.
8. *Harvard Dictionary of Music*, 1972 ed., s.v. "Jeune France, La," 444.
9. Griffiths, *Messiaen and the Music of Time*, 90.
10. Messiaen, "Olivier Messiaen analyse ses œuvres: *Quatuor pour la fin du Temps*," in *Hommage à Olivier Messiaen: November–December 1978*, Claude Samuel, artistic director (France: La Recherche Artistique, 1978), 31.
11. Antoine Goléa, *Rencontres avec Olivier Messiaen* (Paris: René Juilliard, 1960), 63.
12. Griffiths, *Messiaen and the Music of Time*, 90.
13. Olivier Messiaen, *Quatuor pour la fin du Temps*, miniature score (Paris: Durand, 1942), title page.
14. Malcolm Hayes, "Instrumental, Orchestral and Choral Works to 1948," in *The Messiaen Companion*, ed. Peter Hill (Portland, Ore.: Amadeus Press, 1995), 180.
15. Griffiths, *Messiaen and the Music of Time*, 91.

CHAPTER 1. THE QUARTET BEGINS

1. Griffiths, *Messiaen and the Music of Time*, 90.
2. Messiaen, in Goléa, *Rencontres*, 59.
3. Pasquier, interview, 6 June 1994.
4. Ibid.
5. "Trio Pasquier," press release (New York: Colbert-LaBerge Concert Management, n.d.).
6. Alain Pâris, ed. *Dictionnaire des Interprètes et de l'Interprétation Musicale au XXe Siècle* (Paris: Robert Laffont, 1989), s.v. "Trio Pasquier," 1047. Pierné based

the melodies of his *Trois pièces en trio* upon the names of the Trio Pasquier, Jean, Pierre, and Etienne.

7. Pasquier, interview, 6 June 1994.

8. Pasquier, interview, 10 June 1994.

9. Yvonne Dran, interview, 22 December 1995.

10. Lucien Akoka, interview, 22 March 1995.

11. At this time, France did not yet enforce labor laws prohibiting or restricting the employment of children.

12. Lucien Akoka, interview, 22 March 1995.

13. Pasquier, interview, 10 June 1994.

14. Pasquier, interview, 19 June 1995.

15. Pasquier, interview, 10 June 1994.

16. Pasquier, interview, 6 June 1994.

17. Pasquier, "Hommage à Olivier Messiaen: Etienne Pasquier," in *Olivier Messiaen: homme de foi: Regard sur son œuvre d'orgue* (Paris: Edition St. Paul, Trinité Média Communication, 1995), 91.

18. Phillipe Akoka, interview, 22 March 1995.

19. Ibid.

20. André Vacellier, Assistant Principal Clarinetist of the Opéra Comique, who performed at the Quartet's Paris premiere and its first recording, had a bright sound similar to that of Akoka. Messiaen retained both these sounds in his memory (Guy Deplus, interview, 17 January 1995).

21. Deplus, interview, 17 January 1995. See also Appendix B: Select Discography.

22. Michel Arrignon, interview, 27 April 1994. See also Appendix B.

23. "Interview with Yvonne Loriod," in Hill, *Messiaen Companion*, 290–91.

24. Jeannette Akoka, interview, 22 December 1995.

25. Lucien Akoka, interview, 22 March 1995.

26. Philippe Akoka, interview, 22 March 1995.

27. Messiaen, quoted in Goléa, *Rencontres*, 60.

28. Loriod, quoted in Hill, *Messiaen Companion*, 291.

29. "Olivier Messiaen: La Liturgie de l'Arc-en-Ciel," in Patrick Szersnovicz, *Le Monde de la Musique* (July–August 1987): 33.

30. Messiaen, quoted in Goléa, *Rencontres*, 62.

31. Ibid.

32. Anthony Pople, *Messiaen: Quatuor pour la fin du Temps* (Cambridge: Cambridge University Press, 1998), 9.

33. Messiaen, quoted in Goléa, *Rencontres*, 62.

34. Loriod to author, 13 May 1995.

35. Pasquier, interview, 21 March 1995.

36. Pople, 10–11.

CHAPTER 2. THE QUARTET IN PRISON

1. Robert Paxton, *Vichy France: Old Guard and New Order: 1940–1944*, Morningside ed. (1972; reprint, New York: Columbia University Press, 1982), 19.

2. Ibid.

3. Pasquier, interview, 21 March 1995.

4. Hannalore Lauerwald, "*Quartett auf das Ende der Zeiten:* Olivier Messiaen als Kriegsgefangener in Görlitz," *Das Orchester* (May 1995): 17.

5. The image of prisoners being stripped naked and deprived of their possessions is one frequently associated with the preparation of Jews for the gas chambers. But Stalag VIII A was not an extermination camp. One of hundreds of POW camps scat-

tered all over Germany and occupied Europe, Stalag VIII A was a camp for prisoners of war of enlisted rank. For the most part, these POW camps were simply places of temporary confinement and labor, where stripping prisoners was apparently standard German procedure. This is not to imply that prisoners of war did not suffer from hunger, cold, and nervous depression and that they were not sometimes severely mistreated, or that some prison camps were not more desirable than others. Because of differences in geographical location, climate, and enforcement of regulations, Stalag VIII A, for example, had a better reputation than Stalag VIII C, approximately 150 miles to the north. On the whole, however, the prison camps were remarkably similar. (Jean Brossard to Hannalore Lauerwald, 16 February 1992, copy courtesy of Lauerwald.)

6. Messiaen, quoted in Goléa, *Rencontres*, 61.

7. Messiaen, in Leo Samama, "Entretien avec Olivier Messiaen," in *Messiaen: Quartet for the End of Time*, dir. Astrid Wortelboer, 60 min., Amaya, 1993, videocassette.

8. Yvonne Loriod, interview, 25 November 1993.

9. Lauerwald, "*Dokumentation Kriegsgefangene in Deutschland 1939–1945: Stalag VIII A Görlitz-Moys*," Lauerwald personal collection, Görlitz, Germany, 9.

10. Ibid., 6.

11. Comité International de la Croix-Rouge to Lauerwald, 16 March 1992, copy courtesy of Lauerwald.

12. Lauerwald, "*Quartett auf das Ende der Zeiten*," 17.

13. Lauerwald, "Dokumentation Kriegsgefangene," 6.

14. Loriod, interview, 25 November 1993.

15. Pasquier, interview, 10 June 1994.

16. Pasquier, interview, 6 June 1994.

17. Loriod, interview, 25 November 1993.

18. Lauerwald, "Dokumentation Kriegsgefangene," 10. Pierre Messiaen had been without news of his son for several months until Olivier had been allowed to send him a card. In response, Pierre wrote to Pasquier's wife in October, 1940, Suzanne, hoping that she might be able to help get Olivier liberated. Unfortunately, Mme. Pasquier was powerless to do anything for her own husband, let alone for one of his friends, even if that friend happened to be a renowned composer.

19. Lauerwald, "Dokumentation Kriegsgefangene," 6.

20. Ibid., 7.

21. Pasquier, interview, Paris, 19 June 1995.

22. Lauerwald, "*Quartett auf das Ende der Zeiten*," 17. Figure 10 cites an occupancy of 126–222 prisoners.

23. Charles Jourdanet, "Messiaen créait *Quatuor pour la fin du Temps* au stalag," *Nice-matin*, 15 January 2001.

24. Messiaen, in "Entretien avec Olivier Messiaen." by Samama.

25. Pasquier, interview, Paris, 19 June 1995.

26. Lauerwald, "Dokumentation Kriegsgefangene," 7.

27. Ibid., 20.

28. This plan depicts the camp *after* Messiaen's departure, with his barrack 19A now occupied by Russians and Italians.

29. Lauerwald, "Dokumentation Kriegsgefangene," 11, 15.

30. Lauerwald, "*Quartett auf das Ende die Zeiten*," 18.

31. Lauerwald, "Dokumentation Kriegsgefangene," 11. One interesting example of the anti-Semitism of the times is a short story written by a prisoner in the camp, "*Entretien nocturne*" (Nocturnal Meeting), in which the French narrator describes his meeting with a stereotypical Jew who turns out to be a messenger of the devil. To

the narrator's apparent surprise, the Jew disclaims responsibility for the war and for the suffering inflicted upon all the peoples of Europe. O'Bole, "Entretien nocturne," *Le lumignon: Journal mensuel du Stalag VIII A*, July 1942, 8, Lauerwald personal collection, Görlitz.

32. Jules Lefebure, in "Les Stalags: Enquête concernant les P.G." (Paris: Archives Nationales, 29 June 1956), 72AJ298,6C.

33. Lauerwald, "Dokumentation Kriegsgefangene," 9.

34. Pasquier, interview, 19 June 1995. Interestingly, figure 14 does not indicate the Polish barracks.

35. Philippe Akoka, interview, 22 March 1995.

36. Lucien Akoka, interview, 22 March 1995.

37. Jean Martinon (1910–1976) was most famous for serving as music director of the Chicago Symphony Orchestra from 1963 to 1968. He conducted numerous orchestras in Europe, including the Orchestre National de France.

38. Lucien Akoka, interview, 22 March 1995.

39. Loriod, interview, 25 November 1993.

40. Alex Ross, "In Music, Though, There Were No Victories," *New York Times*, 20 August 1995, 25. Ross writes:

Some of the most talented younger Czech composers arrived in Theresienstadt and were allowed to continue their work. A film was made, "The Führer Presents the Jews With a City," in which the ghetto residents appear to engage in happy labor. The film shows Karel Ancerl conducting Pavel Haas' *Study for Strings*. The music's forceful fugal motion speaks of a defiant spirit. But this astounding vigor is diabolically twisted around for propaganda purposes: the music communicates an illusion of Jewish safety. Haas died a month later in Auschwitz.

41. Lauerwald, "*Quartett auf das Ende die Zeiten*," 17.

42. Pasquier, interview, 10 June 1994.

43. Pasquier, interview, 19 June 1995.

44. Loriod, interview, 25 November 1993.

45. Messiaen, in Samama, "Entretien avec Olivier Messiaen."

46. Jourdanet, "Messiaen créait."

47. Pasquier, interview, 6 June 1994.

48. Loriod, interview, 25 November 1993.

49. Pasquier, interview, 6 June 1994.

50. Messiaen, quoted in Goléa, *Rencontres*, 61–62.

51. Messiaen, in Samama, "Entretien avec Olivier Messiaen."

52. David Gorouben, letter to author, 8 August 1995.

53. Jean Le Boulaire, interview, 3 March 1995.

54. Gorouben, letter to author, 8 August 1995.

55. Paxton, *Vichy France*, 174. The law "excluded Jews from elected bodies, from positions of responsibility in the civil service, judiciary, and military services, and from positions influencing cultural life (teaching in public schools, newspaper reporting or editing, direction of films or radio programs)."

56. Lauerwald, "Dokumentation Kriegsgefangene," 23.

57. Paxton, *Vichy France*, 181.

CHAPTER 3. PREPARING THE PREMIERE

1. Le Boulaire, letter to author, 20 March 1995.

2. Le Boulaire, letter to author, 31 July 1995.

3. Le Boulaire, interview, 3 March 1995.
4. Le Boulaire, letter to author, 20 March 1995.
5. Le Boulaire, interview, 3 March 1995.
6. Le Boulaire, letter to author, 31 July 1995.
7. Le Boulaire, interview, 3 March 1995.
8. Le Boulaire, letter to author, 7 June 1995.
9. Le Boulaire, interview, 3 March 1995.
10. Lauerwald, "Dokumentation Kriegsgefangene," 11.
11. Le Boulaire, interview, 3 March 1995.
12. Brossard, memoirs to Lauerwald, p. 3, copy courtesy of Lauerwald.
13. Brossard, letter to Lauerwald, 13 March 1992, copy courtesy of Lauerwald.
14. Lauerwald, "Dokumentation Kriegsgefangene," 9.
15. Pasquier, interview, 10 June 1994.
16. Pasquier, interview, 21 March 1995.
17. Ibid.
18. Messiaen, in Goléa, *Rencontres,* 62.
19. Ibid. As explained in Chapter 1, Messiaen did not specify the order in which the other movements were composed or rehearsed. Musicologist Anthony Pople (*Messiaen,* p. 11) speculates that the first movement was probably composed last, given its complexity and demands on the performers.
20. Lauerwald, "*Quartett auf das Ende die Zeiten,*" 18.
21. Marty and Vial painted *Jeanne aux Fers,* a reproduction of which hangs in the crypt of the Basilica of Domrémy near Toulouse, France. Ibid.
22. Jourdanet, "Messiaen créait."
23. Lauerwald, "*Quartett auf das Ende die Zeiten,*" 18.
24. Jourdanet, "Messiaen créait."
25. Lauerwald, "*Quartett auf das Ende die Zeiten,*" 18.
26. Pasquier, interview, 6 June 1994.
27. Pasquier, interview, 19 June 1995. Lauerwald, "*Quartett auf das Ende die Zeiten,*" 18, speculates that the arts may have helped to prevent depression and nervous breakdowns in a camp in which the suicide rate was already quite high.
28. Pasquier, interview, 6 June 1994; Le Boulaire, letter to author, 7 June 1995.
29. Jourdanet, "Messiaen créait."
30. Pasquier, interview, 6 June 1994.
31. Lauerwald, "Dokumentation Kriegsgefangene," 13.
32. Messiaen, quoted in Goléa, *Rencontres,* 62–63.
33. Messiaen, quoted in Brigitte Massin, *Olivier Messiaen: Une poétique du merveilleux* (Aix-en-Provence: Editions Alinéa, 1989), 154.
34. Brossard, letter to Lauerwald, 13 March 1992.
35. Messiaen, quoted in Goléa, *Rencontres,* 63.
36. Pasquier, "Hommage à Olivier Messiaen," 91–92.
37. Brossard, letter to Lauerwald, 4 November 1992, copy courtesy of Lauerwald.
38. Pasquier, interview, 6 June 1994.
39. Pasquier, interview, 19 June 1995.
40. Pasquier, interview, 10 June 1994.
41. Pasquier, interview, 19 June 1995.
42. Pasquier, "Hommage à Olivier Messiaen," 92.
43. Pasquier, interview, 6 June 1994.
44. Le Boulaire, letter to author, 3 August 1995.
45. Le Boulaire, interview, 3 March 1995.
46. Le Boulaire, letter to author, 3 August 1995.
47. Le Boulaire, interview, 3 March 1995.

48. Messiaen, *Quatuor pour la fin du Temps*, iv.
49. Le Boulaire, interview, 3 March 1995.
50. Ibid.
51. Pasquier, interview, 6 June 1994.
52. Pasquier, interview, 21 March 1995.
53. Pasquier, interview, 6 June 1994.
54. Pasquier, interview, 21 March 1995.
55. Messiaen, quoted in "Olivier Messiaen analyse ses œuvres," 31.
56. Le Boulaire, interview, 3 March 1995.
57. Ibid.
58. Pasquier, interview, 6 June 1994.
59. Pasquier, quoted in Gérard Condé, "Les souvenirs d'Etienne Pasquier," *Le monde*, 3 August 1995, 22.
60. Pasquier, interview, 6 June 1994.
61. Pasquier, interview, 21 March 1995.
62. Pasquier, interview, 6 June 1994.
63. Le Boulaire, interview, 3 March 1995.
64. Ibid.
65. Ibid.
66. Ibid.
67. Ibid.
68. Pasquier, interview, 10 June 1994.
69. Pasquier, interview, 6 June 1994.
70. Pasquier, interview, 10 June 1994.
71. Messiaen, quoted in Massin, *Olivier Messiaen*, 154.
72. Pasquier, interview, 6 June 1994.
73. Le Boulaire, interview, 3 March 1995.
74. Ibid.
75. Pasquier, interview, 10 June 1994.
76. Lucien Akoka, interview, 22 March 1995.
77. Ibid.
78. Yvonne Dran, letter to author, 10 October 1996; Jeannette Akoka, interview, Nice, 22 December 1995. Charles was the actor who organized the variety shows in the Stalag theater. Pasquier credited Charles with helping him get transferred from the *commando* where he had to engage in heavy labor to his comfortable post in the camp kitchen.
79. Lucien Akoka, interview, 22 March 1995.
80. Le Boulaire, interview, 3 March 1995.
81. Pasquier, interview, 10 June 1994.
82. Lucien Akoka, interview, 22 March 1995. For this reason, Lucien never attempted to escape from his prison camp, Stalag IX A in Ziegenhain, remaining there until the Americans liberated him and his fellow prisoners of war in April 1945.
83. Pasquier, interview, 10 June 1994.
84. Pasquier, interview, 6 June 1994.
85. Lucien Akoka, interview, 22 March 1995.
86. Philippe Akoka, interview, 22 March 1995.
87. Pasquier, interview, 10 June 1994.
88. Dran, interview, 22 December 1995; Lucien Akoka, interview, 22 March 1995.
89. Dran, interview, 22 December 1995.
90. Deplus, interview, 17 January 1995.
91. Lucien Akoka, interview, 22 March 1995.

92. Philippe Akoka, interview, 22 March 1995.

93. Philippe Akoka, interview, 15 July 2002.

94. Henri took the French baccalauréat (a difficult exam required to obtain the French equivalent of a high school diploma) at the age of thirty just to prove to himself that he could do it; he passed. Ibid.

95. Lucien Akoka, interview, 22 March 1995.

96. Pasquier, interview, 10 June 1994.

CHAPTER 4. *INTERMÈDE*

1. Messiaen, quoted in Samuel, *Olivier Messiaen: Music and Color,* 20–21.

2. Loriod, interview, 25 November 1993.

3. Messiaen, *Quatuor pour la fin du Temps,* i.

4. Roger Nichols, *Messiaen,* 2d ed. (Oxford: Oxford University Press, 1986), 29.

5. Messiaen, in Goléa, *Rencontres,* 64.

6. Messiaen, quoted in Massin, *Messiaen,* 154.

7. Messiaen, in Samama, "Entretien avec Olivier Messiaen."

8. The latter refers to the *Imitation of Christ* by Thomas à Kempis.

9. Messiaen, quoted in Massin, *Messiaen,* 154.

10. Messiaen, in Samama, "Entretien avec Olivier Messiaen."

11. Messiaen, quoted in Goléa, *Rencontres,* 65.

12. Ibid., 64.

13. Messiaen, quoted in Samuel, "Olivier Messiaen analyse ses œuvres," 31.

14. André Boucourechliev, "Messiaen, Olivier," in *The New Grove Dictionary of Music and Musicians,* ed. Stanley Sadie (London: Macmillan, 1980), 205.

15. Messiaen, "Address Delivered at the Conferring of the Praemium Erasmianum on 25 June 1971, in Amsterdam," in Almut Rössler, *Contributions to the Spiritual World of Olivier Messiaen,* trans. Barbara Dagg et al. (Duisberg, Germany: Gilles and Francke, 1986), 40.

16. Loriod, interview, 25 November 1993. Rubato refers to a flexible tempo involving subtly speeding up and slowing down according to the contour of the phrase—frequently employed in performances of Romantic music. Literally, in Italian, "to rob"; that is, to subtract tempo from one area and add it to another. Opponents of rubato claim that it "robs" the music of rhythm.

17. Messiaen, "Address Delivered at the Conferring of the Praemium Erasmianum," 40–41.

18. Messiaen, in Samuel, "Olivier Messiaen analyse ses œuvres," 40.

19. Messiaen, quoted in Goléa, *Rencontres,* 65.

20. Messiaen, quoted in Claude Samuel, *Conversations with Olivier Messiaen,* trans. by Felix Aprahamian (London: Stainer and Bell, 1976), 43.

21. Messiaen, quoted in Samuel, "Olivier Messiaen analyse ses œuvres," 40.

22. Messiaen, quoted in Samuel, *Olivier Messiaen: Music and Color,* 80.

23. Griffiths, *Messiaen and the Music of Time,* 91.

24. Messiaen, quoted in Goléa, *Rencontres,* 64.

25. Messiaen, *Quatuor pour la fin du Temps,* i.

26. Griffiths, *Messiaen and the Music of Time,* 101.

27. Messiaen, *Quatuor pour la fin du Temps,* i.

28. Messiaen, "Address Delivered at the Conferring of the Praemium Erasmianum," 40.

29. Messiaen, *Quatuor pour la fin du Temps,* i.

30. Messiaen, "Address Delivered at the Conferring of the Praemium Erasmianum," 42–43.

31. Messiaen, in Samuel, *Olivier Messiaen: Music and Color*, 62.

32. Ibid., 61.

33. Boucourechliev, "Messiaen," in *New Grove Dictionary*, 206.

34. Messiaen, quoted in Samuel, *Olivier Messiaen: Music and Color*, 64.

35. Messiaen, in Samuel, "Messiaen analyse ses œuvres," 40.

36. Messiaen, in Samuel, *Conversations with Olivier Messiaen*, 18.

37. Boucourechliev, "Messiaen," in *New Grove Dictionary*, 206.

38. Messiaen, in Samuel, *Olivier Messiaen: Music and Color*, 43. Delaunay's aesthetic application of the rhythmical interplay of abstract colored form greatly influenced the development of abstract art. Kenneth E. Silver and Romy Golan, *The Circle of Montparnasse Jewish Artists in Paris: 1905–1945* (New York: Universe Books, 1985), 98.

39. Messiaen, "Conférence de Notre Dame Delivered on 4 December 1977," in Rössler, *Contributions to the Spiritual World*, 60.

40. Messiaen, "Conversation with Olivier Messiaen on 23 April 1979, in Paris," ibid., 78.

41. Messiaen, quoted in Samuel, *Conversations with Olivier Messiaen*, 17–18.

42. Messiaen, "Address Delivered at the Conferring of the Praemium Erasmianum," 43–44.

43. Messiaen, "Conversation with Olivier Messiaen on 23 April 1979, in Paris," 79.

44. "Dans mes rêves, j'entends et vois accords et mélodies classés, couleurs et formes connues; puis, après ce stade transitoire, je passe dans l'irréel et subis avec extase un tournoiement, une compénétration giratoire de sons et couleurs surhumains. Ces épées de feu, ces coulées de lave bleu-orange, ces brusques étoiles: voilà le fouillis, voilà les arcs-en-ciel!" Messiaen, *Quatuor pour la fin du Temps*, ii.

45. Messiaen, "Address Delivered at the Conferring of the Praemium Erasmianum," 44.

46. Robert Sherlaw Johnson, "Birdsong," in Hill, *Messiaen Companion*, 249.

47. Messiaen, quoted in Samuel, *Olivier Messiaen: Music and Color*, 85.

48. Johnson, "Birdsong," 249.

49. Griffiths, *Messiaen and the Music of Time*, 166.

50. Trevor Hold, "Messiaen's Birds," *Music and Letters* 52, no. 2 (April 1971): 113.

51. Johnson, "Birdsong," 249.

52. Messiaen, quoted in Samuel, *Olivier Messiaen: Music and Color*, 97.

53. Ibid., 86–87.

54. Griffiths, *Messiaen and the Music of Time*, 170.

55. Hold, "Messiaen's Birds," 114.

56. Messiaen, quoted in Samuel, *Olivier Messiaen: Music and Color*, 88.

57. Ibid., 95.

58. Johnson, "Birdsong," 249.

59. Messiaen, *Quatuor pour la fin du Temps*, i.

60. Ibid., 1.

61. Johnson, "Birdsong," 251.

62. Ibid., 252.

63. Messiaen, quoted in Samuel, "Olivier Messiaen analyse ses œuvres," 40.

64. Messiaen, *Quatuor pour la fin du Temps*, i.

65. Iain Matheson, "The End of Time: A Biblical Theme in Messiaen's *Quatuor*," in Hill, *Messiaen Companion*, 235.

66. See Appendix B.

67. Michel Arrignon, interview, 27 April 1994.

68. Messiaen, quoted in Hold, "Messiaen's Birds," 122.
69. Ibid.

CHAPTER 5. THE PREMIERE

1. Pasquier, interview, 6 June 1994.
2. Loriod, quoting a letter from Breton in 1968, to author, 13 May 1995. Breton later became director of the Bureau of Art Education in Paris.
3. Pasquier, interview, 6 June 1994. Judging from a similar document in Pasquier's possession, Breton must have made the invitations individually by hand, for not only are they slightly different in design, they are marred by occasional spelling and copying errors: Pasquier's copy lists the pianist as "Messian," while Loriod's version contains the correct spelling. Pasquier's version contains the correct title, while Loriod's reads *Quatuor de la fin du Temps*.
4. Pasquier, interview, 19 June 1995.
5. Pasquier, interview, 6 June 1994.
6. Loriod, letter to author, 13 May 1995.
7. In an interview with Samama, Messiaen remarked, "There was an enormous audience, maybe not all the prisoners in the camp, still thousands of prisoners." At another time, the composer cited the figure 5,000 (Goléa, *Rencontres*, 63). Loriod estimated that there were 3,000 present (interview, 25 November 1993).
8. Pasquier, quoted in Lafon, "Etienne Pasquier, le dernier témoin," in *Le monde de la musique* (July–August 1997): 60; Pasquier, quoted in Lauerwald, "Er musizierte mit Olivier Messiaen als Kriegsgefangener," in *Das Orchester* 47, 1 (1999): 22.
9. Le Boulaire, letter to author, 20 March 1995.
10. Pasquier, quoted in "Hommage à Olivier Messiaen," 92.
11. Lauerwald, "*Quartett auf das Ende der Zeiten*," 18.
12. Brossard, quoted in Lauerwald, "*Quartett auf das Ende der Zeiten*," 19.
13. Le Boulaire, interview, 3 March 1995.
14. Lauerwald, "*Quartett auf das Ende der Zeiten*," 18.
15. Pasquier, interview, 10 June 1994.
16. Aleksander Lyczewski, quoted by Charles Bodman Rae in Malcolm Hayes, "Instrumental and Choral Works to 1948," Hill, *Messiaen Companion*, 199–200.
17. Messiaen, quoted in Goléa, *Rencontres*, 63.
18. Pasquier, interview, 19 June 1995.
19. Le Boulaire, interview, 3 March 1995.
20. Messiaen, quoted in Goléa, *Rencontres*, 63.
21. Le Boulaire, interview, 3 March 1995.
22. Messiaen, quoted in Goléa, *Rencontres*, 64.
23. M. H. [Marcel Haedrich], "Une grande première au Stalag VIII C [sic]: Olivier Messiaen présente son *Quatuor pour la fin des [sic] Temps*," *Le Figaro* (28 January 1942): 2.
24. Messiaen probably meant to say the A string; there is no E string on the cello.
25. Messiaen, in Samama, "Entretien avec Olivier Messiaen."
26. Pasquier, interview, 21 March 1995.
27. Pasquier, interview, 6 June 1994.
28. Pasquier, interview, 19 June 1995.
29. Pasquier, in Lauerwald, "Er musizierte mit Olivier Messiaen," 23.
30. Lauerwald, "*Quartett auf das Ende der Zeiten*," 18.
31. Leslie Sprout, "Messiaen's *Quatuor pour la fin du Temps*: Modernism, Representation, and a Soldier's Wartime Tale" (paper presented at the annual meeting of the American Musicological Society, Columbus, Ohio, 3 November 2002), 11.

32. Loriod, interview, 25 November 1993.

33. Rae, quoted in Hayes, "Instrumental and Choral Works to 1948," in Hill, *Messiaen Companion*, 199–200.

34. Jourdanet, "Messiaen créait."

35. Lucien Akoka, interview, 22 March 1995.

36. Roman Vlad, *Stravinsky*, trans. Frederick and Ann Fuller, 2nd ed. (London: Oxford University Press, 1967), 28. Stravinsky described this famous premiere as follows:

> Mild protests against the music could be heard from the very beginning of the performance. Then, when the curtain opened on the group of knock-kneed and long-braided Lolitas jumping up and down (*Danse des adolescentes*), the storm broke. Cries of "*Ta gueule*" [Shut your traps!] came from behind me. I heard Florent Schmitt shout, "*Taisez-vous garces du seizième*" [Shut up, bitches from the sixteenth!]; the "garces" of the sixteenth arrondissement were, of course, the most elegant ladies in Paris. The uproar continued, however, and a few minutes later I left the hall in a rage.

Igor Stavinsky and Robert Craft, *Expositions and Developments* (Garden City, N.Y.: Doubleday, 1962), 143.

37. Brossard, letter to Lauerwald, 13 March 1992.

38. Le Boulaire, interview, 3 March 1995.

39. Haedrich, 2.

40. Messiaen, quoted in Goléa, *Rencontres*, 63.

41. Messiaen, in Samama, "Entretien avec Olivier Messiaen."

42. Sprout, 10.

43. Pasquier, "Hommage à Olivier Messiaen," 92.

44. Pasquier, interview, 6 June 1994.

45. Haedrich, 2.

46. Pasquier, interview, 6 June 1994.

47. Autograph in the possession of Loriod.

CHAPTER 6. THE QUARTET FREE

1. Alain Périer, *Messiaen* (France: Editions du Seuil, 1979) 61.

2. Pasquier, interview, 21 March 1995. In his interview with Samama, however, Messiaen claimed that the premiere took place "just a few days before [his] liberation." In any case, writes Sprout, "we can be sure Messiaen was in Neussargues by 10 March 1941 at the latest, from a letter he sent to fellow composer and former Conservatoire classmate, Claude Arrieu, on that date" (Sprout, "Messiaen's *Quatuor pour la fin du Temps*," 5). Messiaen claimed that he began teaching at the Paris Conservatory in April 1941. Nigel Simeone, "Messiaen and the Concerts de la Pléiade: 'A Kind of Clandestine Revenge against the Occupation'," *Music and Letters* 81, no. 4 (November 2000): 556–57. However, Bouvin and numerous other sources confirm that he actually began teaching there in May 1941, with his titular post going into effect the following autumn. Jean Bouvin, *La Classe de Messiaen* (France: Christian Bourgois, 1995), 32.

3. Bouvin, 32.

4. Brossard to Lauerwald, 13 March 1992.

5. Lauerwald, "*Quartett auf das Ende der Zeiten*," 19.

6. Sprout, "Messiaen's *Quatuor pour la fin du Temps*," 6.

7. Pasquier, interview, 6 June 1994.

8. See figure 17.

9. Pasquier, interview, 19 June 1995.

10. Ibid.

11. Ibid.

12. Pasquier, interview, 21 March 1995.

13. Le Boulaire to author, 7 June 1995.

14. Pasquier, interview, 19 June 1995.

15. Pasquier, interview, 21 March 1995.

16. Pasquier, interview, 26 June 1995.

17. Dran to author, 10 October 1996.

18. "Henri used to amuse us by saying that at the moment of his circumcision, the *mohel* [ritual circumciser] missed, and that his penis was as it was because of overuse and sexual abuse. That was his humor." Dran to author, 10 October 1996.

19. Dran, interview, 22 December 1996.

20. Lucien Akoka, interview, 22 March 1995.

21. Dran, interview, 22 December 1995.

22. Pasquier, interview, 19 June 1995.

23. Pasquier, interview, 6 June 1994.

24. Loriod, interview, 25 November 1993.

25. Hayes, "Instrumental and Choral Works to 1948," in Hill, *Messiaen Companion,* 187.

26. Michael R. Marrus and Robert O. Paxton, *Vichy France and the Jews* (New York: Basic Books, 1981), 3.

27. Loriod, in Bouvin, *La classe de Messiaen,* 31–32.

28. "Interview with Yvonne Loriod," in Hill, *Messiaen Companion,* 289.

29. Loriod, interview, 25 November 1993.

30. Dran, interview, 22 December 1995.

31. Lucien Akoka, interview, 22 March 1995.

32. Dran, interview, 22 December 1995.

33. Philippe Akoka, interview, 22 March 1995.

34. Dran, interview, 14 December 1995.

35. Philippe Akoka, interview, 22 March 1995.

36. Pasquier, interview, 10 June 1994. He did not remember the name of the doctor.

37. Antoinette-Angéli Akoka, *"C'est surement un Juif," dit Papa* (Paris: Editions Lescaret), 59.

38. Lucien Akoka, interview, 22 March 1995.

39. Dran, interview, 22 March 1995.

40. Dran, interview, 22 December 1995.

41. Messiaen, "Quatuor pour la fin du Temps" (score) (Paris: Editeurs Durand, 1941), postage stamp reference.

42. Messiaen, *Quatuor pour la fin du Temps,* miniature score; Messiaen, "Quatuor pour la fin du Temps" (score). The current tempo marking of the first movement, 54, was originally 66; the principal tempo of the third movement, 44, was initially 63; that of the fourth movement, now 96, was originally 88; that of the fifth movement, now 44, was originally 50; that of the sixth movement, now 176, was originally 160; that of the seventh movement, now 50, was originally 60, and that of the eighth movement, now 36, was originally 44.

43. Loriod, interview, 25 November 1995. Loriod actually miscited the date of the premiere as 24 June 1942. The correct date is 24 June 1941. It is the date cited in Delannoy's review in *Les Nouveaux Temps,* as well as in the 1941 concert listings for *L'Information musicale.* Sprout, e-mail, 28 April 2003. Numerous other sources have misdated the premiere as well, so Loriod's error is understandable. Catherine Massip

claimed it was 26 June 1941. Massip, *Portrait(s) d'Olivier Messiaen* (Paris: Bibliothèque national de France, 1996), 12. Simeone cited it as 26 June 1942. Nigel Simeone, *Olivier Messiaen: A Bibliographical Catalogue of Messiaen's Works: First Editions and First Performances, with Illustrations of the Title Pages, Programmes, and Documents* (Tutzing: H. Schneider, 1998), np. Zinke-Bianchini cited the month and year only as June 1942, and also misdated Messiaen's appointment to the Paris Conservatory as 1942. Virginie Zinke-Bianchini, ed. *Olivier Messiaen, compositeur de musique et rhythmicien: Notice biographique, catalogue détaillé des œuvres éditées* (Paris: L'Emancipatrice, 1949), p. 71.

44. Messiaen, *The Technique of My Musical Language*, trans. John Satterfield (Paris: Alphonse Leduc, 1956), 8.

45. Loriod, interview, 25 November 1993.

46. Ibid.

47. Sprout, "Messiaen's *Quatuor pour la fin du Temps*," 6–7.

48. Serge Moreux, "Théâtre des Mathurins: Oeuvres de Messiaen," *L'Information musicale 33* (11 July 1941): 759.

49. Ibid.

50. "Les Six was a name applied in 1920 to a group of six French composers—Louis Durey, Arthur Honegger, Darius Milhaud, Germaine Tailleferre, Georges Auric, and Francis Poulenc—who c. 1916 formed a loose association based on their acceptance of the aesthetic ideals of Erik Satie. Although their individual styles differed considerably, they all opposed the vagueness of impressionism and endorsed the simplicity, clarity, and other characteristics of the then dawning neoclassic movement." *Harvard Dictionary of Music*, second edition, 1972, 779.

51. Arthur Honegger, "Olivier Messiaen," *Comoedia* (12 July 1941): 3.

52. Ibid.

53. Marcel Delannoy, "Depuis le mysticisme jusqu'au sport," *Les Nouveaux Temps* (13 July 1941): 2.

54. Ibid.

55. Simeone, "Messiaen and the Concerts de la Pléiade," 557.

56. Griffiths, *Messiaen and the Music of Time*, 91, 107.

57. Paxton, *Vichy France*, 175.

58. Marrus and Paxton, *Vichy France and the Jews*, 6–7.

59. Though France surrendered to the Germans in June 1940, General Charles de Gaulle, who had escaped to England, urged the French to continue the fight in a radio broadcast on 18 June. Those who answered his call became known as the Free French.

60. Dran to author, 10 October 1996.

61. Lucien Akoka, interview, 22 March 1995.

62. Antoinette-Angéli Akoka, *"C'est surement un Juif," dit Papa*, 47. Antoinette was the wife of Yvonne's brother Georges Akoka, who was a member of the French Resistance. She married Georges in the Free Zone in 1942 against the will of her parents, who, fearing for their daughter's safety, pleaded with her to wait until the war was over. Her book recounts her experience under the German Occupation.

63. Susan Zucotti, *The Holocaust, the French, and the Jews* (New York: Basic Books, 1993), 89.

64. Dran, interview, 22 December 1995.

65. Serge Klarsfeld, *Mémorial de la Déportation des Juifs de France* (Paris: Beate and Serge Klarsfeld, 1979), unpaginated.

66. Le Boulaire, interview, 3 March 1995.

67. Escapes apparently occurred quite often in Stalag VIII A, due to a frequent lack of surveillance, claimed Richard Pascal Sanos, a prisoner there: "The lack of surveillance during worktime made escapes somewhat easy. The difficulty, in our case,

was to reach the frontier. . . . The majority of the escapees (8 out of 10) were caught." Richard Pascal Sanos, quoted in *"Questionnaire pour les anciens prisonniers de guerre internés en Stalag,"* Archives Nationales, Document 72AJ298.

68. Le Boulaire to author, 31 July 1995.

69. Le Boulaire, interview, 3 March 1995.

70. Ibid.

71. Ibid.

72. In his private life, he was known by both names.

73. Ibid.

74. Ibid.

CHAPTER 7. AFTER THE QUARTET

1. Paxton, *Vichy France,* 316.

2. Dran, interview, 14 December 1995.

3. Dran, interview, 22 December 1995.

4. Dran, interview, 14 December 1995.

5. Ibid.

6. Antoinette-Angéli Akoka, *"C'est sûrement un juif," dit Papa,* 60.

7. Lucien Akoka, interview, 22 March 1995.

8. Alain Pâris, *Dictionnaire des interprètes et de l'interprétation musicale au xxᵉ siècle,* s.v. "Trio Pasquier," 1047.

9. Pasquier, interview, 10 June 1994.

10. Messiaen, quoted in Bouvin, *La classe de Messiaen,* 46. Messiaen dedicated his *Technique of My Musical Language* (1944) to Delapierre.

11. Messiaen, quoted in Bouvin, *La classe de Messiaen,* 46; and Loriod, quoted in Hill, *Messiaen Companion,* 291. Though he was slandered and defamed, Stravinsky claimed that he was not completely outlawed by the Nazis. In fact, in his memoir, *Themes and Episodes,* coauthored with Robert Kraft (New York: Alfred A. Knopf, 1966), 36, he stated that in 1942, the Nazis actually organized a gala performance of *The Rite of Spring* at the Paris Conservatory.

12. Goléa, *Rencontres,* 60.

13. Loriod, quoted in Hill, *Messiaen Companion,* 291.

14. Griffiths, 108.

15. Ibid., 108, 266–67.

16. Nigel Simeone, "Messiaen and the Concerts de la Pléiade: 'A Kind of Clandestine Revenge Against the Occupation'" *Music and Letters,* 81, 4 (November 2000): 551.

17. Sprout, "Messiaen's *Quatuor pour la fin du Temps,*" 4–5.

18. Ibid., 5–6.

19. Ibid., 7.

20. Sprout, "Music for a 'New Era': Composers and National Identity in France, 1936–1946" (Ph.D diss., University of California, Berkeley, 2000), 176–77.

21. Sprout, "Messiaen's *Quatuor pour la fin du Temps,*" 7.

22. Bouvin, 45; Simeone, "Messiaen and the Concerts de la Pléiade," 566.

23. Sprout, "Messiaen's *Quatuor pour la fin du Temps,*" 7.

24. Ibid., 8.

25. Sprout, "Messiaen's *Quatuor pour la fin du Temps,*" 8; Sprout, "Music for a 'New Era,'" 185.

26. Messiaen, in Goléa, *Rencontres* 67.

27. See figure 32.

28. Lucien Akoka, interview, 22 March 1995.

29. Dran, interview, 22 December 1995.
30. Jeannette Akoka, interview, 22 December 1995.
31. Lucien Akoka, interview, 22 March 1995.
32. Pasquier, interview, 10 June 1994.
33. Pasquier, interview, 6 June 1994. No recording or copyright date is available for this LP. Records show that the Bibliothèque Nationale received it in May 1957. As most recordings are usually filed there almost immediately upon release, one can assume that the recording was done sometime that year.
34. Loriod, interview, 25 November 1993.
35. See Appendix B.
36. Pasquier, interview, 21 March 1995.
37. Messiaen to Vacellier, autograph in the hand of Vacellier's son; copy courtesy Deplus. Note Messiaen's misquote of the date of the Paris premiere as 1942 rather than 1941. Vacellier died in December 1994. Deplus, interview, 17 January 1995.
38. Pasquier, interview, 10 June 1994.
39. Lyczewski to Messiaen, December 1984, copy courtesy Loriod.
40. Gorouben to author, 8 August 1995.
41. Gorouben to Messiaen, 21 September 1968, copy courtesy Loriod.
42. Gorouben to author, 8 July 2002.
43. Loriod to author, 13 May 1995.
44. Lucien Akoka, interview, 22 March 1995.
45. Jeannette Akoka, interview, 22 December 1995.
46. Lucien Akoka, interview, 22 March 1995.
47. Ibid.
48. Philippe Akoka, interview, 22 March 1995.
49. Antoinette-Angéli Akoka, "C'est sûrement un juif," dit Papa, 59.
50. Messiaen to Jeannette Akoka, 5 December 1975; copy courtesy of Jeannette Akoka.
51. Boucourechliev, "Messiaen," in New Grove, 204.
52. Griffiths, 255.
53. Bouvin, La classe de Messiaen, 410–32.
54. Catherine Massip, ed., Portrait(s) d'Olivier Messiaen (Paris: Bibliothèque Nationale de France, 1996), 173.
55. Maurice Werner to Lauerwald, 19 December 1990, copy courtesy Lauerwald.
56. Lauerwald, "Quartett auf das Ende der Zeiten," 56.
57. Paul Dorne to Yvonne Loriod-Messiaen, 16 February 1989, copy courtesy Loriod.
58. Lauerwald, "Quartett auf das Ende der Zeiten," 19.
59. Loriod, interview, 25 November 1993.
60. Loriod, quoted in Hill, Messiaen Companion, 301–2, 545.
61. Ibid., 284–85.
62. The seven volumes of this Treatise on Rhythm, Color, and Ornithology (Tráite de rythme, de couleur. et d'ornithologie) were published between 1994 and 2002.
63. Loriod, interview, 25 November 1993.
64. Fondation Olivier Messiaen (Paris: Fondation de France, 1994), 6–7.
65. Loriod, interview, 25 November 1993.

CHAPTER 8. INTO ETERNITY

1. Messiaen, Quatuor pour la fin du Temps, i.
2. François Lafon, "Etienne Pasquier: Le dernier témoin," in Le monde de la musique (July–August 1997), 58.

3. Pasquier, interview, 6 June 1994.
4. Pasquier, interview, 10 June 1994.
5. Pasquier, interview, 21 March 1995.
6. Ibid.
7. Ibid.
8. Pasquier, interview, 19 June 1995.
9. Pasquier, interview, 10 June 1994.
10. Pasquier, interview, 6 June 1994.
11. Pasquier, interview, 19 June 1995.
12. Pasquier, interview, 10 June 1994.
13. Ibid.
14. Pasquier, interview, 19 June 1995.
15. *PARC MONCEAU*

> J'étais là, admiratif, ému, dans ce jardin superbe,
> en pleine évolution printanière.
> J'avais une très jeune petite voisine,
> qui s'amusait à donner des miettes aux pigeons.
> Cet enfant était la grâce même.
> Casquée d'or fin (toute blonde) et possédant les yeux les plus beaux du
> monde enfantin dont elle semblait être la petite reine.
> Merveille de l'enfance
> qui n'a pas connu encore la pollution de l'esprit.

16. Pasquier, interview, 10 June 1994.
17. Ibid.
18. When the Trio Pasquier retired in 1974, it was succeeded by a new generation of Pasquiers—the Nouveau Trio Pasquier—consisting of cellist Roland Pidoux and violist Pierre Pasquier's sons Régis (violinist) and Bruno (violist), both international soloists as well as orchestral players and teachers at the Paris Conservatory (Pâris, *Dictionnaire des interprètes et de l'interprétation musicale au XXe siècle*, s.v. "Trio Pasquier, 1047; "Nouveau Trio Pasquier," 1045).
19. Obituary, "Etienne Pasquier," *Le monde*, Paris, 17 December 1997, 16.
20. Lanier to author, 12 January 1995.
21. Unless otherwise noted, all quotations of Lanier are from this interview, 3 March 1995.
22. Lanier to author, 20 March 1995.
23. Ibid.
24. Lanier to author, 7 June 1995.
25. Yvette Lanier, interview, 9 July 1997.
26. Ibid.
27. Jacques Joel, "Un café avec l'auteur (le faux) ou Qui est Jean Lanier?" in program for *Faits Divers* (Brussels: Théâtre Royal des Galeries, n.d.), unpaginated.
28. Unless otherwise noted, all quotations of Lucien Akoka are from the interview of 22 March 1995.
29. Most of the other occupied countries of Europe could be said to have collaborated with the Nazis in the general sense that they obeyed orders; they yielded to the Nazis' demand for the deportation of the Jews. In fact, some countries, notably Latvia, Lithuania, and the Ukraine, actively aided the Germans in the slaughtering of the Jews (see Daniel Jonah Goldhagen, *Hitler's Willing Executioners: Ordinary Germans and the Holocaust* [New York: Alfred A. Knopf, 1996], 409). However, France was the only country that collaborated in the political sense: it established a government specifically designed to aid and abet the occupying power.
30. Lucien did not recall the title of the book.

31. Philippe Akoka, interview, 22 March 1995.

32. Lucien Akoka, interview, 22 March 1995.

33. Dran, interview, 22 December 1995.

34. Jeannette Akoka, interview, 22 December 1995.

35. Dran, interview, 22 December 1995.

36. As of 7 June 1942, Jews over the age of six in the Occupied Zone had to wear, on the left side of their outer garment, a yellow Star of David, upon which was written in black letters the word *Juif* or *Juive* (Marrus and Paxton, *Vichy France and the Jews*, 236).

37. Dran, interview, 22 December 1995.

38. Performance of works by Jewish composers such as Mendelssohn was banned in Vichy France (Simeone, 551). The source of the quote about Loriod has requested to remain anonymous.

39. Messiaen, in Goléa, *Rencontres*, 67.

40. Dran, interview, 22 December 1995.

41. Jeannette Akoka, interview, 22 December 1995.

42. Unless otherwise noted, all quotations of Loriod are from the interview of 25 November 1993.

43. It is important to remember, however, said one of Messiaen's colleagues (who has requested to remain anonymous), that despite his suffering early on, Messiaen was a serenely happy man who was universally admired as an artist and human being and blessed with an extremely happy marriage.

44. Loriod, interview, 25 November 1993.

45. Messiaen, quoted in Patrick Szersnovicz, "Olivier Messiaen: La liturgie de l'arc-en-ciel," 33.

46. See Appendix B.

47. Quoted in interview with Loriod, 25 November 1993.

48. "Interview with Yvonne Loriod," in Hill, *Messiaen Companion*, 295.

49. Loriod, interview, 25 November 1993.

50. Pasquier, interview, 10 June 1994.

APPENDIX A

1. Messiaen conflated Revelation 10:1–7 and made slight changes. Although the most familiar reading of verse 6 is *"Il' n'y aura plus de délai"* [There will be no more delay], Messiaen chose a less common version, in which *"délai"* is replaced by the word *"temps"* [time]. Support of such a reading, for example, can be found in *The Abingdon Bible Commentary* (1929), where we find "There shall be time no longer" (p. 1384); in a French bible of 1861, *"Il n'y aurait plus de temps"* (*La Sainte Bible*, London); and in an updated Oxford Bible, "There shall be time no longer."

2. Messiaen's phrase, "d'un halo de trilles" (by a halo of trills) is actually an error. The solo blackbird and nightingale lines played by the clarinet and violin, respectively, are surrounded by a halo of harmonics in the cello, not by a halo of trills. Subsequently, Messiaen corrected this error in his more comprehensive analysis of the *Quartet* published in Claude Samuel's *Hommage à Olivier Messiaen*, in which he wrote: "d'un halo d'harmoniques." Messiaen, quoted in Samuel, "Olivier Messiaen analyse ses oeuvres, 40."

APPENDIX B

1. This recording was one of a set of seventeen compact discs reissued twice by Erato, once to commemorate the composer's eightieth birthday and a second time after his death.

Bibliography

INTERVIEWS BY THE AUTHOR

Akoka, Dominique. 22 March 1995.
Akoka, Jeannette. 22 December 1995.
Akoka, Lucien. 22 March 1995.
Akoka, Philippe. 22 March 1995, 15 July 2002.
Arrignon, Michel. 27 April 1994.
Deplus, Guy. 6 May 1994, 17 January 1995.
Dran, Yvonne. 22 March, 14 December, 22 December 1995
Lanier, Jean [Jean Le Boulaire]. 3 March 1995.
Lanier, Yvette. 9 July 1997.
Loriod, Yvonne. 25 November 1993.
Muraro, Roger. 8 May 1994.
Nagano, Kent. 21 May 1995.
Pasquier, Etienne. 6 June, 10 June 1994, 21 March, 19 June, 26 June 1995.

UNPUBLISHED SOURCES

Brossard, Jean. Letters to Hannalore Lauerwald, 16 February, 13 March, 4 November 1992.
———. Memoirs to Hannalore Lauerwald.
Comité International de la Croix-Rouge. Letter to Hannalore Lauerwald, 16 March 1992.
Dorne, Paul. Letter to Yvonne Loriod-Messiaen, 16 February 1989.
Dran, Yvonne. Letter to author, 10 October 1996.
Gorouben, David. Letters to author, 8 August 1995, 8 July 2002.
———. Letter to Olivier Messiaen, 21 September 1968.
Lanier, Jean. Letters to author, 12 January, 20 March, 7 June, 31 July, 3 August 1995.
Lanier, Jean and Yvette. "Partial List of Dramatic Productions Featuring Jean Lanier, 1995.
Lauerwald, Hannalore. "Dokumentation Kriegsgefangene in Deutschland 1939–1945: Stalag VIII A Görlitz-Moys."

Loriod, Yvonne. Letters to author, 25 January, 13 May, 2 June 1995.

Lyczewski, Aleksander. Letter to Olivier Messiaen, December 1984.

Messiaen, Olivier. Letter to Jeannette Akoka, 5 December 1975.

Messiaen, Pierre. Letter to Suzanne Pasquier, 3 October 1940.

Sprout, Leslie. E-mails to author, 28 and 29 April 2003.

Werner, Maurice. Letter to Hannalore Lauerwald, 19 December 1990.

PRIMARY SOURCES

Boulez, Pierre, Alain Louvier, and Serge Nigg. "L'hommage des compositeurs au pédagogue: témoignages." In *L'hommage du Conservatoire à Olivier Messiaen: Saison 1987–8*. Paris: Centre de Documentation de la Musique Contemporaine, 1988.

"Fondation Olivier Messiaen" (pamphlet). Paris: Fondation de France, 1994.

Goléa, Antoine. *Rencontres avec Olivier Messiaen*. Paris: René Juilliard, 1960.

Haedrich, Marcel. "Une grande première au Stalag VIII C [sic]: Olivier Messiaen présente son Quatuor pour la fin des [sic] Temps." *Le Figaro*, 28 January 1942, 2.

Hill, Peter. "Interview with Yvonne Loriod." In *The Messiaen Companion*. Portland, Ore.: Amadeus Press, 1995.

Joel, Jacques. "Un café avec l'auteur (le faux) ou Qui est Jean Lanier?" Program for *Faits Divers* by Aimé Declercq. Brussels: Théâtre Royal des Galéries, n.d.

Jourdanet, Charles. "Messiaen créait *Quatuor pour la fin du temps* au stalag." *Nice-matin*, 15 January 2001, Nice, France, 9.

"Kammerkonzert in der Krypta der Peterskirche": *Quatuor pour la fin du Temps* (program). St. Peters Church, Görlitz, 15 January 1991.

Lafon, François. "Etienne Pasquier, le dernier témoin." *Le monde de la musique* (July–August 1997): 58–60.

Lauerwald, Hannalore. "Er musizierte mit Olivier Messiaen als Kriegsgefangener." *Das Orchester* (47:1), 1999: 21–23.

Messiaen, Olivier. "*Quatuor pour la fin du Temps*." Score. 1941. Editeurs Durand, Paris.

———. *Quatuor pour la fin du Temps*. Miniature score. Paris: Editeurs Durand, 1942.

———. *The Technique of My Musical Language*. Trans. John Satterfield. Paris: Alphonse Leduc, 1956. Originally published as *Technique de mon langage musical*. Paris: Alphonse Leduc, 1944.

O'Bole. "Entretien nocturne." *Le lumignon: Journal mensuel du Stalag VIIIA* (July 1942): 8.

Pasquier, Etienne. "Hommage à Olivier Messiaen: Etienne Pasquier." In

Olivier Messiaen: homme de foi: Regard sur son œuvre d'orgue, 91–92. Paris: Edition St. Paul, Trinité Média Communication, 1995.

Rössler, Almut, ed. *Contributions to the Spiritual World of Olivier Messiaen: With Original Texts by the Composer*. Trans. Barbara Dagg, Nancy Poland, Timothy Tikker, and Almut Rössler. Duisburg, Germany: Gilles and Francke, 1986.

Samama, Leo. "Entretien avec Olivier Messiaen." In *Messiaen: Quartet for the End of Time*. Dir. Astrid Wortelboer. 60 min. Amaya, 1993. Videocassette.

Samuel, Claude. *Conversations with Olivier Messiaen*. Trans. Felix Aprahamian. Paris: Editions Pierre Belfond, 1967; London: Stainer and Bell, 1976.

———. "Olivier Messiaen analyse ses œuvres: *Quatuor pour la fin du Temps*." In *Hommage à Olivier Messiaen*. Paris: La Recherche Artistique, 1978.

———. *Olivier Messiaen: Music and Color: Conversations with Claude Samuel*. Trans. E. Thomas Glasow. Portland, Ore.: Amadeus Press, 1986.

"Les Stalags: Enquête concernant les P.G." In *Séries modernes et contemporaines, Série AJ, Second guerre mondiale: La captivité de guerre*. Paris: Archives nationales de France, 72AJ298, 6C.

Szersnovicz, Patrick. Olivier Messiaen: La Liturgie de l'Arc-en-Ciel. *Le Monde de la Musique* (July–August 1987): 29–35.

Stravinsky, Igor, and Robert Craft. *Expositions and Developments*. 1st ed. Garden City, N.Y.: Doubleday, 1962.

"Trio Pasquier" (press release for Pasquier Trio). New York: Colbert-LaBerge Concert Management, date unlisted.

Le Trio Pasquier. Paris: Bureau de Concerts Marcel de Valmalette, n.d.

SECONDARY SOURCES

Akoka, Antoinette-Angéli. *"C'est sûrement un juif," dit Papa*. Paris: Editions Lescaret, n.d.

Bell, Carla Huston. *Olivier Messiaen*. Boston: Twayne Publishers, 1984.

Bouvin, Jean. *La classe de Messiaen*. France: Christian Bourgois, 1995.

Condé, Gérard. "Les souvenirs d'Etienne Pasquier." *Le monde*, 3 August 1995, 22.

Delannoy, Marcel. "Depuis le mysticisme jusqu'au sport." *Les Nouveaux temps*, 13 July 1941, 2.

Durand, Yves. *La vie quotidienne des prisonniers de guerre dans les Stalags, les Oflags et les Kommandos, 1939–1945*, France: Hachette, 1987.

"Etienne Pasquier" (obituary). *Le Monde*, 17 December 1997, 16.

Goldhagen, Daniel Jonah. *Hitler's Willing Executioners: Ordinary Germans and the Holocaust*. New York: Alfred A. Knopf, 1996.

Griffiths, Paul. *Olivier Messiaen and the Music of Time*. Ithaca, N.Y.: Cornell University Press, 1985.

Hayes, Malcolm. "Instrumental, Orchestral and Choral Works to 1948." In *The Messiaen Companion*, ed. Peter Hill. Portland, OR: Amadeus Press, 1995.

Hold, Trevor. "Messiaen's Birds." *Music and Letters* 52, no. 2 (April 1971): 113–122.

Honegger, Arthur. "Olivier Messiaen." *Comœdia*, 12 July 1941, 3.

Hull, A. Eaglefield. *The Great Russian Tone-Poet Scriabin*. New York: AMS Press, 1916.

Johnson, Robert Sherlaw. "Birdsong." In *The Messiaen Companion*, ed. Peter Hill. Portland, Ore.: Amadeus Press, 1995.

———. *Messiaen*. Berkeley: University of California Press, 1975; reprinted 1980; first paperback printing 1989.

Kelly, Thomas Forest. *First Nights: Five Musical Premieres*. New Haven, Conn.: Yale University Press, 2000.

Klarsfeld, Serge. *Memorial de la Déportation des Juifs de France*. Paris: Beate and Serge Klarsfeld, 1979.

Lauerwald, Hannalore. *Im Fremdem Land: Kriegsgefangene im Stalag VIIIA Görlitz 1939–1945*. Görlitz, Germany: Viadukt Verlag, 1996.

———. "*Quartett auf das Ende der Zeiten*: Olivier Messiaen als Kriegsgefangener in Görlitz." *Das Orchester* 43, no.5 (1995): 17–19.

Marrus, Michael R., and Robert O. Paxton. *Vichy France and the Jews*. New York: Basic Books, 1981.

Massin, Brigitte. *Olivier Messiaen: Une poétique du merveilleux*. Aix-en-Provence: Editions Alinéa, 1989.

Massip, Catherine, ed. *Portrait(s) d'Olivier Messiaen*. Paris: Bibliothèque Nationale de France, 1996.

Matheson, Iain. "The End of Time: A Biblical Theme in Messiaen's *Quatour*." In *The Messiaen Companion*, ed. Peter Hill. Portland, Ore.: Amadeus Press, 1995.

"Messiaen, Olivier." *Diapason catalogue général classique* (1997): 255–257.

"Messiaen, Olivier." *Schwann Opus* 8, no. 3 (Summer 1997): 546–548.

Moreux, Serge. "Théâtre des Mathurins: Oeuvres de Messiaen." *L'Information musicale 33*, 11 July 1941, 759.

Nichols, Roger. *Messiaen*. 2nd ed. Oxford Studies of Composers. Oxford: Oxford University Press, 1986.

Paxton, Robert. *Vichy France: Old Guard and New Order: 1940–1944*. 1972; reprint, New York: Columbia University Press, 1982.

Périer, Alain. *Messiaen*. Paris: Editions du Seuil, 1979.

Pople, Anthony. *Messiaen: Quatuor pour la fin du Temps*. Cambridge: Cambridge University Press, 1998.

Ross, Alex. "In Music, Though, There Were No Victories." *New York Times*, 20 August 1995, 25–31.

Silver, Kenneth E., and Romy Golan. *The Circle of Montparnasse Jewish Artists in Paris: 1905–1945*. New York: Universe Books, 1985.

Simeone, Nigel. "Messiaen and the Concerts de la Pléiade: 'A Kind of Clandestine Revenge against the Occupation.'" *Music and Letters* 81 (November 2000): 551–84.

———. *Olivier Messiaen: A Bibliographical Catalogue of Messiaen's Works: First Editions and First Performances, with Illustrations of the Title Pages, Programmes, and Documents*. Tutzing: H. Schneider, 1998.

Sprout, Leslie. "Messiaen's *Quatuor pour la fin du Temps*: Modernism, Representation, and a Soldier's Wartime Tale." Paper presented at the annual meeting of American Musicological Society, Columbus, Ohio, 3 November 2002.

———. "Music for a 'New Era': Composers and National Identity in France, 1936–1946." Ph.D diss., University of California, Berkeley, 2000.

Vlad, Roman. *Stravinsky*. Trans. Frederick and Ann Fuller. 2nd ed. London: Oxford University Press, 1967.

Zinke-Bianchini, Virginie. *Olivier Messiaen, compositeur de musique et rhythmicien: Notice biographique, catalogue détaillé des oeuvres éditeés*. Paris: L'Emancipatrice, 1949.

Zucotti, Susan. *The Holocaust, the French, and the Jews*. New York: Basic Books, 1993.

Index